Multimedia Security:
Steganography and Digital Watermarking Techniques for Protection of Intellectual Property

Chun-Shien Lu
Institute of Information Science
Academia Sinica, Taiwan, ROC

IDEA GROUP PUBLISHING
Hershey • London • Melbourne • Singapore

Acquisitions Editor: Mehdi Khosrow-Pour
Senior Managing Editor: Jan Travers
Managing Editor: Amanda Appicello
Development Editor: Michele Rossi
Copy Editor: Ingrid Widitz
Typesetter: Jennifer Wetzel
Cover Design: Lisa Tosheff
Printed at: Yurchak Printing Inc.

Published in the United States of America by
Idea Group Publishing (an imprint of Idea Group Inc.)
701 E. Chocolate Avenue, Suite 200
Hershey PA 17033
Tel: 717-533-8845
Fax: 717-533-8661
E-mail: cust@idea-group.com
Web site: http://www.idea-group.com

and in the United Kingdom by
Idea Group Publishing (an imprint of Idea Group Inc.)
3 Henrietta Street
Covent Garden
London WC2E 8LU
Tel: 44 20 7240 0856
Fax: 44 20 7379 3313
Web site: http://www.eurospan.co.uk

Library of Congress Cataloging-in-Publication Data

Multimedia security : steganography and digital watermarking techniques for protection of intellectual property / Chun-Shien Lu, Editor.
p. cm.
ISBN 1-59140-192-5 -- ISBN 1-59140-275-1 (ppb) -- ISBN 1-59140-193-3 (ebook)
1. Computer security. 2. Multimedia systems--Security measures. 3. Intellectual property. I. Lu, Chun-Shien.
QA76.9.A25M86 2004
005.8--dc22

2004003775

British Cataloguing in Publication Data
A Cataloguing in Publication record for this book is available from the British Library.

Multimedia Security:
Steganography and Digital Watermarking Techniques for Protection of Intellectual Property

Table of Contents

Preface

In this digital era, the ubiquitous network environment has promoted the rapid delivery of digital multimedia data. Users are eager to enjoy the convenience and advantages that networks have provided. Meanwhile, users are eager to share various media information in a rather cheap way without awareness of possibly violating copyrights. In view of these, digital watermarking technologies have been recognized as a helpful way in dealing with the copyright protection problem in the past decade. Although digital watermarking still faces some challenging difficulties for practical uses, there are no other techniques that are ready to substitute it. In order to push ahead with the development of digital watermarking technologies, the goal of this book is to collect both comprehensive issues and survey papers in this field so that readers can easily understand state of the art in multimedia security, and the challenging issues and possible solutions. In particular, the authors that contribute to this book have been well known in the related fields. In addition to the invited chapters, the other chapters are selected from a strict review process. In fact, the acceptance rate is lower than 50%.

There are eight chapters contained in this book. The first two chapters provide a general survey of digital watermarking technologies. In Chapter I, an extensive literature review of the multimedia copyright protection is thoroughly provided. It presents a universal review and background about the watermarking definition, concept and the main contributions in this field. Chapter II focuses on the discussions of perceptual properties in image watermarking. In this chapter, a detailed description of the main phenomena regulating the HVS will be given and the exploitation of these concepts in a data hiding system will be considered. Then, some limits of classical HVS models will be highlighted and some possible solutions to get around these problems pointed out. Finally, a complete mask building procedure, as a possible exploitation of HVS characteristics for perceptual data hiding in still images will be described.

From Chapter III through Chapter V, audio watermarking plays the main role. In Chapter III, the main theme is to propose a methodology, including performance metrics, for evaluating and comparing the performance of digital audio watermarking schemes. This is because the music industry is facing several challenges as well as opportunities as it tries to adapt its business to the new medium. In fact, the topics discussed in this chapter come not only from printed sources but also from very productive discussions with some of the active researchers in the field. These discussions have been conducted via e-mail, and constitute a rich complement to the still low number of printed sources about this topic. Even though the annual number of papers published on watermarking has been nearly doubling every year in the last years, it is still low. Thus it was necessary to augment the literature review with personal interviews. In Chapter IV, the aim is to provide a comprehensive survey and summary of the technical achievements in the research area of digital audio watermarking. In order to give a big picture of the current status of this area, this chapter covers the research aspects of performance evaluation for audio watermarking, human auditory system, digital watermarking for PCM audio, digital watermarking for wav-table synthesis audio, and digital watermarking for compressed audio. Based on the current technology used in digital audio watermarking and the demand from real-world applications, future promising directions are identified. In Chapter V, a method for embedding a customer identification code into multimedia data is introduced. Specifically, the described method, *active digital fingerprinting,* is a combination of robust digital watermarking and the creation of a collision-secure customer vector. There is also another mechanism often called *fingerprinting* in multimedia security, which is the identification of content with robust hash algorithms. To be able to distinguish both methods, robust hashes are called *passive fingerprinting* and collision-free customer identification watermarks are called *active fingerprinting.* Whenever we write fingerprinting in this chapter, we mean active fingerprinting.

In Chapters VI and VII, the media content authentication problem will be discussed. It is well known that multimedia authentication distinguishes itself from other data integrity security issues because of its unique property of content integrity in several different levels - from signal syntax levels to semantic levels. In Chapter VI, several image authentication issues, including the mathematical forms of optimal multimedia authentication systems, a description of robust digital signature, the theoretical bound of information hiding capacity of images, an introduction of the *Self-Authentication-and-Recovery Image* (SARI) system, and a novel technique for image/video authentication in the semantic level will be thoroughly described. This chapter provides an overview of these image authentication issues. On the other hand, in the light of the possible disadvantages that watermarking-based authentication techniques may result in, Chapter VII has moved focus to labeling-based authentication techniques. In labeling-based techniques, the authentication information is conveyed in a separate file called *label.* A label is additional information associated with the image content and can be used to identify the image. In order to associate the label content with the image content, two different ways can be employed and are stated as follows.

The last chapter describes watermarking methods applied to those media data that receives less attention. With the proliferation of digital media such as images, audio, and video, robust digital watermarking and data hiding techniques are needed for copyright protection, copy control, annotation, and authentication of document images. While many techniques have been proposed for digital color and grayscale images, not all of them can be directly applied to binary images in general and document images in particular. The difficulty lies in the fact that changing pixel values in a binary image could introduce irregularities that are very visually noticeable. Over the last few years, we have seen a growing but limited number of papers proposing new techniques and ideas for binary image watermarking and data hiding. In Chapter VIII, an overview and summary of recent developments on this important topic, and discussion of important issues such as robustness and data hiding capacity of the different techniques is presented.

Acknowledgments

As the editor of this book, I would like to thank all the authors who have contributed their chapters to this book during the lengthy process of compilation. In particular, I truly appreciate Idea Group Inc. for giving me the extension of preparing the final book manuscript. Without your cooperation, this book would not be born.

Chun-Shien Lu, PhD
Assistant Research Fellow
Institute of Information Science, Academia Sinica
Taipei City, Taiwan 115, Republic of China (ROC)
lcs@iis.sinica.edu.tw
http://www.iis.sinica.edu.tw/~lcs

Chapter I

Digital Watermarking for Protection of Intellectual Property

Mohamed Abdulla Suhail, University of Bradford, UK

ABSTRACT

Digital watermarking techniques have been developed to protect the copyright of media signals. This chapter aims to provide a universal review and background about the watermarking definition, concept and the main contributions in this field. The chapter starts with a general view of digital data, the Internet and the products of these two, namely, the multimedia and the e-commerce. Then, it provides the reader with some initial background and history of digital watermarking. The chapter presents an extensive and deep literature review of the field of digital watermarking and watermarking algorithms. It also highlights the future prospective of the digital watermarking.

INTRODUCTION

Digital watermarking techniques have been developed to protect the copyright of media signals. Different watermarking schemes have been suggested for multimedia content (images, video and audio signal). This chapter aims to provide an extensive literature review of the multimedia copyright protection. It presents a universal review and background about the watermarking definition, concept and the main contributions in this field. The chapter consists of four main sections.

The first section provides a general view of digital data, the Internet and the products of these two, namely multimedia and e-commerce. It starts this chapter by providing the reader with some initial background and history of digital watermarking. The second section gives an extensive and deep literature review of the field of digital watermarking. The third section reviews digital-watermarking algorithms, which are classified into three main groups according to the embedding domain. These groups are spatial domain techniques, transform domain techniques and feature domain techniques. The algorithms of the frequency domain are further subdivided into wavelet, DCT and fractal transform techniques. The contributions of the algorithms presented in this section are analyzed briefly. The fourth section discusses the future prospective of digital watermarking.

DIGITAL INTELLECTUAL PROPERTY

Information is becoming widely available via global networks. These connected networks allow cross-references between databases. The advent of multimedia is allowing different applications to mix sound, images, and video and to interact with large amounts of information (e.g., in e-business, distance education, and human-machine interface). The industry is investing to deliver audio, image and video data in electronic form to customers, and broadcast television companies, major corporations and photo archivers are converting their content from analogue to digital form. This movement from traditional content, such as paper documents, analogue recordings, to digital media is due to several advantages of digital media over the traditional media. Some of these advantages are:

1. The quality of digital signals is higher than that of their corresponding analogue signals. Traditional assets degrade in quality as time passes. Analogue data require expensive systems to obtain high quality copies, whereas digital data can be easily copied without loss of fidelity.
2. Digital data (audio, image and video signals) can be easily transmitted over networks, for example the Internet. A large amount of multimedia data is now available to users all over the world. This expansion will continue at an even greater rate with the widening availability of advanced multimedia services like electronic commerce, advertising, interactive TV, digital libraries, and a lot more.
3. Exact copies of digital data can be easily made. This is very useful but it also creates problems for the owner of valuable digital data like precious digital images. Replicas of a given piece of digital data cannot be distinguished and their origin cannot be confirmed. It is impossible to determine which piece is the original and which is the copy.
4. It is possible to hide some information within digital data in such a way that data modifications are undetectable for the human senses.

E-Commerce

Modern electronic commerce (e-commerce) is a new activity that is the direct result of a revolutionary information technology, digital data and the Internet. E-commerce is defined as the conduct of business transactions and trading over a common information systems (IS) platform such as the Web or Internet. The amount of information being offered to public access grows at an amazing rate with current and new technologies. Technology used in e-commerce is allowing new, more efficient ways of carrying out existing business and this has had an impact not only on commercial enterprises but also on social life. The e-commerce potential was developed through the World Wide Web (WWW) in the 1990s.

E-commerce can be divided into *e-tailing, e-operations* and *e-fulfillment,* all supported by an *e-strategy. E-tailing* involves the presentation of the organization's selling wares (goods/services) in the form of electronic catalogues (e-catalogues). *E-catalogues* are an Internet version of the information presentation about the organization, its products, and so forth. *E-operations* cover the core transactional processes for production of goods and delivery of services. *E-fulfillment* is an area within e-commerce that still seems quite blurred. It complements e-tailing and e-operations as it covers a range of post-retailing and operational issues. The core of e-fulfillment is payment systems, copyright protection of intellectual property, security (which includes privacy) and order management (i.e., supply chain, distribution, etc.). In essence, fulfillment is seen as the fuel to the growth and development of e-commerce.

The owners of copyright and related rights are granted a range of different rights to control or be remunerated for various types of uses of their property (e.g., images, video, audio). One of these rights includes the right to exclude others from reproducing the property without authorization. The development of digital technologies permitting transmission of digital data over the Internet has raised questions about how these rights apply in the new environment. How can digital intellectual property be made publicly available while guaranteeing ownership of the intellectual rights by the rights-holder and free access to information by the user?

Copyright Protection of Intellectual Property

An important factor that slows down the growth of multimedia networked services is that authors, publishers and providers of multimedia data are reluctant to allow the distribution of their documents in a networked environment. This is because the ease of reproducing digital data in their exact original form is likely to encourage copyright violation, data misappropriation and abuse. These are the problems of theft and distribution of intellectual property. Therefore, creators and distributors of digital data are actively seeking reliable solutions to the problems associated with copyright protection of multimedia data.

Moreover, the future development of networked multimedia systems, in particular on open networks like the Internet, is conditioned by the development of efficient methods to protect data owners against unauthorized copying and redistribution of the material put on the network. This will guarantee that their rights are protected and their assets properly managed. Copyright protection of multimedia data has been accomplished by means of cryptography algorithms to provide control over data access and to make data unreadable to non-authorized users. However, encryption systems do not completely solve the problem, because once encryption is removed there is no more control on the dissemination of data.

The concept of digital watermarking arose while trying to solve problems related to the copyright of intellectual property in digital media. It is used as a means to identify the owner or distributor of digital data. Watermarking is the process of encoding hidden copyright information since it is possible today to hide information messages within digital audio, video, images and texts, by taking into account the limitations of the human audio and visual systems.

Digital Watermarking: What, Why, When and How?

It seems that digital watermarking is a good way to protect intellectual property from illegal copying. It provides a means of embedding a message in a piece of digital data without destroying its value. Digital watermarking embeds a known message in a piece of digital data as a means of identifying the rightful owner of the data. These techniques can be used on many types of digital data including still imagery, movies, and music. This chapter focuses on digital watermarking for images and in particular invisible watermarking.

What is Digital Watermarking?

A digital watermark is a signal permanently embedded into digital data (audio, images, video, and text) that can be detected or extracted later by means of computing operations in order to make assertions about the data. The watermark is hidden in the host data in such a way that it is inseparable from the data and so that it is resistant to many operations not degrading the host document. Thus by means of watermarking, the work is still accessible but permanently marked.

Digital watermarking techniques derive from *steganography,* which means covered writing (from the Greek words *stegano* or "covered" and *graphos* or "to write"). Steganography is the science of communicating information while hiding the existence of the communication. The goal of steganography is to hide an information message inside harmless messages in such a way that it is not possible even to detect that there is a secret message present. Both steganography and watermarking belong to a category of information hiding, but the objectives and conditions for the two techniques are just the opposite. In watermarking, for example, the important information is the "external" data (e.g., images, voices, etc.). The "internal" data (e.g., watermark) are additional data for protecting the external data and to prove ownership. In steganography, however, the external data (referred to as a vessel, container, or dummy data) are not very important. They are just a carrier of the important information. The internal data are the most important.

On the other hand, watermarking is not like encryption. Watermarking does not restrict access to the data while encryption has the aim of making messages unintelligible to any unauthorized persons who might intercept them. Once encrypted data is decrypted, the media is no longer protected. A watermark is designed to permanently reside in the host data. If the ownership of a digital work is in question, the information can be extracted to completely characterize the owner.

Why Digital Watermarking?

Digital watermarking is an enabling technology for e-commerce strategies: conditional and user-specific access to services and resources. Digital watermarking offers several advantages. The details of a good digital watermarking algorithm can be made public knowledge. Digital watermarking provides the owner of a piece of digital data the means to mark the data invisibly. The mark could be used to serialize a piece of data as it is sold or used as a method to mark a valuable image. For example, this marking allows an owner to safely post an image for viewing but legally provides an embedded copyright to prohibit others from posting the same image. Watermarks and attacks on watermarks are two sides of the same coin. The goal of both is to preserve the value of the digital data. However, the goal of a watermark is to be robust enough to resist attack but not at the expense of altering the value of the data being protected. On the other hand, the goal of the attack is to remove the watermark without destroying the value of the protected data. The contents of the image can be marked without visible loss of value or dependence on specific formats. For example a bitmap (BMP) image can be compressed to a JPEG image. The result is an image that requires less storage space but cannot be distinguished from the original. Generally, a JPEG compression level of 70% can be applied without humanly visible degradation. This property of digital images allows insertion of additional data in the image without altering the value of the image. The message is hidden in unused "visual space" in the image and stays below the human visible threshold for the image.

When Did the Technique Originate?

The idea of hiding data in another media is very old, as described in the case of steganography. Nevertheless, the term *digital watermarking* first appeared in 1993, when Tirkel et al. (1993) presented two techniques to hide data in images. These methods were based on modifications to the *least significant bit* (LSB) of the pixel values.

How Can We Build an Effective Watermarking Algorithm?

The following sections will discuss further answering this question. However, it is desired that watermarks survive image-processing manipulations such as rotation, scaling, image compression and image enhancement, for example. Taking advantage of the discrete wavelet transform properties and robust features extraction techniques are the new trends that are used in the recent digital image watermarking methods. Robustness against geometrical transformation is essential since image-publishing applications often apply some kind of geometrical transformations to the image, and thus, an intellectual property ownership protection system should not be affected by these changes.

DIGITAL WATERMARKING CONCEPT

This section aims to provide the theoretical background about the watermarking field but concentrating mainly on digital images and the principles by which watermarks are implemented. It discusses the requirements that are needed for an effective watermarking system. It shows that the requirements are application-dependent, but some of them are common to most practical applications. It explains also the challenges facing the researchers in this field from the digital watermarking requirement viewpoint. Swanson, Kobayashi and Tewfik (1998), Busch and Wolthusen (1999), Mintzer, Braudaway and Yeung (1997), Servetto, Podilchuk and Ramchandran (1998), Cox, Kilian, Leighton and Shamoon (1997), Bender, Gruhl, Morimoto and Lu (1996), Zaho, and Silvestre and Dowling (1997) include discussions of watermarking concepts and principles and review developments in transparent data embedding for audio, image, and video media.

Visible vs. Invisible Watermarks

Digital watermarking is divided into two main categories: visible and invisible. The idea behind the visible watermark is very simple. It is equivalent to stamping a watermark on paper, and for this reason is sometimes said to be digitally stamped. An example of visible watermarking is provided by television channels, like BBC, whose logo is visibly superimposed on the corner of the TV picture. Invisible watermarking, on the other hand, is a far more complex concept. It is most often used to identify copyright data, like author, distributor, and so forth.

Though a lot of research has been done in the area of invisible watermarks, much less has been done for visible watermarks. Visible and invisible watermarks both serve to deter theft but they do so in very different ways. Visible watermarks are especially useful for conveying an immediate claim of ownership (Mintzer, Braudaway & Yeung, 1997). Their main advantage, in principle at least, is the virtual elimination of the commercial value of a document to a would-be thief, without lessening the document's utility for legitimate, authorized purposes. Invisible watermarks, on the other hand, are more of an aid in catching a thief than for discouraging theft in the first place (Mintzer et al., 1997; Swanson et al., 1998). This chapter focuses on the latter category, and the phrase "watermark" is taken to mean the invisible watermark, unless otherwise stated.

Watermarking Classification

There are different classifications of invisible watermarking algorithms. The reason behind this is the enormous diversity of watermarking schemes. Watermarking approaches can be distinguished in terms of watermarking host signal (still images, video signal, audio signal, integrated circuit design), and the availability of original signal during extraction (non-blind, semi-blind, blind). Also, they can be categorized based on the domain used for watermarking embedding process, as shown in Figure 1. The watermarking application is considered one of the criteria for watermarking classification. Figure 2 shows the subcategories based on watermarking applications.

Figure 1. Classification of watermarking algorithms based on domain used for the watermarking embedding process

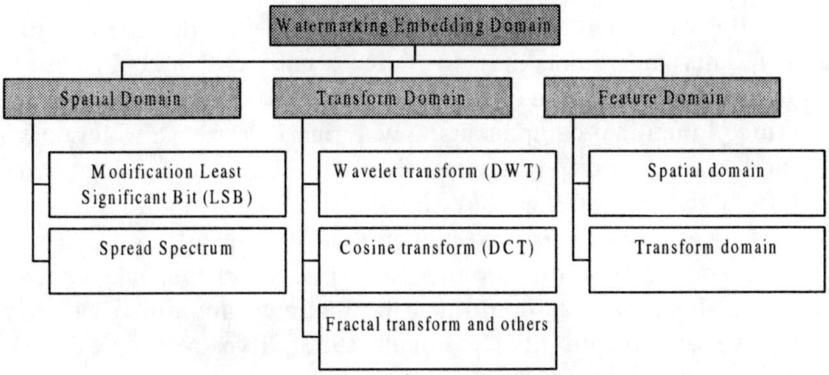

Figure 2. Classification of watermarking technology based on applications

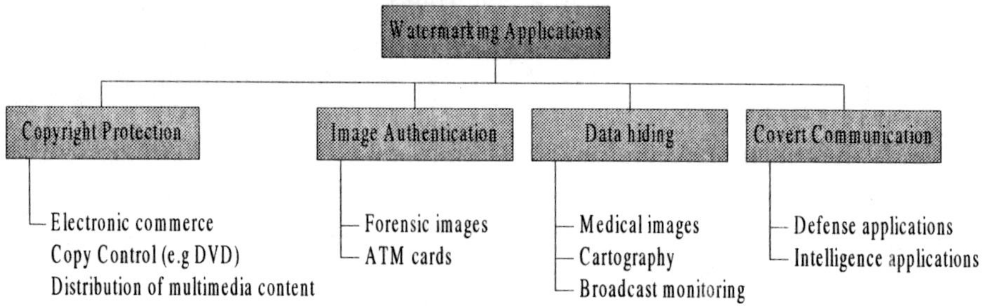

Digital Watermarking Application

Watermarking has been proposed in the literature as a means for different applications. The four main digital watermarking applications are:

1. Copyright protection
2. Image authentication
3. Data hiding
4. Covert communication

Figure 2 shows the different applications of watermarking with some examples for each of these applications. Also, digital watermarking is proposed for tracing images in the event of their illicit redistribution. The need for this has arisen because modern digital networks make large-scale dissemination simple and inexpensive. In the past, infringement of copyrighted documents was often limited by the unfeasibility of large-scale photocopying and distribution. In principle, digital watermarking makes it possible to uniquely mark each image sold. If a purchaser then makes an illicit copy, the illicit duplication may be convincingly demonstrated (Busch & Wolthusen, 1999; Swanson et al., 1998).

Watermark Embedding

Generally, watermarking systems for digital media involve two distinct stages: (1) watermark embedding to indicate copyright and (2) watermark detection to identify the owner (Swanson et al., 1998). Embedding a watermark requires three functional components: a watermark carrier, a watermark generator, and a carrier modifier. A watermark carrier is a list of data elements, selected from the un-watermarked signal, which are modified during the encoding of a sequence of noise-like signals that form the watermark. The noise signals are generated pseudo-randomly, based on secret keys, independently of the carrier. Ideally, the signal should have the maximum amplitude, which is still below the level of perceptibility (Cox et al., 1997; Silvestre & Dowling, 1997;

Figure 3. Embedding and detecting systems of digital watermarking

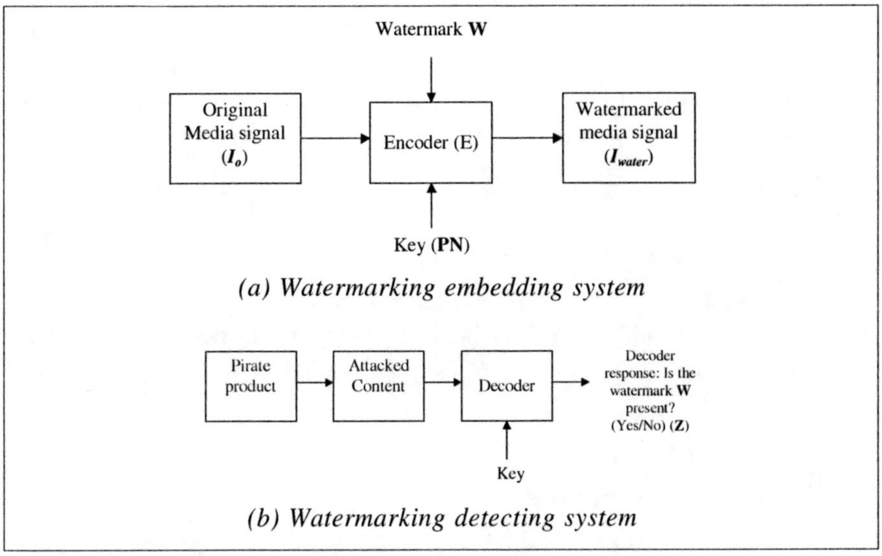

(a) Watermarking embedding system

(b) Watermarking detecting system

Swanson et al., 1998). The carrier modifier adds the generated noise signals to the selected carrier. To balance the competing requirements for low perceptibility and robustness of the added watermark, the noise must be scaled and modulated according to the strength of the carrier.

Embedding and detecting operations proceeds as follows. Let I_{orig} denote the original multimedia signal (an image, an audio clip, or a video sequence) before watermarking, let W denote the watermark that the copyright owner wishes to embed, and let I_{water} denote the signal with the embedded watermark. A block diagram representing a general watermarking scheme is shown in Figure 3. The watermark W is encoded into I_{orig} using an embedding function E:

$$E(I_{orig}, W) = I_{water} \qquad \textbf{(1)}$$

The embedding function makes small modifications to I_{orig} related to W. For example, if $W = (w1, w2, ...)$, the embedding operation may involve adding or subtracting a small quantity a from each pixel or sample of I_{orig}. During the second stage of the watermarking system, the detecting function D uses knowledge of W, and possibly I_{orig}, to extract a sequence W' from the signal R undergoing testing:

$$D(R, I_{orig}) = W' \qquad \textbf{(2)}$$

The signal R may be the watermarked signal I_{water}, it may be a distorted version of I_{water} resulting from attempts to remove the watermark, or it may be an unrelated signal. The extracted sequence W' is compared with the watermark W to determine whether R is watermarked. The comparison is usually based on a correlation measure ρ, and a threshold λ_0 used to make the binary decision (Z) on whether the signal is watermarked or not. To check the similarity between W, the embedded watermark and W', the extracted one, the correlation measure between them can be found using:

$$\rho(W,W') = \frac{W \cdot W'}{\sqrt{W' \cdot W'}} \tag{3}$$

where W, W' is the scalar product between these two vectors. However, the decision function is:

$$Z(W',W) = \begin{cases} 1, & \rho \geq \lambda_0 \\ 0 & otherwise \end{cases} \tag{4}$$

where ρ is the value of the correlation and λ_0 is a threshold. A *1* indicates a watermark was detected, while a *0* indicates that a watermark was not detected. In other words, if W and W' are sufficiently correlated (greater than some threshold λ_0), the signal R has been verified to contain the watermark that confirms the author's ownership rights to the signal. Otherwise, the owner of the

Figure 4. Detection threshold experimentally (of 600 random watermark sequences studied, only one watermark — which was origanally inserted — has a higher correlation output above others) (Threshold is set to be 0.1 in this graph.)

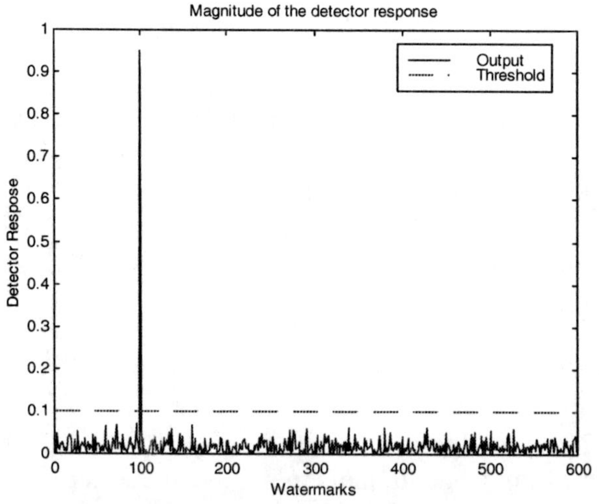

watermark W has no rights over the signal R. It is possible to derive the detection threshold λ_0 analytically or empirically by examining the correlation of random sequences. Figure 4 shows the detection threshold of 600 random watermark sequences studied, and only one watermark, which was originally inserted, has a significantly higher correlation output than the others. As an example of an analytically defined threshold, τ can be defined as:

$$\tau = \frac{\alpha}{3N_c} \sum^{N_c} | I_{water}(m,n) | \quad \textbf{(5)}$$

where α is a weighting factor and N_c is the number of coefficients that have been marked. The formula is applicable to square and non-square images (Hernadez & Gonzalez, 1999). One can even just select certain coefficients (based on a pseudo-random sequence or a *human visual system* (HVS) model). The choice of the threshold influences the false-positive and false- negative probability. Hernandez and Gonzalez (1999) propose some methods to compute predictable correlation thresholds and efficient watermark detection systems.

A Watermarking Example

A simple example of the basic watermarking process is described here. The example is very basic just to illustrate how the watermarking process works. The discrete cosine transform (DCT) is applied on the host image, which is represented by the first block (8x8 pixel) of the "trees" image shown in Figure 5. The block is given by:

Figure 5. 'Trees' image with its first 8x8 block

Block B_1 of 'trees' image

B_1

0.7232	0.8245	0.6599	0.7232	0.6003	0.6122	0.6122	0.5880
0.7745	0.7745	0.7745	0.7025	0.7745	0.7025	0.7745	0.7025
0.7745	0.7745	0.7025	0.7745	0.7745	0.7025	0.7025	0.7025
0.7025	0.7025	0.7025	0.7025	0.7025	0.7745	0.7025	0.7025
0.7745	0.7025	0.7745	0.7025	0.7025	0.7025	0.7025	0.7025
0.7025	0.7025	0.7025	0.7745	0.7025	0.7745	0.7025	0.7025
0.7025	0.7745	0.7025	0.7025	0.7745	0.7025	0.7745	0.7025
0.7025	0.7025	0.7745	0.7745	0.7745	0.7025	0.7025	0.7025

$$B_1 = \begin{bmatrix} 0.7232 & 0.8245 & 0.6599 & 0.7232 & 0.6003 & 0.6122 & 0.6122 & 0.5880 \\ 0.7745 & 0.7745 & 0.7745 & 0.7025 & 0.7745 & 0.7025 & 0.7745 & 0.7025 \\ 0.7745 & 0.7745 & 0.7025 & 0.7745 & 0.7745 & 0.7025 & 0.7025 & 0.7025 \\ 0.7025 & 0.7025 & 0.7025 & 0.7025 & 0.7025 & 0.7745 & 0.7025 & 0.7025 \\ 0.7745 & 0.7025 & 0.7745 & 0.7025 & 0.7025 & 0.7025 & 0.7025 & 0.7025 \\ 0.7025 & 0.7025 & 0.7025 & 0.7745 & 0.7025 & 0.7745 & 0.7025 & 0.7025 \\ 0.7025 & 0.7745 & 0.7025 & 0.7025 & 0.7745 & 0.7025 & 0.7745 & 0.7025 \\ 0.7025 & 0.7025 & 0.7745 & 0.7745 & 0.7745 & 0.7025 & 0.7025 & 0.7025 \end{bmatrix}$$

Applying DCT on B_1, the result is:

$$DCT(B_1) = \begin{bmatrix} 5.7656 & 0.1162 & -0.0379 & 0.0161 & -0.0093 & -0.0032 & -0.0472 & -0.0070 \\ -0.0526 & 0.1157 & 0.0645 & 0.0104 & -0.0137 & -0.0114 & -0.0415 & -0.0336 \\ -0.0354 & 0.0739 & -0.0136 & -0.0410 & -0.0081 & -0.0187 & -0.0871 & 0.0063 \\ -0.0953 & 0.0436 & 0.0379 & -0.0090 & -0.0394 & 0.0182 & -0.0031 & -0.0589 \\ -0.1066 & 0.0500 & 0.0034 & -0.0355 & -0.0093 & 0.0147 & 0.0526 & -0.0278 \\ -0.0790 & -0.0064 & 0.0088 & 0.0240 & -0.0200 & -0.0361 & -0.0586 & -0.0731 \\ -0.0422 & 0.0366 & -0.0460 & -0.0150 & 0.0518 & 0.0141 & 0.0105 & -0.0980 \\ 0.0025 & 0.0697 & 0.0327 & -0.0140 & 0.0286 & -0.0084 & -0.0422 & 0.0329 \end{bmatrix}$$

Notice that most of the energy of the DCT of B_1 is compact at the DC value (DC coefficient =5.7656).

The watermark, which is a pseudo-random real number generated using random number generator and a seed value (key), is given by:

$$W = \begin{bmatrix} 1.6505 & 0.2759 & -0.8579 & -1.6130 & -1.0693 & 0.2259 & -0.4570 & 0.7167 \\ 0.7922 & -0.6320 & 0.8350 & -0.3888 & 0.4993 & 0.2174 & -1.6095 & -0.9269 \\ 0.7319 & 0.7000 & 1.6191 & -0.0870 & 0.7859 & 0.1870 & -0.3633 & 2.5061 \\ 0.9424 & 0.8966 & -0.0246 & -1.4165 & 0.5422 & 0.1539 & -1.1958 & 0.0374 \\ 0.2059 & 1.8204 & 0.5224 & -0.9099 & -1.6061 & -0.7764 & -0.8054 & -1.0894 \\ -0.1303 & -0.3008 & 1.6732 & -1.1281 & -0.3946 & 0.8294 & -0.0007 & -0.7952 \\ 0.0509 & -1.7409 & 1.1233 & 0.3541 & 0.1994 & -0.0855 & 0.1278 & -0.6312 \\ -0.1033 & -1.7087 & 0.5532 & 0.2068 & 2.5359 & 1.7004 & -0.6811 & -0.7771 \end{bmatrix}$$

Applying DCT on W, the result is:

Figure 6. Basic block diagram of the watermarking process

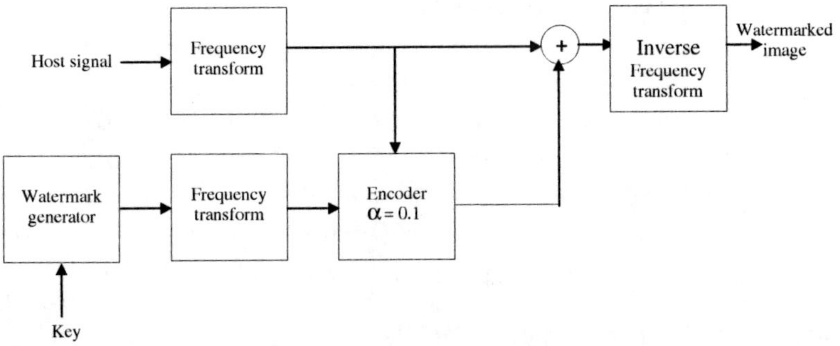

$$DCT(W) = \begin{bmatrix} 0.2390 & 1.5861 & 0.1714 & 0.7187 & -0.3163 & -1.0925 & 2.6675 & 1.3164 \\ 0.1255 & 0.8694 & 2.8606 & -0.2411 & 0.6162 & -1.1665 & -0.1335 & -0.8266 \\ 0.0217 & -1.4093 & -1.3448 & 1.3837 & 1.3513 & 1.0022 & 0.8743 & 0.3735 \\ -1.7482 & 0.8337 & 1.5394 & -0.0076 & -1.7946 & 1.1027 & -0.4434 & -0.5771 \\ -0.7653 & 0.5313 & 0.9799 & 1.2930 & -0.0309 & -0.9858 & -0.9079 & -0.8152 \\ 0.4222 & -0.9041 & 1.2626 & -0.0979 & 0.6200 & 0.1858 & -0.1021 & 0.1452 \\ 1.4724 & -1.1217 & 0.7449 & -0.2921 & -0.3144 & -0.7244 & 0.4119 & 0.0535 \\ 0.4453 & 0.0380 & 0.9942 & -1.5048 & 0.0656 & 0.4169 & -0.7046 & -0.5278 \end{bmatrix}$$

B_1 is watermarked with W as shown in the block diagram in Figure 6 according to:

$$f_w = f + \alpha \cdot w \cdot f \qquad \textbf{(6)}$$

where f is a DCT coefficient of the host signal (B_1), w is a DCT coefficient of the watermark signal (W) and α is the watermarking energy, which is taken to be 0.1 (α=0.1). The DC value of the host signal is not modified. This is to minimize the distortion of the watermarked image. Therefore, the DC value will be kept un-watermarked.

The above equation can be rewritten in matrix format as follows:

$$DCT(B_{1w}) = \begin{cases} DCT(B_1) + \alpha \cdot DCT(W) \cdot DCT(B_1) & \textit{for all } \text{coefficient } \textit{except DC value} \\ DCT(B_1) & \textit{for DC value} \end{cases} \qquad \textbf{(7)}$$

where B_{1w} is the watermarked signal of B_1. The result after applying the above equation can be calculated as:

$$DCT(B_{1w}) = \begin{bmatrix} 5.7656 & 0.1346 & -0.0386 & 0.0172 & -0.0090 & -0.0028 & -0.0598 & -0.0079 \\ -0.0532 & 0.1258 & 0.0830 & 0.0101 & -0.0145 & -0.0101 & -0.0409 & -0.0308 \\ -0.0355 & 0.0635 & -0.0117 & -0.0467 & -0.0092 & -0.0206 & -0.0947 & 0.0066 \\ -0.0786 & 0.0472 & 0.0438 & -0.0090 & -0.0323 & 0.0202 & -0.0029 & -0.0555 \\ -0.0984 & 0.0527 & 0.0037 & -0.0400 & -0.0092 & 0.0132 & 0.0478 & -0.0255 \\ -0.0823 & -0.0058 & 0.0099 & 0.0238 & -0.0212 & -0.0368 & -0.0580 & -0.0742 \\ -0.0485 & 0.0325 & -0.0494 & -0.0146 & 0.0502 & 0.0131 & 0.0109 & -0.0985 \\ 0.0026 & 0.0700 & 0.0360 & -0.0119 & 0.0288 & -0.0088 & -0.0392 & 0.0312 \end{bmatrix}$$

Notice that the DC value of $DCT(B_{1w})$is the same as the DC value of $DCT(B_1)$. To construct the watermarked image, the inverse DCT of the above two-dimensional array is computed to give:

$$B_{1w} = \begin{bmatrix} 0.7331 & 0.8361 & 0.6609 & 0.7228 & 0.5991 & 0.6026 & 0.6175 & 0.5922 \\ 0.7818 & 0.7809 & 0.7735 & 0.7011 & 0.7712 & 0.6955 & 0.7755 & 0.6998 \\ 0.7734 & 0.7746 & 0.6973 & 0.7682 & 0.7663 & 0.7002 & 0.6956 & 0.6920 \\ 0.7064 & 0.7093 & 0.7045 & 0.7037 & 0.7013 & 0.7692 & 0.6986 & 0.6933 \\ 0.7872 & 0.7100 & 0.7789 & 0.7081 & 0.7067 & 0.7012 & 0.7013 & 0.6996 \\ 0.7051 & 0.7032 & 0.7026 & 0.7801 & 0.7078 & 0.7741 & 0.7015 & 0.6978 \\ 0.7017 & 0.7765 & 0.7002 & 0.7067 & 0.7765 & 0.7026 & 0.7736 & 0.6992 \\ 0.6877 & 0.7048 & 0.7712 & 0.7800 & 0.7793 & 0.7001 & 0.7044 & 0.6974 \end{bmatrix}$$

It is easy to compare B_{1w} and B_1 and see the very slight modification due to the watermark.

Robust Watermarking Scheme Requirements

In this section, the requirements needed for an effective watermarking system are introduced. The requirements are application-dependent, but some of them are common to most practical applications. One of the challenges for researchers in this field is that these requirements compete with each other. Such general requirements are listed below. Detailed discussions of them can be found in Petitcolas (n.d.), Voyatzis, Nikolaidis and Pitas (1998), Ruanaidh, Dowling and Boland (1996), Ruanaidh and Pun (1997), Hsu and Wu (1996), Ruanaidh, Boland and Dowling (1996), Hernandez, Amado and Perez-Gonzalez (2000), Swanson, Zhu and Tewfik (1996), Wolfgang and Delp (1996), Craver, Memon, Yeo and Yeung (1997), Zeng and Liu (1997), and Cox and Miller (1997).

Security

Effectiveness of a watermark algorithm cannot be based on the assumption that possible attackers do not know the embedding process that the watermark went through (Swanson et al., 1998). The robustness of some commercial products is based on such an assumption. The point is that by making the technique very robust and making the embedding algorithm public, this actually reduces the computational complexity for the attacker to remove the watermark. Some of the techniques use the original non-marked image in the extraction process. They use a secret key to generate the watermark for security purpose.

Invisibility

Perceptual Invisibility. Researchers have tried to hide the watermark in such a way that the watermark is impossible to notice. However, this requirement conflicts with other requirements such as robustness, which is an important requirement when facing watermarking attacks. For this purpose, the characteristics of the human visual system (HVS) for images and the *human auditory system* (HAS) for audio signal are exploited in the watermark embedding process.

Statistical Invisibility. An unauthorized person should not detect the watermark by means of statistical methods. For example, the availability of a great number of digital works watermarked with the same code should not allow the extraction of the embedded mark by applying statistically based attacks. A possible solution is to use a content dependent watermark (Voyatzis et al., 1998).

Robustness

Digital images commonly are subject to many types of distortions, such as lossy compression, filtering, resizing, contrast enhancement, cropping, rotation and so on. The mark should be detectable even after such distortions have occurred. Robustness against signal distortion is better achieved if the watermark is placed in perceptually significant parts of the image signal (Ruanaidh et al., 1996). For example, a watermark hidden among perceptually insignificant data is likely not to survive lossy compression. Moreover, resistance to geometric manipulations, such as translation, resizing, rotation and cropping is still an open issue. These geometric manipulations are still very common.

Watermarking Extraction: False Negative/Positive Error Probability

Even in the absence of attacks or signal distortions, false negative error probability (the probability of failing to detect the embedded watermark) and of detecting a watermark when, in fact, one does not exist (false positive error probability), must be very small. Usually, statistically based algorithms have no problem in satisfying this requirement.

Capacity Issue (Bit Rate)

The watermarking algorithm should embed a predefined number of bits to be hidden in the host signal. This number will depend on the application at hand.

Figure 7. Digital watermarking requirements triangle

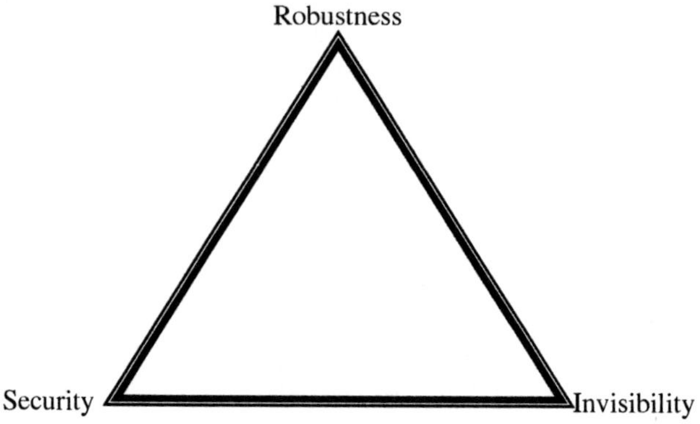

There is no general rule for this. However, in the image case, the possibility of embedding into the image at least 300-400 bits should be guaranteed. In general, the number of bits that can be hidden in data is limited. Capacity issues were discussed by Servetto et al. (1998).

Comments

One can understand the challenge to researchers in this field since the above requirements compete with each other. The important test of a watermarking method would be that it is accepted and used on a large, commercial scale, and that it stands up in a court of law. None of the digital techniques have yet to meet all of these requirements. In fact the first three requirements (security, robustness and invisibility) can form sort of a triangle (Figure 7), which means that if one is improved, the other two might be affected.

DIGITAL WATERMARKING ALGORITHMS

Current watermarking techniques described in the literature can be grouped into three main classes. The first includes the transform domain methods, which embed the data by modulating the transform domain signal coefficients. The second class includes the spatial domain techniques. These embed the watermark by directly modifying the pixel values of the original image. The transform domain techniques have been found to have the greater robustness, when the watermarked signals are tested after having been subjected to common signal distortions. The third class is the feature domain technique. This technique takes into account region, boundary and object characteristics. Such watermarking methods may present additional advantages in terms of detection and recovery from geometric attacks, compared to previous approaches.

In this chapter, the algorithms in this survey are organized according to their embedding domain, as indicated in Figure 1. These are grouped into:

1. spatial domain techniques
2. transform domain techniques
3. feature domain techniques

However, due to the amount of published work in the field of watermarking technology, the main focus will be on wavelet-based watermarking technique papers. The wavelet domain is the most efficient domain for watermarking embedding so far. However, the review considers some other techniques, which serve the purpose of giving a broader picture of the existing watermarking algorithms. Some examples of spatial domain and fractal-based techniques will be reviewed.

Spatial Domain Techniques

This section gives a brief introduction to the spatial domain technique to give the reader some background information about watermarking in this domain. Many spatial techniques are based on adding fixed amplitude pseudo noise (PN) sequences to an image. In this case, *E* and *D* (as introduced in previous section) are simply the addition and subtraction operators, respectively. PN sequences are also used as the "spreading key" when considering the host media as the noise in a spread spectrum system, where the watermark is the transmitted message. In this case, the PN sequence is used to spread the data bits over the spectrum to hide the data.

When applied in the spatial or temporal domains, these approaches modify the least significant bits (LSB) of the host data. The invisibility of the watermark is achieved on the assumption that the LSB data are visually insignificant. The watermark is generally recovered using knowledge of the PN sequence (and perhaps other secret keys, like watermark location) and the statistical properties of the embedding process. Two LSB techniques are described in Schyndel, Tirkel and Osborne (1994). The first replaces the LSB of the image with a PN sequence, while the second adds a PN sequence to the LSB of the data. In Bender et al. (1996), a direct sequence spread spectrum technique is proposed to embed a watermark in host signals. One of these, LSB-based, is a statistical technique that randomly chooses n pairs of points (a_i, b_i) in an image and increases the brightness of a_i by one unit while simultaneously decreasing the brightness of b_i. Another PN sequence spread spectrum approach is proposed in Wolfgang and Delp (1996), where the authors hide data by adding a fixed amplitude PN sequence to the image. Wolfgang and Delp add fixed amplitude 2D PN sequence obtained from a long 1D PN sequence to the image. In Schyndel et al. (1994) and Pitas and Kaskalis (1995), an image is randomly split into two subsets of equal size. The mean value of one of the subsets is increased by a constant factor *k*. In effect, the scheme adds high frequency noise to the image.

In Tanaka, Nakamura and Matsui (1990), the watermarking algorithms use a predictive coding scheme to embed the watermark into the image. Also, the watermark is embedded into the image by dithering the image based on the statistical properties of the image. In Bruyndonckx, Quisquater and Macq (1995), a watermark for an image is generated by modifying the luminance values inside 8x8 blocks of pixels, adding one extra bit of information to each block. The encoder secretly makes the choice of the modified block. The Xerox Data Glyph technology (Swanson et al., 1998) adds a bar code to its images according to a predetermined set of geometric modifications. Hirotsugu (1996) constructs a watermark by concealing graph data in the LSBs of the image.

In general, approaches that modify the LSB of the data using a fixed magnitude PN sequence are highly sensitive to signal processing operations and are easily corrupted. A contributing factor to this weakness is the fact that the watermark must be invisible. As a result, the magnitude of the embedded noise is limited by the portions of the image or audio for example, smooth regions, that most easily exhibit the embedded noise.

Transform Domain Techniques

Many transform-based watermarking techniques have been proposed. To embed a watermark, a transformation is first applied to the host data, and then modifications are made to the transform coefficients.

The work presented in Ruanaidh, Dowling and Boland (1996), Ruanaidh, Boland and Dowling (1996), Bors and Pitas (1996), Nikolaidis and Pitas (1996), Pitas (1996), Boland, Ruanaidh and Dautzenberg (1995), Cox et al. (1995, 1996), Tilki and Beex (1996) and Hartung and Girod (1996) can be considered to be the pioneering work that utilizes the transform domain for the watermarking process. These papers were published at early stages of development of watermarking algorithms, so they represent a basic framework for this research. Therefore, the details of these papers will not be described since most of them discuss the basic algorithms that are not robust enough for watermarking copyright protection. They are mentioned here for those readers who are interested in the historical background of the watermarking research field. In this section, the state of the art of the current watermarking algorithms using the transform domain is presented. The section has three main parts, including discussions of wavelet-based watermarking, DCT-based watermarking and fractal domain watermarking.

Digital Watermarking Using Wavelet Decomposition

Many papers propose to use the wavelet transform domain for watermarking because of a number of advantages that can be gained by using this approach. The work described in many of the works referenced in this chapter implement watermarking in the wavelet domain. The wavelet-based watermarking algorithms that are most relevant to the proposed method are discussed here.

A perceptually based technique for watermarking images is proposed in Wei, Quin and Fu (1998). The watermark is inserted in the wavelet coefficients and its amplitudes are controlled by the wavelet coefficients so that watermark noise does not exceed the just-noticeable difference of each wavelet coefficient. Meanwhile, the order of inserting watermark noise in the wavelet coefficients is the same as the order of the visual significance of the wavelet coefficients (Wei et al., 1998). The invisibility and the robustness of the digital watermark may be guaranteed; however, security is not, which is a major drawback of these algorithms.

Zhu et al. (1998) proposed to implement a four-level wavelet decomposition using a watermark of a Gaussian sequence of pseudo-random real numbers. The detail sub-band coefficients are watermarked. The watermark sequence at different resolution levels is nested:

$$\ldots \subset W_3 \subset W_2 \subset W_1 \quad \textbf{(8)}$$

where W_j denotes the watermark sequence w_i at resolution level j. The length of W_j used for an image size of MxM is given by

$$N_j = 3 \cdot \frac{M^2}{2^{2.j}} \quad \textbf{(9)}$$

This algorithm can easily be built into video watermarking applications based on a 3-D wavelet transform due to its simple structure. The hierarchical nature of the wavelet representation allows multi-resolutional detection of the digital watermark, which is a Gaussian distributed random vector added to all the high pass bands in the wavelet domain. It is shown that when subjected to distortion from compression, the corresponding watermark can still be correctly identified at each resolution in the DWT domain. Robustness against rotation and other geometric attacks are not investigated in this chapter. Also, the watermarking is not secure because one can extract the watermark statistically once the algorithm is known by the attackers.

The approach used in Wolfgang, Podlchuk and Delp (1998, 1999) is four-level wavelet decomposition using 7/9-bi-orthogonal filters. To embed the watermarking, the following model is used:

$$f'(m,n) = \begin{cases} f(m,n) + j(m,n) \cdot w_i & \text{if} \quad f(m,n) > j(m,n) \\ f(m,n) & \text{otherwise} \end{cases} \quad \textbf{(10)}$$

Only transform coefficients $f(m, n)$ with values above their corresponding JND threshold $j(m, n)$ are selected. The JND used here is based on the work of Watson et al. (1997). The original image is needed for watermarking extraction. Also, Wolfgang et al. (1998) compare the robustness of watermarks embedded in the DCT vs. the DWT domain when subjected to lossy compression attack. They found that it is better to match the compression and watermarking domains. However, the selection of coefficients does not include the perceptual significant parts of the image, which may lead to loss of the watermarking coefficient inserted in the insignificant parts of the host image. Also, low-pass filtering of the image will affect the watermark inserted in the high-level coefficients of the host signal.

Dugad et al. (1998) used a Gaussian sequence of pseudo-random real numbers as a watermark. The watermark is inserted in a few selected significant coefficients. The wavelet transform is a three-level decomposition with Daubechies-8 filters. The algorithm selects coefficients in all detail sub-bands whose magnitude is above a given threshold T_1 and modifies these coefficients according to:

$$f'(m, n) = f(m, n) + \alpha \cdot |f(m, n)| \cdot w_i \tag{11}$$

During the extraction process, only coefficients above the detection threshold $T_1 > T_2$ are taken into consideration. The visual masking in Dugad et al. (1998) is done implicitly due to the time-frequency localization property of the DWT. Since the detail sub-bands where the watermark is added contain typically edge information, the signature's energy is concentrated in the edge areas of the image. This makes the watermark invisible because the human eye is less sensitive to modifications of texture and edge information. However, these locations are considered to be the easiest locations to modify by compression or other common signal processing attacks, which reduces the robustness of the algorithm.

Inoue et al. (1998, 2000) suggested the use of a three-level decomposition using 5/3 symmetric short kernel filters (SSKF) or Daubechies-16 filters. They classify wavelet coefficients as insignificant or significant by using zero-tree, which is defined in the embedded zero-tree wavelet (EZW) algorithm. Therefore, wavelet coefficients are segregated as significant or insignificant using the notion of zero-trees (Lewis & Knwles, 1992; Pitas & Kaskalis, 1995; Schyndel et al., 1994; Shapiro, 1993). If the threshold *is* T, then a DWT coefficient $f(m, n)$ is said to be insignificant:

$$\text{if } |f(m, n)| < T \tag{12}$$

If a coefficient and all of its descendants[1] are insignificant with respect to T, then the set of these insignificant wavelet coefficients is called a zero-tree for the threshold T.

This watermarking approach considers two main groups. One handles significant coefficients where all zero-trees Z for the threshold T are chosen. This group does not consider the approximation sub-band (LL). All coefficients of zero-tree Z_i are set as follows:

$$f'(m,n) = \begin{cases} -m & if \quad w_i = 0 \\ +m & if \quad w_i = 1 \end{cases} \tag{13}$$

The second group manipulates significant coefficients from the coarsest scale detail sub-bands (LH_3, HL_3, HH_3). The coefficient selection is based on:

$$T_1 < |f(m, n)| < T_2, \text{ where } T_2 > T_1 > T \tag{14}$$

The watermark here replaces a selected coefficient via quantization according to:

$$f'(m,n) = \begin{cases} T_2 & w_i = 1 \text{ and } f(m,n) > 0 \\ T_1 & w_i = 0 \text{ and } f(m,n) > 0 \\ -T_2 & w_i = 1 \text{ and } f(m,n) < 0 \\ -T_1 & w_i = 0 \text{ and } f(m,n) < 0 \end{cases} \tag{15}$$

To extract the watermark in the first group, the average coefficient value M for the coefficients belonging to zero-tree Z_i is first computed as follows:

$$w_i = \begin{cases} 0 & Mi < 0 \\ 1 & Mi \geq 0 \end{cases} \tag{16}$$

However, for the second group, the watermark w_i is detected from a significant coefficient $f^*(m, n)$ according to:

$$w_i = \begin{cases} 0 & |f^*(m,n)| < (T_1 + T_2)/2 \\ 1 & |f^*(m,n)| \geq (T_1 + T_2)/2 \end{cases} \tag{17}$$

This approach makes use of the positions of zero-tree roots to guide the extraction algorithms. Experimental results showed that the proposed method gives the watermarked image of better quality compared to other existing systems at that time and is robust against JPEG compression. On the other hand, the proposed approach may lose synchronization because it depends on insignificant coefficients, which of course harms the robustness of the watermarking embedding process.

The watermark is added to significant coefficients in significant sub-bands in Wang and Kuo (1998a, 1998b). First, the multi-threshold wavelet code (MTWC) is used to achieve the image compression purpose. Unlike other embedded wavelet coders, which use a single initial threshold in their successive approximate quantization (SAQ), MTWC adopts different initial thresholds in different sub-bands. The additive embedding formula can be represented as:

$$f_s'(m,n) = f_s(m,n) + \alpha_s \cdot T_s \cdot w_i \tag{18}$$

where α_s is the scaling factors for the sub-band *s, and* β_s is used to weight the sub-bands. $T_{s,i}$ is the current sub-band threshold. The initial threshold of a sub-band s is defined by:

$$T_{s,0} = \beta_s \frac{\max |f_s|}{2} \tag{19}$$

This approach picks out coefficients whose magnitude is larger than the current sub-band threshold, $T_{s,i}$. The sub-band's threshold is divided by two after watermarking a sub-band. Figure 8 shows the watermarking scheme by Wang.

Xie et al. developed a watermarking approach that decomposes the host image to get a low-frequency approximation representation (Xie & Arce, 1998). The watermark, which is a binary sequence, is embedded in the approximation image (*LL* sub-band) of the host image. The coefficients of a non-overlapping 3x1 sliding window are selected each time. First, the elements b_1, b_2, b_3 of the local sliding window are sorted in ascending order. They can be seen in Figure 9. Then the range between min $|b_j|$ and max $|b_j|$, $j = 1 \ldots 3$ is divided into intervals of length:

$$\Delta = \alpha \cdot \frac{\max |b_j| - \min |b_j|}{2} \tag{20}$$

Next, the median of the coefficient of these elements is quantized to a multiple of D. The median coefficient is altered to represent the watermark information bit. This coefficient is updated in the host image's sub-band. The extraction by this algorithm is done blindly without referring to the original image.

This algorithm is designed for both image authentication applications and copyright protection. The number of decomposition steps of this algorithm

Figure 8. Pyramid two-level wavelet decomposition structure of the Wang algorithm

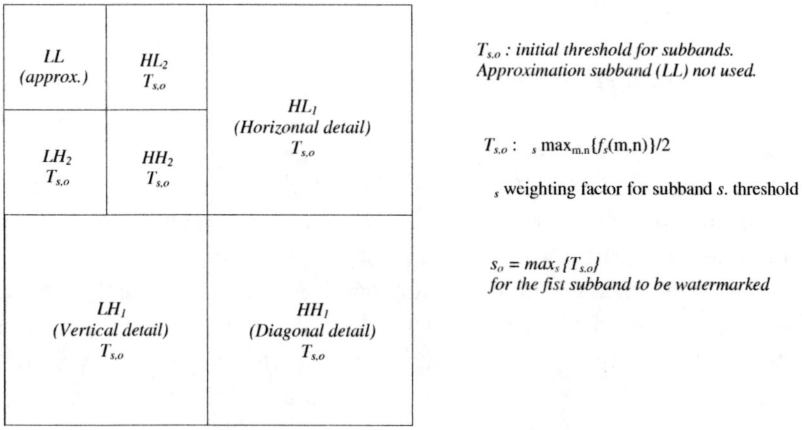

Figure 9. Xie watermarking block diagram (The elements b_1, b_2, b_3 *of the local sliding window are sorted in ascending order.)*

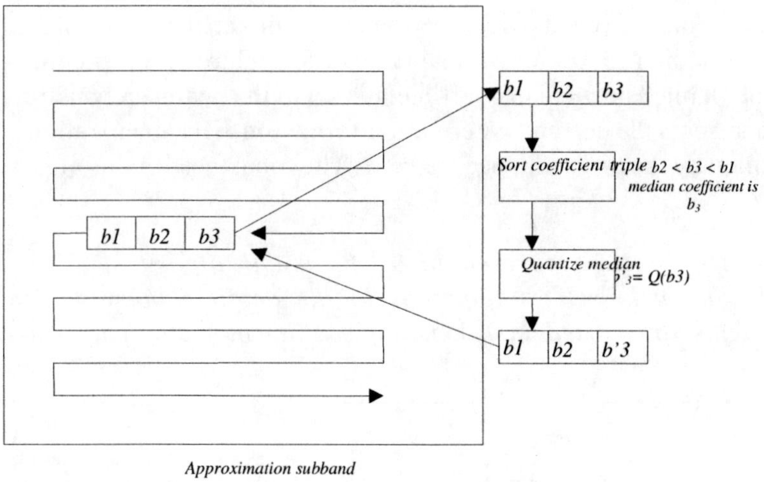

determines its robustness. Very good robustness can be achieved by employing five-level wavelet decomposition, which is costly from a computation point of view.

Xia et al. (1997) proposed an algorithm using a two-level decomposition with Haar wavelet filters. Pseudo-random codes are added to the large coefficients at the high and middle frequency bands of the DWT of an image. The watermark coefficients are embedded using:

$$f(m,n)' = f(m,n) + \alpha \cdot f(m,n)^{\beta} \cdot w_i \quad \textbf{(21)}$$

The *LL* sub-band does not carry any watermark information. α is the weighting or watermarking energy factor as explained before, and β indicates the amplification of large coefficients. Therefore, this algorithm merges most of the watermarking energy in edges and texture, which represents most of the coefficients in the detail sub-bands. This will enhance invisibility of the watermarking process because the human eye is less sensitive to changes in edge and texture information, compared to changes in low-frequency components that are concentrated in the *LL* sub-band. Also, it is shown that this method is robust to some common image distortions. However, low pass and median filters will affect the robustness of the algorithm since most of the watermarking coefficients are in the high frequency coefficients of the host signal.

Kundur and Hatzinakos proposed to apply the Daubechies family of orthogonal wavelet filters to decompose the original image to a three-level multi-resolution representation (1998). Figure 10 shows the scheme representation of this algorithm.

The algorithm pseudo-randomly selects locations in the detail sub-bands. The selected coefficients are sorted in ascending coefficient magnitude order. Then the median coefficient is quantized to designate the information of a single watermark bit. The median coefficient is set to the nearest reconstruction point that represents the current watermark information. The quantization step size is controlled by the bin width parameter Δ. The robustness of this algorithm is not

Figure 10. Scheme representation of Kundur algorithm (The algorithm pseudo-randomly selects locations in the detail subbands. The selected coefficients are sorted in ascending coefficient magnitude order.)

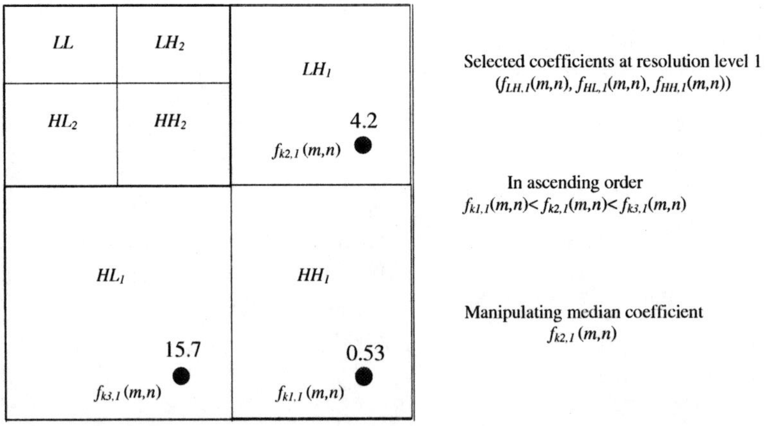

good enough; therefore, the authors suggest an improvement to the algorithm in Kundur and Hatzinakos (1999). Coarser quantization in this algorithm enhances robustness. However, this also increases distortion in the watermarked signal.

Also, Kundur and Hatzinakos (1998) proposed a fragile watermark. They call such a technique a telltale tamper-proofing method. Their design embeds a fragile watermark in the discrete wavelet domain of the signal by quantizing the corresponding coefficients with user-specified keys. The watermark is a binary signature, which is embedded into key-selected detail sub-band coefficients. This algorithm is built on the quantization method (Kundur & Hatzinakos, 1998). An integer wavelet transform is introduced to avoid round-off errors during the inverse transform, because round-off may be considered as a tampering attempt. This algorithm is just an extension of Kundur and Hatzinakos (1998); however, it is not used for copyright protection, just for tamper proofing.

Kundur and Hatzinakos also developed an algorithm for still image watermarking in which the watermark embedding process employs multi-resolution fusion techniques and incorporates a model of the human visual system (Kundur & Hatzinakos, 1997). The watermark in Kundur and Hatzinakos (1997) is a logo image, which is decomposed using the DWT. The watermark is chosen to be a factor of 2^M smaller than the host image. Both the original image and the watermark are transformed into the DWT domain. The host image is decomposed in L steps (L is an integer, $L \leq M$). The watermark is embedded in all detail sub-bands. Kundur presented rules to select all parameters of the HVS model and the scaling parameters. Simulation results demonstrated robustness of the algorithm to common image distortions. The algorithm is not robust to rotation.

Podilchukand Zeng (1998) proposed two watermarking techniques for digital images that are based on utilizing visual models, which have been developed in the context of image compression. Specifically, they proposed watermarking schemes where visual models are used to determine image-dependent upper bounds on watermark insertion. They propose perceptually based watermarking schemes in two frameworks: the block-based discrete cosine transform and multi-resolution wavelet framework, and discuss the merits of each one. Their schemes are shown to provide very good results both in terms of image transparency and robustness.

Chae et al. (1998a, 1998b) proposed a grayscale image, with as much as 25% of the host image size to be used as a watermark. They suggested using a one-level decomposition on both the host and the logo image. Each coefficient of the original signal is modified to insert the logo image. The block diagram of this scheme can be seen in Figure 11. The coefficients have to be expanded due to the size of the logo image, which is 25% of the host image. For the logo image, *A, B, C* stand for the most significant byte (MSB), the middle byte, and the least significant byte (LSBe) respectively. A, B, C represent a 24-bits per coefficient. Three 24-bit numbers A', B', C' are produced by considering A, B and C as their

Figure 11. Chae watermarking process (The coefficients have to be expanded due to the size of the logo image, which is 25% of the host image.)

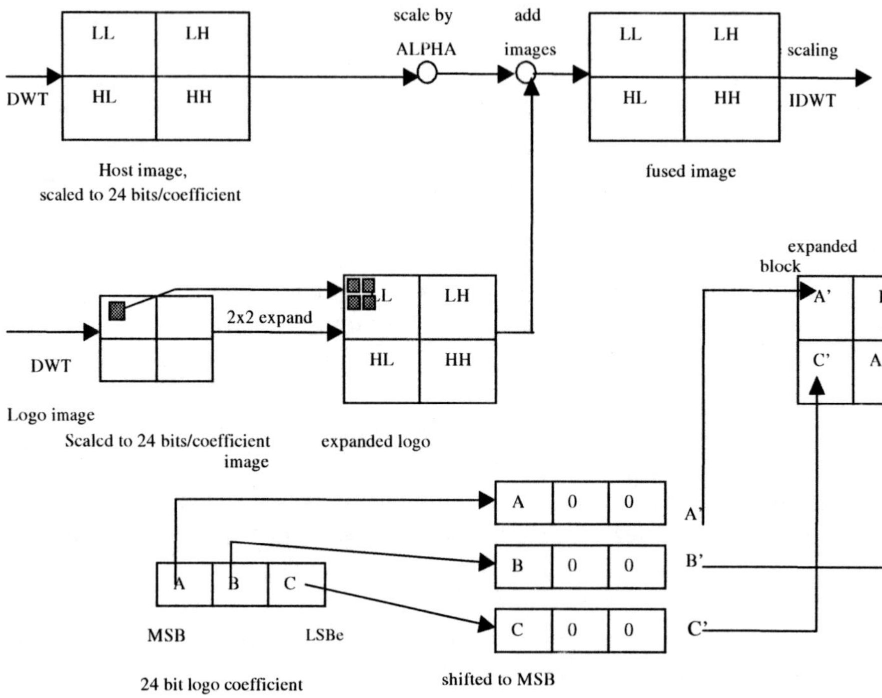

most significant byte, respectively. Also, the middle and least significant bytes are set to zero. Then a block of 2x2 is built. The logo image is added to the original image by:

$$f'(m, n) = \alpha\ f(m, n) + w(m, n) \qquad \textbf{(22)}$$

where $f(m,n)$ is the DWT coefficient of the original image and the DWT coefficients of the logo image are given by $w(m, n)$. This algorithm is limited to logo images that are 25% of the size of the host image. Also, there is another constraint. It is difficult to use higher wavelet decomposition steps since the watermark is a logo image. Also, their experimental results show that the watermarked image is transparent to embedding and the quality of the extracted signature is high even when the watermarked image is subjected to wavelet compression and JPEG lossy compression. On the other hand, geometric attacks were not studied in this work. The capacity issue with this scheme can be considered as trade-off between the quantity of hidden data and the quality of the watermarked image. Murkherjee et al. (1998) and Chae et al. (1998) also introduced a watermark sequence w_i of p-ary symbols. Similar to the work of

Chae et al. (1998), a one-level DWT decomposition of both the original and watermark image is calculated and the coefficients are quantized into p-levels. Four transform coefficients are arranged together to form an n-vector. The coefficients of the approximation sub-band of the logo image are inserted in the corresponding approximation sub-band of the host image. The same method is applied for the detail sub-bands of the watermark and the host signals. The embedding process of the DWT host vector coefficients (v) is given by:

$$v' = v + \alpha \cdot C(w_i) \qquad \textbf{(23)}$$

$C(w_i)$ is the codeword of the watermark coefficients of w_i. To detect the watermark, the original image is required. The error vector:

$$e = \frac{v^* - v}{\alpha} \qquad \textbf{(24)}$$

is used in a nearest-neighbor search against the codebook to reconstruct the embedded information according to:

$$w_i = \min_{wi} \| C(w_i) - e \| \qquad \textbf{(25)}$$

Examine Figure 12 for an illustration of the vector quantization process. The vector quantization approach is more flexible than that of Chae et al. (1998). It is possible to control robustness using the embedding strength (α) and adjust quality of the embedded logo image via the quantization level (p). However, this quantization algorithm has to find the closest vector in the codebook; this is computationally expensive if the codebook is large.

A method for multi-index decision (maximizing deviation method) based watermarking is proposed in Zhihui and Liang (2000). This watermarking technique is designed and implemented in the DCT domain as well as the wavelet domain utilizing HVS (Human Visual System) models. Their experimental results show that the watermark based on the wavelet transform more closely approaches the maximum data hiding capacity in the local image compared to other frequency transform domains. Tsekeridou and Pitas presented watermarks that are structured in such a way as to attain spatial self-similarity with respect to a Cartesian grid. Their scheme is implemented in the wavelet domain. They use self-similar watermarks (quasi scale-invariant), which are expected to be robust against scaling but not other geometric transformation (Tsekeridou & Pitas, 2000). On the other hand, hardware architecture is presented for the embedded zero-tree wavelet (EZW) algorithm in Hsai et al. (2000). This hardware architecture alleviates the communication overhead without sacrificing PSNR (signal-to-noise ratio).

Figure 12. Vector quantization procedure — There is a representative set of sequences called the codebook (Given a source sequence or source vector, it is represented with one of the elements in the codebook.))

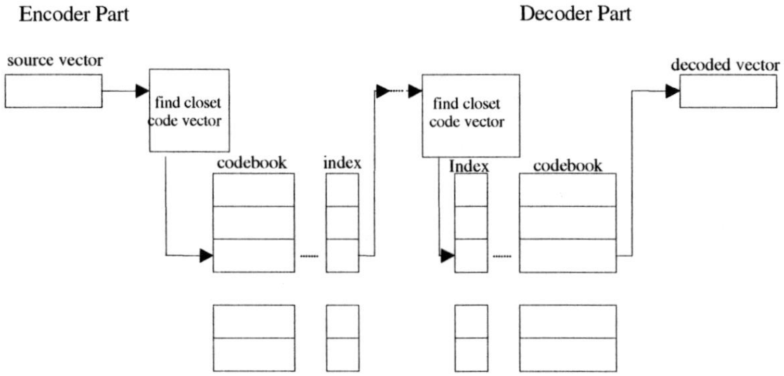

Loo and Kingsbury proposed a watermarking algorithm in the complex wavelet domain (2000). They model watermarking as a communication process. It is shown in Loo and Kingsbury (2000) that the complex wavelet domain has relatively high capacity for embedding information in the host signal. They concluded that the complex wavelet domain is a good domain for watermarking. However, it is computationally very expensive.

The watermark and the host image are decomposed into a multi-resolution representation in the work of Hsu and Wu (1996, 1998, 1999). The watermark is a logo binary image. The size of the watermark image is 50% of the size of the original image. Daubechies six-filter is used to decompose the original image; however, the binary logo image is decomposed with the resolution-reduction (RR) function of the joint binary image experts group (JBIG) compression standard. It is more appropriate for bi-level images such as text or line drawings than normal images; that is, it is not practical for normal images. A differential layer is obtained from subtraction of an up-scaled version of the residual from the original watermark pattern. The differential layer and the residual of the watermark are inserted into the detail sub-bands of the host image at the same resolution. The even columns of the watermark components are hidden into the HL_i sub-bands. On the other hand, the odd columns are embedded into the LH_i sub-bands. There are no watermarking components inserted in the approximation image to avoid visible image distortion. Also, the HH_i sub-bands are not modified due to the low robustness in this sub-band. The residual mask shown in Figure 13 is used to alter the neighboring relationship of host image coefficients. During extraction, the original image is required. Using any compression filters that pack most of the image's energy in the approximation image will

Figure 13. Scheme for binary watermarking embedding algorithm proposed by Hsu's

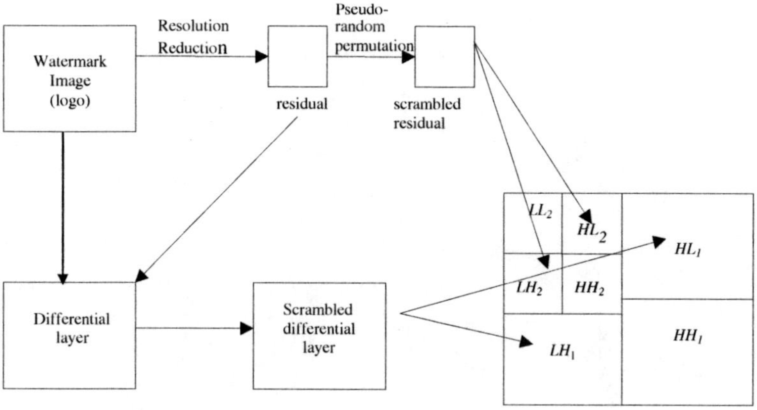

seriously damage the robustness of this algorithm. This is because the watermark information is embedded in the detail sub-band.

Ejima and Miyazki suggested using a wavelet packet of image and video watermarking (2000). Figure 14 depicts the wavelet packet representation used by Ejima. The energy for each sub-band $B_{i,j}$ is calculated. Then, certain sub-bands are pseudo-randomly selected according to their energy. The mean absolute coefficient value of each selected sub-band is quantized and used to encode one bit of watermark information. Finally, pseudo-randomly selected coefficients of that sub-band are manipulated to reflect the quantized coefficient mean value. This type of algorithm generates redundant information since the wavelet packet generates details and approximation sub-band for each resolution, which adds to the computation overhead.

Kim et al. (1999) proposed to insert a watermark into the large coefficients in each DWT band of L=3, except the first level sub-bands. The number of watermark elements w_i in each of the detail sub-bands is proportional to the energy of that sub-band. They defined this energy by:

$$e_s = \frac{1}{M \cdot N} \sum_{m=0}^{M-1} \sum_{n=0}^{N-1} f(m,n)^2 \qquad \textbf{(26)}$$

where M, N denotes the size of the sub-band. The watermark (w_i) is also a Gaussian sequence of pseudo-random real numbers. In the detail sub-bands, 4,500 coefficients are modified but only 500 are modified in the approximation sub-band. Before inserting the watermark coefficients, the host image DWT

Figure 14. Wavelet packet decomposition proposed by Ejima's

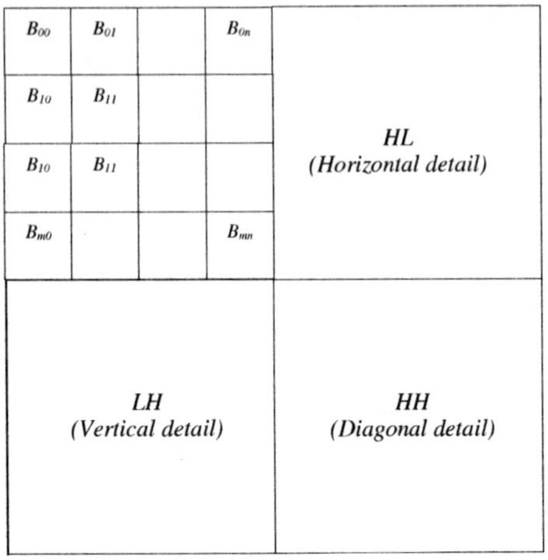

coefficients are sorted according to their magnitude. Experiments described in Kim et al. (1999) show that the proposed three-level wavelet based watermarking method is robust against attacks like JPEG compression, smoothing, and cropping. These references do not mention robustness against geometric distortions such as resizing and rotation.

Perceptually significant coefficients are selected applying the level-adaptive thresholding scheme in by Kim and Moon (1999). The proposed approach in Kim and Moon (1999) decomposes the original image into three levels ($L=3$), applying bi-orthogonal filters. The watermark is a Gaussian sequence of pseudo-random real numbers with a length of 1,000. A level-adaptive thresholding scheme is used by selecting perceptually significant coefficients for each sub-band. The watermark is detected taking into account the level-adaptive scaling factor, which is used during the insertion process. The experimental results presented in Kim and Moon (1999) show that the proposed watermark is invisible to human eyes and robust to various attacks but not geometric transformations. The paper does not address the possibilities of repetitive watermark embedding or watermark weighting to increase robustness.

Discrete Cosine Transform-Based Digital Watermarking

Several watermarking algorithms have been proposed to utilize the DCT. However, the Cox et al. (1995, 1997) and the Koch and Zhao (1995) algorithms are the most well-known DCT-based algorithms. Cox et al. (1995) proposed the most well-known spread spectrum watermarking schemes. Figure 15 shows the block diagram of the Cox algorithm. The image is first subjected to a global DCT. Then, the 1,000 largest coefficients in the DCT domain are selected for watermarking. They used a Gaussian sequence of pseudo-random real numbers

Figure 15. Cox embedding process which classifies DCT coefficients into significant and rejected coeffecients

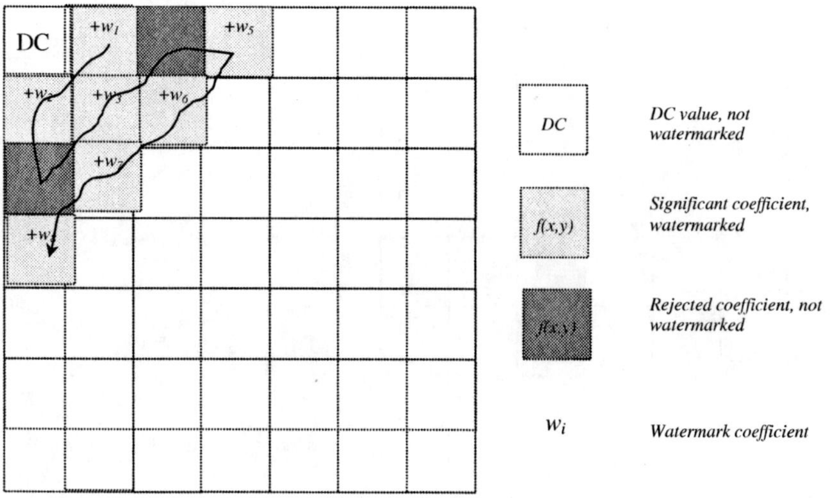

of length 1,000 as a watermark. This approach achieves good robustness against compression and other common signal processing attacks. This is a result of the selection of perceptually significant transform domain coefficients. However, the algorithm is in a weak position against the invariability attack proposed by Craver (1997). Also, the global DCT employed on the image is computationally expensive.

Koch and Zhao (1995) proposed to use a sequence of binary values, $w \in \{0, 1\}$, as a watermark. This approach modifies the difference between randomly selected mid-frequency components in random image blocks. They chose pseudo-randomly 8x8 DCT coefficient blocks. From each block b_i, two coefficients from the mid-frequency range are pseudo-randomly selected. Figure 16 shows the block diagram of this scheme. Each block is quantized using the JPEG quantization matrix and a quantization factor Q. Then, if $f_b(m_1,n_1)$, $f_b(m_2,n_2)$ are the selected coefficients from an 8x8 DCT coefficient block, the absolute difference between them can be represented by:

$$\Delta_b = |f_b(m_1,n_1)| - |f_b(m_2,n_2)| \qquad \textbf{(27)}$$

One bit of watermark information, w_i, is inserted in the selected block b_i by modifying the coefficient pair $f_b(m_1,n_1)$, $f_b(m_2,n_2)$ such that the distance becomes

Figure 16. Koch watermarking process (It operates on 8x8 DCT coefficient blocks and manipulates a pair of coefficients to embed a single bit of watermark information.)

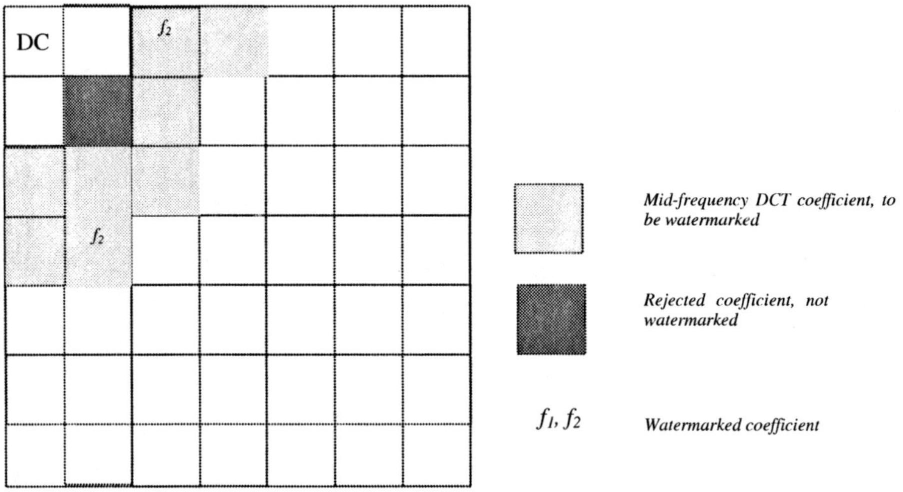

$$\Delta_b = \begin{cases} \geq q & \text{if } w_i = 1 \\ \leq -q & \text{if } w_i = 0 \end{cases} \quad \textbf{(28)}$$

where q is a parameter controlling the embedding strength. This is not a robust algorithm because two coefficients are watermarked from each block. The algorithm is not robust against scaling or rotation because the image dimension is used to generate an appropriate pseudo-random sequence. Also, visible artifacts may be produced because the watermark is inserted in 8x8 DCT domain coefficient blocks. These artifacts may be seen more in smooth regions than in edge regions.

The DCT has been applied also in many other watermarking algorithms. The reader can refer for examples of these different DCT techniques to Bors and Pitas (1996), Piva et al. (1997), Tao and Dickinson (1997), Kankanhalli and Ramakrishnan (1999), Huang and Shi (1998), Kang and Aoki (1999), Goutte and Baskurt (1998), Tang and Aoki (1997), Barni et al. (1997), Duan et al. (1998) and Kim et al. (1999).

Fractal Transform-Based Digital Watermarking

Though a lot of work has been done in the area of invisible watermarks using the DCT and the wavelet-based methods, relatively few references exist for invisible watermarks based on the fractal transform. The reason for this might be the computational expense of the fractal transform. Discussions of fractal watermarking methods are presented in Puate and Jordan (1996), Roche and Dugelay (1998) and Bas et al. (1998). Puate and Jordan (1996) used fractal compression analysis to embed a signature in an image. In fractal analysis, similar patterns are identified in an image and only a limited amount of binary code can be embedded using this method. Since fractal analysis is computationally expensive and some images do not have many large self-similar patterns, the techniques may not be suitable for general use.

Feature Domain Techniques (Second Generation Watermarking)

First generation watermarking (1GW) methods have been mainly focused on applying the watermarking on the entire image/video domain. However, this approach is not compatible with novel approaches for still image and video compression. JPEG2000 and MPEG4/7 standards are the new techniques for image and video compression. They are region- or object-based, as can be seen in the compression process. Also, the 1GW algorithms proposed so far do not satisfy the watermarking requirements.

Second generation watermarking (2GW) was developed in order to increase the robustness and invisibility and to overcome the weaknesses of 1GW. The 2GW methods take into account region, boundary and object characteristics and give additional advantages in terms of detection and recovery from geometric attacks compared to first generation methods. This is achieved by exploiting salient region or object features and characteristics of the image. Also, 2GW methods may be designed so that selective robustness to different classes of attacks is obtained. As a result, watermark flexibility will be improved considerably *(http://www.tsi.enst.fr/~maitre/tatouage//icip2000.html).*

Kutter et al. (1999) published the first second-generation paper in ICIP1999. Kutter et al. used feature point extraction and the Voronoi diagram as an example to define region of interest (ROI) to be watermarked (1995). The feature extraction process is based on a decomposition of the image using Mexican-Hat wavelet mother, as shown in Figure 17. In two dimensions the Mexican-Hat wavelet can be represented as:

$$\Re(\varpi) = \sigma \cdot e^{(\frac{-\varpi^2}{2})} \cdot (1-\varpi^2)$$

$$\sigma = \frac{2}{\sqrt{3} \cdot \pi^{1/4}} \qquad \textbf{(29)}$$

where ϖ is the two-dimensional coordinate of a pixel (refer to Figure 18). Then the wavelet in the spatial-frequency domain can be written as

Figure 17. Mexican-hat mother wavelet function for 1D

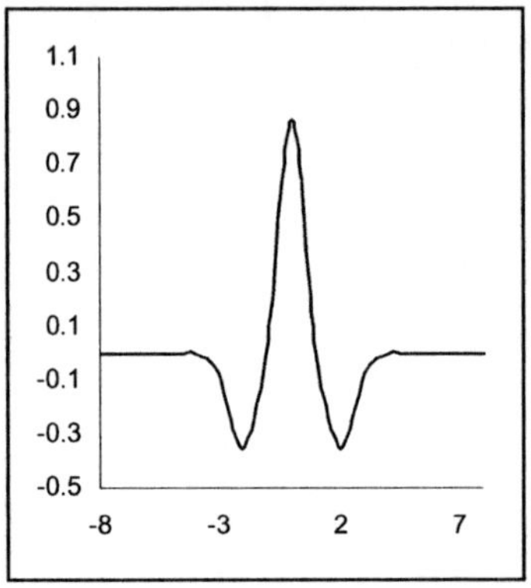

Figure 18. 2D Mexican-hat mother wavelet function in spatial domain (left) and in transform domain (right)

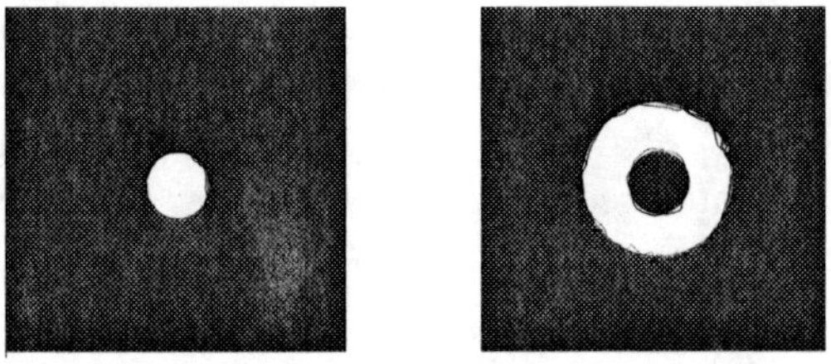

$$\hat{\Re}_H(\vec{k}) = (\vec{k} \cdot \vec{k}) \cdot e^{-1/(\vec{k} \cdot \vec{k})} \quad \textbf{(30)}$$

where $\vec{k}$ is the 2D spatial-frequency variable. The Mexican Hat is always centered at the origin in the frequency domain, which means that the response of a Mexican Hat wavelet is invariant to rotation. However, the stability of the method proposed in Kutter's work depends on the features points. These extracted features have the drawback that their location may change by some pixels because of attack or during the watermarking process. Changing the location of the extracted feature points will cause problems during the detecting process.

Later in 2000, ICIP organized a special session on second-generation digital watermarking algorithms (Baudry et al., 2000; Eggers et al., 2000; Furon & Duhamel, 2000; Loo & Kingsbury, 2000; Lu & Liao, 2000; Miller et al., 2000; Piva et al., 2000; Solachidis et al., 2000). Eight papers were presented in this session. This special session was intended to provide researchers with the opportunity of presenting the latest research results on second-generation digital watermarking Kutter et al. (1999) show that rather than looking at the image from a signal (waveform) point of view, one can try to exploit the objects, or the semantic content, of the image to insert and retrieve the watermark.

In Solachidis (2000), the properties of the Fourier descriptors are utilized in order to devise a blind watermarking scheme for vector graphics images. With this approach, the watermarking method will be robust to a multitude of geometric manipulations and smoothing. But, it is still not robust to polygonal line cropping and insertion/deletion of vertices. The method should be improved more in this direction.

A new modulation (embedding) scheme was proposed by Lu, Liao and Sze (2000) and Lu and Liao (2000). Half of the watermark is positively embedded and the other half is negatively embedded. The locations for the two watermarks are interleaved by inserting complementary watermarks into the host signal. Both the wavelet coefficients of the host signal and the Gaussian watermark sequence are sorted independently in increasing order based on their magnitude. Each time, a pair of wavelet coefficients $(f_{positive}, f_{negative})$ is fetched from the top and bottom of the sorted host image coefficient (f) sequence and a pair of watermark values (w_{top}, w_{bottom}) is fetched the top and the bottom of the sorted watermark sequence, w. The following modulation rules apply for positive modulation:

$$f' = \begin{cases} f_{positive} + J \cdot w_{bottom} \cdot \alpha, & f_{positive} \geq 0 \\ f_{positive} + J \cdot w_{top} \cdot \alpha, & f_{positive} < 0 \end{cases} \tag{31}$$

and negative modulation,

$$f' = \begin{cases} f_{negative} + J \cdot w_{top} \cdot \alpha, & f_{negative} \geq 0 \\ f_{negative} + J \cdot w_{bottom} \cdot \alpha, & f_{negative} < 0 \end{cases} \tag{32}$$

J represents the just noticeable difference value of the selected wavelet coefficient based on the visual model (Wolfgang et al., 1999). α is the weighting factor, which controls the maximum possible modification. It is determined differently for approximation and detail sub-bands. Extraction is achieved by re-ordering the transform coefficients and applying the inverse formula,

$$w^* = \frac{f^* - f}{J - \alpha} \quad \textbf{(33)}$$

This proposed complementary modulation approach can be applied to all spread spectrum watermarking algorithms in other domains. It performs better than random insertion because modulation of one of the two marks will be significantly stronger after attack by simultaneously embedding two complimentary watermarks. Security issues and geometric attacks were not considered in the design of this algorithm. Also, Lu and Liao (2000) used the same approach to propose a semi-blind watermark extraction. The original image is not required at the detection side; only a set of image-dependent parameters is needed. These parameters describe the wavelet coefficient probability distribution that originally has been embedded. The host image coefficient selection is limited to detail sub-bands because only the high frequency bands can be accurately modeled using this approach. More research should focus on the analysis of accuracy of independent component analysis (ICA). This is because ICA is used to represent the host image in this work. Also, the accuracy of automatic segmentation is one of the drawbacks of this method.

Piva et al. proposed a method for a DWT-based object watermarking system for MPEG-4 video streams. Their method relies on an image-watermarking algorithm, which embeds the code in the discrete wavelet transform of each frame. They insert the watermark before compression, that is, frame by frame, for this to be robust against format conversions. However, analysis of the proposed system against a larger set of attacks is not considered in Piva et al. (2000).

The host image is decomposed using the dual tree complex-wavelet transform (DT-CWT) to obtain a three-level multi-resolution representation in Loo and Kingsbury (2000). The mark is a bipolar, $w_i \in \{-1, 1\}$ pseudo-random bitmap. The 1,000 largest coefficients in the DCT domain are selected in a similar manner to the Cox et al. algorithm (1997). However, the embedding is done in the wavelet transform domain. The watermark coefficient is inserted according to:

$$f'(m,n) = f(m,n) + \sqrt{\alpha \cdot \zeta(m,n)^2 + \beta^2} \cdot w_i \quad \textbf{(34)}$$

where α and β are level-dependent weights. ζ(m,n) is the average magnitude in a 3x3 neighborhood around the coefficient location. The DT-CWT has a 4:1 redundancy for $2D$ signals. The proposed transform overcomes two drawbacks of the DWT. These are directional selectivity of diagonal features and lack of shift invariance. Real DWT filters do not capture the direction of diagonal features. As a result of that, the local image activity is not optimally represented, also limiting the energy of the signal that can be embedded imperceptibly. Shift invariance means that small shifts in the input signal do not cause major variations in the distribution of energy between wavelet coefficients at different scales. On the other hand, due to the redundancy in the transform domain, some embedded information might be lost in the inverse transform process or during image compression, which affects the robustness of the algorithm.

Comments on the Existing Algorithms

From the literature review in this section, it is apparent that digital watermarking can be achieved by using either transform techniques and embedding the watermark data into the frequency domain representation of the host image or by directly embedding the watermark into the spatial domain data of the image. The review also shows there are several requirements that the embedding method has yet to satisfy. Creating robust watermarking methods is still a challenging research problem. These algorithms are robust against some attacks but not against most of them. As an example, they cannot withstand geometric attacks such as rotation or cropping. Also, some of the current methods are designed to suit only specific application, which limits their widespread use.

Moreover, there are drawbacks in the existing algorithms associated with the watermark-embedding domain. These drawbacks vary from system to system. Watermarking schemes that modify the LSB of the data using a fixed magnitude PN sequence are highly sensitive to signal processing operations and are easily corrupted. Some transform domain watermarking algorithms cannot survive most image processing operations and geometric manipulations. This will limit their use in large numbers of applications. Using fractal transforms, only a limited amount of binary code can be embedded. Since fractal analysis is computationally expensive, and some images do not have many large, self-similar patterns, fractal-based algorithms may not be suitable or practical for general use. Feature domain algorithms suffer from problems of stability of feature points if they are exposed to an attack. For example, the method proposed in Kutter's work depends on the stability of extracted features whose locations may change by several pixels because of attack or because of the watermarking process. This will cause problems during the decoding process. Security is an issue facing most of the algorithms reviewed.

FUTURE OF DIGITAL WATERMARKING

Watermarking technology is still in the evolutionary stages. The watermarking future is promising. While the challenges to realization of this dream are many, a great deal of research effort has already been expended to overcome these challenges. Therefore, the objective of this section is to shed light on important aspects of the future of watermarking technology.

Development Challenges

Watermarking technology will become increasingly important as more vendors wish to sell their digital works on the Internet. This includes all manners of digital data including books, images, music and movies. Progress has been made and lots of developments and improvements have happened in the last seven years. However, despite this development and improvement in the digital image watermarking field, current technologies are far from what the end user is expecting. Lack of standardization and lack of a set of precise and realistic requirements for watermarking systems are two aspects that hinder further developments of digital watermarking techniques and copy protection mechanisms. Also, the lack of agreement on the definition of a common benchmark for method comparison and on the definition of the performance related concept is the third aspect for this hindering.

Digital Watermarking and Image Processing Attacks

Digital watermarking was claimed to be the ultimate solution for copyright protection over the Internet when the concept of digital watermarking was first presented. However, some problems related to robustness and security of watermarking algorithms to intentional or unintentional attacks still remain unsolved. These problems must be solved before digital watermarking can be claimed to be the ultimate solution for copyright ownership protection in digital media. One of these problems is the effect of geometrical transformations such as rotation, translation and scaling on the recovery of the watermark. Another is the security of the watermarking algorithm when intentional attackers make use of knowledge of the watermarking algorithm to destroy or remove the watermark.

Watermarking Standardization Issue

The most important question about watermarking technology is whether watermarking will be standardized and used in the near future. There are several movements to standardize watermarking technology, but no one standard has prevailed at this moment in time. Some researchers have been working to develop a standardized framework for protecting digital images and other multimedia content through technology built into media files and corresponding application software. However, they have lacked a clear vision of what the framework should be or how it would be used.

In addition, there was a discussion about how and whether watermarking should form part of the standard during the standardization process of JPEG2000. The requirements regarding security have been identified in the framework of JPEG2000. However, there has been neither in-depth clarification nor a harmonized effort to address watermarking issues. It is important to deduce what really needs to be standardized for including the watermarking concept in JPEG2000 and to what extent. The initial drafts of the JPEG2000 standard did not mention the issue of watermarking. However, there is a plan to examine how watermarking might be best applied within JPEG2000. The features of a given watermarking scheme are likely to offer designers an opportunity to integrate watermarking technology into JPEG2000 for different application such as distributing images on the Internet. Also, standardization of digital watermarking will influence the progress in imaging standards of JPEG2000 where the data security will be part of this standard. Therefore, the likelihood is that watermarking technology will be used in conjunction with JPEG2000 (Clark, 2000).

Future Highlights

Nevertheless, the future seems bright for digital watermarking. Many companies have already been active in digital watermarking research. For example, Microsoft has developed a prototype system that limits unauthorized playback of music by embedding a watermark that remains permanently attached to audio files. Such technology could be included as a default playback mechanism in future versions of the Windows operating system. If the music industry begins to include watermarks in its song files, Windows would refuse to play copyrighted music released after a certain date that was obtained illegally. Also, Microsoft Research has also invented a separate watermarking system that relies on graph theory to hide watermarks in software.

Normally the security technology is hackable. However, if the technology is combined with proper legal enforcement, industry standards and respects of the privacy of individuals seeking to legitimately use intellectual property, digital watermarking will encourage content creators to trust the Internet more. There is a tremendous amount of money at stake for many firms. The value of illegal copies of multimedia content distributed over the Internet could reach billions of dollars a year. It will be interesting to see how the development and adoption of digital watermarking plays out. With such high stakes involved for entertainment and other multimedia companies, they are likely to keep pushing for (and be willing to pay for) a secure technology that they can use to track and reduce copyright violation and capture some of their foregone revenues. Finally, it is expected that a great deal of effort must still be put into research before digital image watermarking can be widely accepted as legal evidence of ownership.

CHAPTER SUMMARY

This chapter started with a general view of digital data, the Internet and the products of these two, namely, multimedia and e-commerce. It provided the reader with some initial background and history of digital watermarking. The chapter gave an extensive and deep literature review of the field of digital watermarking in the second section. The concept of digital watermarking and the requirements of digital watermarking were discussed. In the third section, digital watermarking algorithms were reviewed. They were grouped into three main collections based on the embedding domain, that is, spatial domain techniques, transform domain techniques or feature domain techniques. The algorithms of the frequency domain were further subdivided into wavelet, DCT and fractal transform techniques. The fourth section highlighted the future prospective of the digital watermarking.

REFERENCES

Barni, M., Bartolini, F., Cappellini, V., & Piva, A. (1997). Robust watermarking of still images for copyright protection. *13th International Conference on Digital Signal Processing Proceedings,* DSP 97, (vol. 1, pp. 499-502).

Bas, P., Chassery, J., & Davoine, F. (1998, October). Using the fractal code to watermark images. *International Conference on Image Processing Proceedings,* ICIP 98, (vol. 1, pp. 469-473).

Baudry, S., Nguyen, P., & Maitre, H. (2000, October). Channel coding in video watermarking: Use of soft decoding to improve the watermark retrieval. *International Conference on Image Processing Proceedings,* ICIP 2000, (vol. 3, pp. 25-28).

Bender, W., Gruhl, D., Morimoto, N., & Lu, A. (1996). Techniques for data hiding. *IBM Systems Journal, 35*(3/4).

Boland, F., Ruanaidh, J.O., & Dautzenberg, C. (1995). Watermarking digital images for copyright protection. *Proceeding of IEE International Conference on Image Processing and Its Applications,* (pp. 321-326).

Bors, A., & Pitas, I. (1996, September). Image watermarking using DCT domain constraints. *International Conference on Image Processing Proceedings,* ICIP 96, (pp. 231-234).

Bruyndonckx, O., Quisquater, J.-J., & Macq, B. (1995). Spatial method for copyright labeling of digital images. *Proceeding of IEEE Nonlinear Signal Processing Workshop,* (pp. 456-459).

Busch, C., & Wolthusen, S. (1999, February). Digital watermarking from concepts to real-time video applications. *IEEE Computer Graphics and Applications,* 25-35.

Chae, J., Mukherjee, D., & Manjunath, B. (1998, January). A robust embedded data from wavelet coefficients. *Proceeding of SPIE, Electronic Imaging, Storage and Retrieval for Image and Video Database, 3312,* (pp. 308-317).

Chae, J.J., Mukherjee, D., & Manjunath, B.S. (1998). A robust data hiding technique using multidimensional lattices. *Proceedings IEEE Interna-*

tional Forum on Research and Technology Advances in Digital Libraries, ADL 98, (pp. 319-326).

Clark, R. (2000). An introduction to JPEG 2000 and watermarking. *IEE Seminar on Secure Images & Image Authentication,* 3/1-3/6.

Cox, I., & Miller, L. (1997, February). A review of watermarking and the importance of perceptual modeling. *Proceeding of SPIE Conference on Human Vision and Electronic Imaging II, 3016,* (pp. 92-99).

Cox, I., Kilian, J., Leighton, F.T., & Shamoon, T. (1995). *Secure spread spectrum watermarking for multimedia.* Technical Report 95-10, NEC Research Institute.

Cox, I., Kilian, J., Leighton, F.T., & Shamoon, T. (1996, September). Secure spread spectrum watermarking for images, audio and video. *International Conference on Image Processing Proceedings,* ICIP 96, (vol. 3, pp. 243-246).

Cox, I., Kilian, J., Leighton, F.T., & Shamoon, T. (1997, December). Secure spread spectrum watermarking for multimedia. *IEEE Transaction Image Processing, 6*(12), 1673-1687.

Craver, S., Memon, N., Yeo, B., & Yeung, M. (1997, October). On the invertibility of invisible watermarking techniques. *International Conference on Image Processing Proceedings,* ICIP 97, (pp. 540-543).

Duan, F., King, I., Chan, L., & Xu, L. (1998). Intra-block algorithm for digital watermarking. *14th International Conference on Pattern Recognition Proceedings,* (vol. 2, pp. 1589-1591).

Dugad, R., Ratakonda, K., & Ahuja, N. (1998, October). A new wavelet-based scheme for watermarking images. *International Conference on Image Processing Proceedings,* ICIP 98, (vol. 2, pp. 419-423).

Eggers, J., Su, J., & Girod, B. (2000, October). Robustness of a blind image watermarking scheme. *International Conference on Image Processing Proceedings,* ICIP 2000, (vol. 3, pp. 17-20).

Ejim, M., & Miyazaki, A. (2000, October). A wavelet-based watermarking for digital images and video. *International Conference on Image Processing,* ICIP 00, (vol. 3, pp. 678-681).

Furon, T., & Duhamel, P. (2000, October). Robustness of asymmetric watermarking technique. *International Conference on Image Processing Proceedings,* ICIP 2000, (vol. 3, pp. 21-24).

Goutte, R., & Baskurt, A. (1998). On a new approach of insertion of confidential digital signature into images. *Proceedings of Fourth International Conference on Signal Processing,* ICSP 98, (vol. 2, pp. 1170-1173).

Hartung, F., & Girod, B. (1996, October). Digital watermarking of raw and compressed video. *Proceeding of the SPIE Digital Computing Techniques and Systems for Video Communication, 2952,* (pp. 205-213).

Hernadez, J., & Gonzalez, F. (1999, July). Statistical analysis of watermarking schemes for copyright protection of images. *Proceeding of the IEEE, Special Issue on Protection of Multimedia Content,* (pp. 1142-1165).

Hernandez, J.R., Amado, M., & Perez-Gonzalez, F. (2000, January). DCT-domain watermarking techniques for still images: Detector performance analysis and a new structure. *IEEE Transactions on Image Processing, 91,* 55-68.

Hirotsugu, K. (1996, September). An image digital signature system with zkip for the graph isomorphism. *International Conference on Image Processing Proceedings,* ICIP 96, (vol. 3, pp. 247-250).

Hsiao, S.F., Tai, Y.C., & Chang, K.H. (2000, June). VLSI design of an efficient embedded zerotree wavelet coder with function of digital watermarking. *International Conference on Consumer Electronics,* ICCE 2000, 186-187.

Hsu, C., & Wu, J. (1996, September). Hidden signatures in images. *International Conference on Image Processing Proceedings,* ICIP 96, 223-226.

Hsu, C., & Wu, J. (1998, August). Multiresolution watermarking for digital images. *IEEE Transactions on Circuits and Systems II, 45*(8), 1097-1101.

Hsu, C., & Wu, J. (1999, January). Hidden digital watermarks in images. *IEEE Transactions on Image Processing*, *8*(1), 58-68. http://www.tsi.enst.fr/~maitre/tatouage//icip2000.html.

Huang, J., & Shi, Y. (1998, April). Adaptive image watermarking scheme based on visual masking. *Electronics Letters, 34*(8), 748-750.

Inoue, H., Miyazaki, A., Yamamoto, A., & Katsura, T. (1998, October). A digital watermark based on the wavelet transform and its robustness on image compression. *International Conference on Image Processing Proceedings,* ICIP 98, (vol. 2, pp. 391-395).

Inoue, H., Miyazaki, A., Yamamoto, A., & Katsura, T. (2000, October). Wavelet-based watermarking for tamper proofing of still images. *International Conference on Image Processing Proceedings, 2000,* ICIP 00, 88-912.

ISO/IEC JTC 1/SC 29/WG 1, ISO/IEC FCD 15444-1. (2000, March). *Information technology - JPEG 2000 image coding system: Core coding system.* WG 1 N 1646 (pp. 1-205). Available online: http://www.jpeg.org/FCD15444-1.htm.

Kang, S., & Aoki, Y. (1999). Image data embedding system for watermarking using Fresnel transform. *IEEE International Conference on Multimedia Computing and Systems, 1,* 885-889.

Kankanhalli, M., & Ramakrishnan, K. (1999). Adaptive visible watermarking of images. *IEEE International Conference on Multimedia Computing and Systems, 1,* 568-573.

Kim, J.R., & Moon, Y.S. (1999, October). A robust wavelet-based digital watermarking using level-adaptive thresholding. *International Conference on Image Processing Proceedings,* ICIP 99, *2,* 226-230.

Kim, S., Suthaharan, S., Lee, H., & Rao, K. (1999). Image watermarking scheme using visual model and BN distribution. *Electronics Letters, 35*(3), 212-214.

Kim, Y.S., Kwon, O.H., & Park, R.H. (1999, March). Wavelet based watermarking method for digital images using the human visual system. *Electronics Letters, 35*(6), 466-468.

Koch, E., & Zhao, J. (1995). Towards robust and hidden image copyright labeling. *Proceeding of IEEE Nonlinear Signal Processing Workshop,* (pp. 452-455).

Kreyszic, E. (1998). *Advanced engineering mathematics.* New York: John Wiley & Sons.

Kundur, D., & Hatzinakos, D. (1997, September). A robust digital image watermarking method using wavelet-based fusion. *International Conference on Image Processing Proceedings,* ICIP 97, (vol. 1, pp. 544-547).

Kundur, D., & Hatzinakos, D. (1998a). Digital watermarking using multiresolution wavelet decomposition. *International Conference on Acoustics, Speech and Signal Processing Proceedings,* (vol. 5, pp. 2969-2972).

Kundur, D., & Hatzinakos, D. (1998b, October). Towards a telltale watermarking technique for tamper-proofing. *International Conference on Image Processing Proceedings,* ICIP 98, (vol. 2, pp. 409-413).

Kundur, D., & Hatzinakos, D. (1999, October). Attack characterization for effective watermarking. *International Conference on Image Processing Proceedings,* ICIP 99, (vol. 2, pp. 240-244).

Kutter, M., Bhattacharjee, S.K., & Ebrahimi, T. (1999, October). Towards second generation watermarking schemes. *International Conference on Image Processing Proceedings,* ICIP 99, (vol. 1, pp. 320-323).

Lewis, A., & Knwles, G. (1992, April). Image compression using 2-D wavelet transform. *IEEE Transactions on Image Processing, 1,* 244-250.

Loo, P., & Kingsbury, N. (2000a, April). Digital watermarking with complex wavelets. *IEE Seminar on Secure Images and Image Authentication,* 10/1-10/7.

Loo, P., & Kingsbury, N. (2000b, October). Digital watermarking using complex wavelets. *International Conference on Image Processing Proceedings,* ICIP 2000, *3,* 29-32.

Lu, C.S., & Liao, H.Y. (2000, October). Oblivious cocktail watermarking by sparse code shrinkage: A regional- and global-based scheme. *International Conference on Image Processing Proceedings,* ICIP 2000, *3,* 13-16.

Lu, C.S., Liao, H.Y., & Sze, C.J. (2000, July). Combined watermarking for image authentication and protection. *IEEE International Conference on Multimedia and Expo,* ICME 2000, *3,* 1415-1418.

Lumini, A., & Maio, D. (2000, March). A wavelet-based image watermarking scheme. *International Conference on Information Technology: Coding and Computing,* 122-127.

Miller, M., Cox, I., & Bloom, J. (2000, October). Informed embedding exploiting image and detector information during watermark insertion. *International Conference on Image Processing Proceedings,* ICIP 2000, *3,* 1-4.

Mintzer, F., Braudaway, G.W., & Yeung, M.M. (1997, October). Effective and ineffective digital watermarks. *International Conference on Image Processing Proceedings,* ICIP 97, *3,* 9-12.

Mukherjee, D., Chae, J.J., & Mitra, S.K. (1998, October). A source and channel coding approach to data hiding with application to hiding speech in video. *International Conference on Image Processing Proceedings,* ICIP 98, *1,* 348-352.

Nikolaidis, N., & Pitas, I. (1996, May). Copyright protection of images using robust digital signatures. *Proceeding of IEEE Conference Acoustics, Speech & Signal Processing '96,* (pp. 2168-2171).

Petitcolas, F. Weakness of existing watermarking schemes. Available online: http://www.cl.cam.ac.uk/~fabb2/watermarking.

Pitas, I. (1996, September). A method for signature casting on digital images. *International Conference on Image Processing Proceedings,* ICIP 96, (vol. 3, pp. 215-218).

Pitas, I., & Kaskalis, T. (1995). Applying signatures on digital images. *Proceeding of IEEE Nonlinear Signal Processing Workshop,* (pp. 460-463).

Piva, A., Barni, M., Bartolini, F., & Cappellini, V. (1997, September). DCT-based watermark recovering without resorting to the uncorrupted original image. *International Conference on Image Processing Proceedings,* ICIP 97, (pp. 520-523).

Piva, A., Caldelli, R., & De Rosa, A. (2000, October). A DWT-based object watermarking system for MPEG-4 video streams. *International Conference on Image Processing Proceedings,* ICIP 2000, (vol. 3, pp. 5-8).

Podilchuk, C.I., & Zeng, C.W. (1998, May). Image-adaptive watermarking using visual models. *IEEE Journal on Selected Areas in Communications, 16*(4), 525-539.

Puate, J., & Jordan, F. (1996, November). Using fractal compression scheme to embed a digital signature into an image. *Proceedings of SPIE Photonics East'96 Symposium.* Available online: http://iswww.epfl.ch/~jordan/watremarking.html.

Roche, S., & Dugelay, J. (1998). Image watermarking based on the fractal transform: A draft demonstration. *IEEE Second Workshop on Multimedia Signal Processing,* 358–363.

Ruanaidh, J.O., Boland, F., & Dowling, W. (1996, September). Phase watermarking of digital images. *International Conference on Image Processing Proceedings,* ICIP 96, 239-242.

Ruanaidh, J.O., Dowling, W.J., & Boland, F.M. (1996, August). Watermarking digital images for copyright protection. *IEE Proceedings on Vision, Signal and Image Processing, 143*(4), 250-256.

Ruanaidh, J.O., & Pun, T. (1997, October). Rotation, scale and translation invariant digital image watermarking. *International Conference on Image Processing Proceedings,* ICIP 97, *1,* 536-539.

Schyndel, R.G., Tirkel, A.Z., & Osborne, C.F. (1994). A digital watermark. *Proceeding of IEEE International Conference on Image,* (vol. 2, pp. 86-90).

Servetto, S.D., Podilchuk, C.I., & Ramchandran, K. (1998, October). Capacity issues in digital image watermarking. *International Conference on Image Processing,* ICIP 98, *1,* 445-449.

Silvestre, G., & Dowling, W. (1997). Image watermarking using digital communication techniques. *International Conference on Image Processing and its Application 1997, 1,* 443-447.

Solachidis, V., Nikolaidis, N., & Pitas, I. (2000, October). Fourier descriptors watermarking of vector graphics images. *International Conference on Image Processing Proceedings,* ICIP 2000, *3,* 9-12.

Swanson, M., Zhu, B., & Tewfik, A. (1996, September). Transparent robust image watermarking. *International Conference on Image Processing Proceedings,* ICIP 96, pp. 211-214.

Swanson, M.D., Kobayashi, M., & Shapiro, J. (1993, December). Embedded image coding using zerotrees of wavelet coefficients. *IEEE Transactions on Signal Processing, 41*(12), 3445-3462.

Tanaka, K., Nakamura, Y., & Matsui, K. (1990). Embedding secret information into a dithered multi-level image. *Proceeding of IEEE Military Communications Conference,* (pp. 216-220).

Tang, W., & Aoki, Y. (1997). A DCT-based coding of images in watermarking. *Proceedings of International Conference on Information, Communications and Signal Processing,* ICICS97, (vol. 1, pp. 510-512).

Tao, B., & Dickinson, B. (1997). Adaptive watermarking in the DCT domain. *IEEE International Conference on Acoustics, Speech, and Signal Processing,* ICASSP 97, *4,* 2985-2988.

Tewfik, A.H. (1998, June). Multimedia data-embedding and watermarking technologies. *Proceedings of the IEEE, 86*(6), 1064–1087.

Tilki, J.F., & Beex, A.A. (1996). Encoding a hidden digital signature onto an audio signal using psychoacoustic masking. *Proceeding of 7th International Conference on Signal Processing Applications and Techniques,* (pp. 476-480).

Tirkel, A., Rankin, G., Schyndel, R., Ho, W., Mee, N., & Osborne, C. (1993). Electronic watermark. *Proceedings of Digital Image Computing, Technology and Applications,* DICTA 93, (pp. 666-673).

Tsai, M., Yu, K., & Chen, Y. (2000, February). Joint wavelet and spatial transformation for digital watermarking. *IEEE Transactions on Consumer Electronics, 46*(1), 237.

Tsekeridou, S., & Pitas, I. (2000, May). Wavelet-based self-similar watermarking for still images. *The IEEE International Symposium on Circuits and Systems,* ISCAS 2000, *1,* 220- 223.

Voyatzis, G., Nikolaidis, N., & Pitas, I. (1998, September). Digital watermarking an overview. *Proceedings EUSIPCO '98,* Rhodes, Greece.

Wang, H.J., & Kuo, C.C. (1998a). Image protection via watermarking on perceptually significant wavelet coefficients. *IEEE Second Workshop on Multimedia Signal Processing*, 279-284.

Wang, H.J., & Kuo, C.C. (1998b). An integrated progressive image coding and watermark system. *International Conference on Acoustics, Speech and Signal Processing Proceedings, 6,* 3721-3724.

Watson, A., Yang, G., Solomom, A., & Villasenor, J. (1997). Visibility of wavelet quantization noise. *IEEE Transaction in Image Processing, 6,* 1164-1175.

Wei, Z.H., Qin, P., & Fu, Y.Q. (1998, November). Perceptual digital watermark of images using wavelet transform. *IEEE Transactions on Consumer Electronics, 44*(4), 1267 –1272.

Wolfgang, P., & Delp, E. (1996, September). A watermark for digital images. *International Conference on Image Processing Proceedings,* ICIP 96, 219-222.

Wolfgang, R., Podlchuk, C., & Delp, E. (1999, July). Perceptual watermarks for digital images and video. *Proceedings of IEEE Special Issue on Identification and Protection of Multimedia Information, 7,* 1108-1126.

Wolfgang, R.B., Podilchuk, C.I., & Delp, E.J. (1998, October). The effect of matching watermark and compression transforms in compressed color images. *International Conference on Image Processing Proceedings,* ICIP 98, *1,* 440-444.

Wu, X., Zhu, W., Xiong, Z., & Zhang, Y. (2000, May). Object-based multiresolution watermarking of images and video. *The 2000 IEEE International Symposium on Circuits and Systems,* ISCAS 2000, *1,* 212-215.

Xia, X., Boncelet, C.G., & Arce, G.R. (1997, September). A multiresolution watermark for digital images. *International Conference on Image Processing Proceedings,* ICIP 97, *1,* 548-551.

Xie, L., & Arce, G.R. (1998, October). Joint wavelet compression and authentication watermarking. *International Conference on Image Processing Proceedings,* ICIP 98, *2,* 427-431.

Zaho, J. *Look it's not there.* Available online: http://www.byte.com/art/9701/sec18/art1.htm.

Zeng, W., & Liu, B. (1997, October). On resolving rightful ownerships of digital images by invisible watermarks. *International Conference on Image Processing Proceedings,* ICIP 97, (pp. 552-555).

Zhihui, W., & Liang, X. (2000, July). An evaluation method for watermarking techniques. *IEEE International Conference on Multimedia and Expo,* ICME 2000, *1,* 373-376.

Zhu, W., Xiong, Z., & Zhang, Y. (1998, October). Multiresolution watermarking for images and video: A unified approach. *International Conference on Image Processing Proceedings,* ICIP 98, *1,* 465-468.

ENDNOTES

[1] Descendants are defined as the coefficients corresponding to the same spatial location but at a finer scale of the same orientation in the DWT subbands.

Chapter II

Perceptual Data Hiding in Still Images

Mauro Barni, University of Siena, Italy

Franco Bartolini, University of Florence, Italy

Alessia De Rosa, University of Florence, Italy

ABSTRACT

The idea of embedding some information within a digital media, in such a way that the inserted data are intrinsically part of the media itself, has aroused a considerable interest in different fields. One of the more examined issues is the possibility of hiding the highest possible amount of information without affecting the visual quality of the host data. For such a purpose, the understanding of the mechanisms underlying Human Vision is a mandatory requirement. Hence, the main phenomena regulating the Human Visual System will be firstly discussed and their exploitation in a data hiding system will be then considered.

INTRODUCTION

In the last 10 years, digital watermarking has received increasing attention, since it is seen as an effective tool for copyright protection of digital data (Petitcolas, Anderson, & Kuhn, 1999), one of the most crucial problems slowing down the diffusion of new multimedia services such as electronic commerce, open access to digital archives, distribution of documents in digital format and so on. According to the watermarking paradigm, the protection of copyrighted data is accomplished by injecting into the data an invisible signal, that is, the watermark, conveying information about data ownership, its provenance or any other information that can be useful to enforce copyright laws.

Recently, the idea of embedding some information within a digital document in such a way that the inserted data are intrinsically part of the document itself has been progressively applied to other purposes as well, including broadcast monitoring, data authentication, data indexing, content labelling, hidden annotation, and so on.

Regardless of the specific purpose, it is general agreed that one of the main requirements a data hiding scheme must satisfy regards invisibility; that is, the digital code must be embedded in an imperceptible way so that its presence does not affect the quality of the to-be-protected data.

As far as the embedding of a hidden signal within a host image is concerned, it is evident that the understanding of the mechanisms underlying human vision is a mandatory requirement (Cox & Miller, 1997; Tewfik & Swanson, 1997; Wolfgang, Podilchuk, & Delp, 1999). All the more that, in addition to the invisibility constraint, many applications require that the embedded information be resistant against the most common image manipulations. This, in turn, calls for the necessity of embedding a watermark whose strength is as high as possible, a task which clearly can take great advantage from the availability of an accurate model to describe the human visual system (HVS) behaviour. In other words, we can say that the goal of perceptual data hiding is twofold: to better hide the watermark, thus making it less perceivable to the eye, and to allow to the use of the highest possible watermark strength, thus influencing positively the performance of the data recovery step.

Many approaches have been proposed so far to model the characteristics of the HVS and to exploit such models to improve the effectiveness of existing watermarking systems (Podilchuk & Zeng, 1998; Wolfgang et al., 1999). Though all the proposed methods rely on some general knowledge about the most important features of HVS, we can divide the approaches proposed so far into theoretical (Kundur & Hatzinakos, 1997; Podilchuk & Zeng, 1998; Swanson, Zhu, & Tewfik, 1998; Wolfgang et al., 1999) and heuristic (Bartolini, Barni, Cappellini & Piva, 1998; Delaigle, Vleeschouwer, & Macq, 1998; Van Schyndel, Tirkel, & Osborne, 1994) ones. Even if a theoretically grounded approach to the problem would be clearly preferable, heuristic algorithms sometimes provide better results due to some problems with HVS models currently in use (Bartolini, 1998; Delaigle, 1998).

In this chapter, we will first give a detailed description of the main phenomena regulating the HVS, and we will consider the exploitation of these concepts in a data hiding system. Then, some limits of classical HVS models will be highlighted and some possible solutions to get around these problems pointed out. Finally, we will describe a complete mask building procedure, as a possible exploitation of HVS characteristics for perceptual data hiding in still images.

BASICS OF HUMAN VISUAL SYSTEM MODELLING

Even if the human visual system is certainly one of the most complex biological devices far from being exactly described, each person has daily experience of the main phenomena that influence the ability of the HVS to perceive (or not to perceive) certain stimuli. In order to exemplify such phenomena, it may very instructive to consider two copies of the same image, one being a disturbed version of the other. For instance, we can consider the two images depicted in Figure 1, showing, on the left, a noiseless version of the *house* image, and, on the right, a noisy version of the same image. It is readily seen that: (1) noise is not visible in high activity regions, for example, on foliage; (2) noise is very visible in uniform areas such as the sky or the street; (3) noise is less visible in correspondence of edges; (4) noise is less visible in dark and bright areas.

As it can be easily experienced, the above observations do not depend on the particular image depicted in the figure. On the contrary, they can be generalised, thus deriving some very general rules: (1) disturbances are less visible in highly textured regions than in uniform areas; (2) noise is more easily perceived around edges than in textured areas, but less easily than in flat regions; (3) the human eye is less sensitive to disturbances in dark and bright regions. In the last decades, several mathematical models have been developed to describe the above basic mechanisms. In the following, the main concepts underlying these models are presented.

Figure 1. Noiseless (left) and noisy (right) versions of the House image

Basically, a model describing the human visual perception is based on two main concepts: the *contrast sensitivity function* and the *contrast masking model.* The first concept is concerned with the sensitivity of the human eye to a sine grating stimulus; as the sensitivity of the eye depends strongly on display background luminance and spatial frequency of the stimulus, these two parameters have to be taken into account in the mathematical description of human sensitivity. The second concept considers the effect of one stimulus on the detectability of another, where the stimuli can be coincident (*iso-frequency masking*), or non- coincident (*non iso-frequency masking*) in frequency and orientation.

Contrast Sensitivity

Contrast represents the dynamic range of luminance in a region of a picture. If we consider an image characterised by a uniform background luminance L and a small superimposed patch of uniform luminance $L+\Delta L$, the contrast can be expressed as:

$$C = \frac{\Delta L}{L}. \qquad \textbf{(1)}$$

For understanding how a human observer is able to perceive this variation of luminance, we can refer to the experiments performed by Weber in the middle of 18th century. According to Weber's experimental set-up, ΔL is increased until the human eye can perceive the difference between the patch and the background. Weber observed that the ratio between the *just noticeable* value of the superimposed stimulus ΔL_{jn} and L is nearly constant to 0.02; the only exception is represented by very low and very high luminance values, a fact that is in complete agreement with the rules listed before, that is, disturbances are less visible in dark and bright areas. Such behaviour is justified by the fact that receptors are not able to perceive luminance changes above and below a given range (saturation effect).

However, a problem with the above experimental set-up is that the case of a uniform luminance stimuli superimposed to a uniform luminance background is not a realistic one: hence, a different definition of the contrast must be given. In particular, by letting $L(x, y)$ be the luminance of a pixel at position (x, y) and L_o the local mean background luminance, a local contrast definition can be written as:

$$C = \frac{L(x,y) - L_o}{L_o}. \qquad \textbf{(2)}$$

This formulation is still a simplification of real images, where more complex texture patterns are present. The easiest way to get closer to the case of real images consists in decomposing the disturbing signal into a sum of sinusoidal signals, and then investigating the HVS behaviour in the presence of a single sinusoidal stimulus, and then considering the combination of more stimuli. To this aim, let us consider an image obtained by summing a sinusoidal stimulus to a uniform background. The spatial luminance of the image is given by:

$$L(x, y) = L_o + \Delta L \cos(2\pi f(x\cos\theta + ysin\theta)), \quad \textbf{(3)}$$

where f, θ and ΔL are, respectively, the frequency, orientation and amplitude of the superimposed stimulus. Note that the frequency f, measured in *cycles/degree,* is a function of the frequency v measured in *cycles/m* and the viewing distance D between the observer and the monitor expressed in meter:

$$f = (\pi D/180)v.$$

In order to evaluate the smallest sinusoid a human eye can distinguish from the background, ΔL is increased until the observer perceives it. We refer to such a threshold value of ΔL as the luminance value of the *just noticeable* sinusoidal stimulus, and we will refer to it as ΔL_{jn}. Instead of ΔL_{jn}, it is usually preferred to consider the minimum contrast necessary to just detect a sine wave of a given frequency f and orientation θ superimposed to a background $L_{o,}$ thus leading to the concept of *just noticeable contrast* (JNC) (Eckert & Bradley, 1998):

$$JNC = \frac{\Delta L_{jn}}{L_o}. \quad \textbf{(4)}$$

The inverse of *JNC* is commonly referred to as the *contrast sensitivity function* (CSF) (Damera-Venkata, Kite, Geisler, Evans, & Bovik, 2000) and gives an indication of the capability of the human eye to notice a sinusoidal stimulus on a uniform background:

$$S_c = \frac{1}{JNC} = \frac{L_o}{\Delta L_{jn}}. \quad \textbf{(5)}$$

By repeating the above experiment for different viewing conditions and different values of f and θ, it is found that the major factors *JNC* (or equivalently S_c) depends upon are: (1) the frequency of the stimulus f, (2) the orientation of the stimulus θ, (3) background luminance L_o, and (4) the viewing angle w, that is, the ratio between the square root of the area A of the monitor and the viewing distance D:

$$w = 180\sqrt{A}/\pi D \cdot$$

Many analytical expressions of *CSF* can be found in the scientific literature. In this chapter, we only consider the one obtained by Barten (1990) by fitting data of psychophysical experiments. According to Barten's model, the factors influencing human vision are taken into account by the following expression:

$$S_c(f,\theta,w,L_o) = a(f,w,L_o) f \exp\left(-\Gamma(\theta) b(L_o) f\right) \cdot \sqrt{1 + c \cdot \exp\left(b(L_o) f\right)}, \quad (6)$$

with:

$$a(f,w,L_o) = \frac{540\left(1+0.7/L_o\right)^{-0.2}}{1+\dfrac{12}{w\cdot\left(1+f/3\right)^2}},$$
$$b(L_o) = 0.3\left(1+100/L_o\right)^{0.15},$$
$$c = 0.06,$$
$$\Gamma(\theta) = 1.08 - 0.08\cos\left(4\theta\right), \quad (7)$$

where the frequency of the stimulus f is measured in *cycles/degree;* the orientation of the stimulus θ in *degrees;* the observer viewing angle w in *degrees,* and the mean local background luminance L_0 in *candelas/m²*. In particular, the term $\Gamma(\theta)$ takes into account that the eye sensitivity is not isotropic.

In fact, psychophysical experiments showed less sensitivity to ±45 degrees oriented stimuli than to vertically and horizontally oriented ones, an effect that is even more pronounced at high frequencies: about -3dB at six *cycles/degree* and -1dB at 1 *cycle/degree* (Comes & Macq, 1990).

In Figures 2, 3 and 4, the plot of S_c against luminance and frequency is shown. In particular, in Figure 2 the plots of *CSF* with respect to frequency are reported for several values of background luminance; results refer to a horizontal stimulus (i.e., $\theta = 0$) and to an observer viewing angle $w = 180/\pi\sqrt{12}$, which is obtained when the monitor is viewed from a distance of four time its height. As it can be seen, all the curves exhibit the same trend for all values of background

Figure 2. Plots of S_c against frequency for values of background luminance of 0.01, 0.1, 1, 10, 100 cd/m² (from bottom to top)

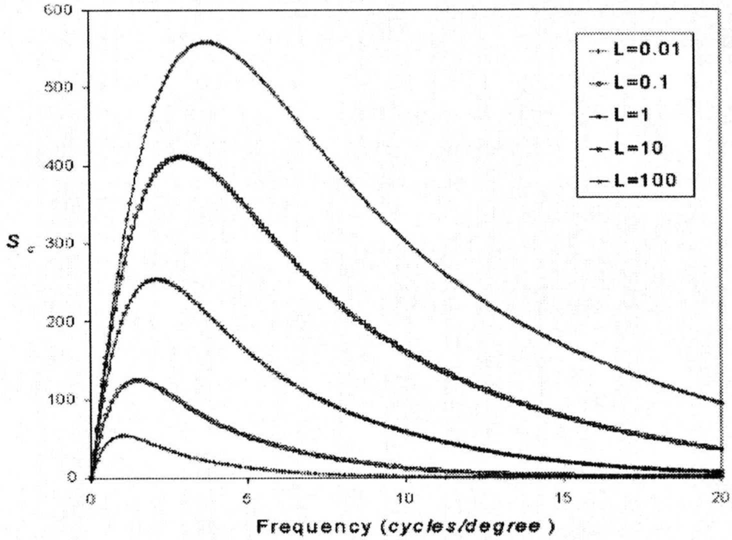

luminance: the maximum sensitivity is reached in the middle range of frequencies, while in the low and high part of the frequency range the HVS has a lower sensitivity.

In Figure 3 the just noticeable stimulus ΔL_{jn} is plotted against luminance L, for a frequency of 15 *cycles/degree*. This plot is consistent with the phenomenon

Figure 3. Plot of the just noticeable stimulus vs. image background luminance, for a frequency of 15 cycles/degree

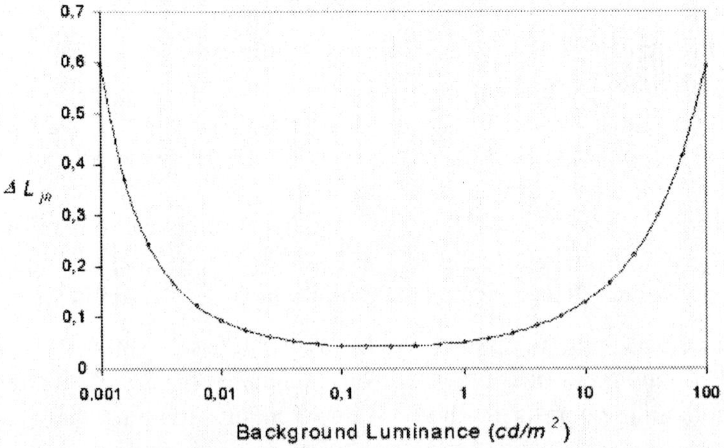

Figure 4. Plots of the S_c with respect to frequency for horizontal and diagonal stimuli and background luminance of 50 cd/m²

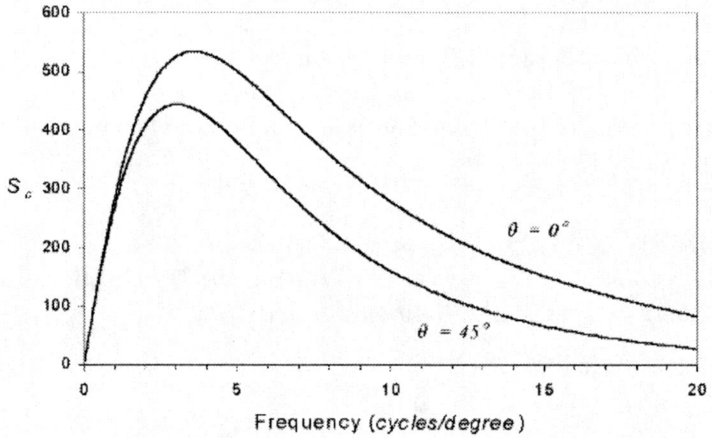

that disturbances are less visible in dark and bright regions and shows the results achieved by following Weber's experiment. Finally, Figure 4 highlights how horizontal (or vertical) stimuli are more visible than those oriented at 45°.

Contrast Masking

The term *masking* is commonly used to refer to any destructive interaction and interference among stimuli that are closely coupled (Legge & Foley, 1980). In this framework we will refer to masking to indicate the visibility reduction of one image component due to the presence of other components.

By referring to the previous analysis regarding the *contrast sensitivity function* let us note that it only considers sinusoidal stimuli superimposed to a uniform background, while in real scenarios stimuli are usually superimposed to a spatially changing background. Such a background can be described again as a combination of sinusoidal stimuli plus a uniform luminance value L_o. Thus, by considering a stimulus of amplitude ΔL_m, frequency f_m and orientation θ_m for describing the background, the spatial luminance of the image can be rewritten as:

$$L(x,y) = L_o + \Delta L_m \cos(2\pi f_m (x\cos\theta_m + y sin\theta_m)) + \\ + \Delta L \cos(2\pi f (x\cos\theta + y sin\theta)). \quad \textbf{(8)}$$

In particular, the stimulus ΔL_m is called *masking stimulus* since its presence usually increases the *JNC* of another stimulus ΔL (e.g., a disturbance). The stimuli can be coincident in frequency and orientation (i.e., $f_m = f$ and $\theta_m = \theta$), leading to *iso-frequency masking,* or non-coincident (i.e. $f_m \neq f$ and $\theta_m \neq \theta$), leading to *non- iso-frequency masking.* In the first case, *JNC* elevation is maximal; in the latter, *JNC* elevation decreases regularly as the masking frequency departs from the stimulus frequency.

In the following both *iso* and *non-iso-frequency masking* will be considered and a *masked just noticeable contrast* function (JNC_m) detailed to model these masking effects.

Iso-Frequency Masking

By relying on the works by Watson (Watson, 1987, 1993),the *masked JNC* can be written as a function of the *non-masked JNC*:

$$JNC_m(f,\theta,w,L_o) = JNC(f,\theta,w,L_o) \cdot \cdot F\left(\frac{C_m(f,\theta,w,L_o)}{JNC(f,\theta,w,L_o)}\right) \tag{9}$$

where F is a non-linear function indicating how much *JNC* increments in presence of a masking signal, and C_m is the contrast of the masking image component, that is, $C_m = \Delta L_m / L_o$.

The function $F(\cdot)$ can be approximated by the following relation (Watson, 1987):

$$F(X) = \max\left\{1, |X|^W\right\}, \tag{10}$$

where W is an exponent lying between 0.4 and 0.95.

Let us note that expression (10) does not take the so-called *pedestal effect* into account (Legge & Foley, 1980). In fact, it assumes that the presence of one stimulus can only decrease the detectability of another stimulus at the same frequency and orientation. Indeed, several studies have shown that a low value of the masking contrast C_m increases noise visibility (Foley & Legge, 1981); in particular, when the masking component is not perceptible, that is, $C_m < JNC$, then a more exact expression for F would also assume values below one. In Figure 5, the trends of the masking function $F(X)$ obtained by fitting experimental results (solid line) and by using equation 10 (dashed line) are shown: the *pedestal effect* is also highlighted.

By inserting equation 10 in equation 9, we get:

Figure 5. Plot of the masking function F(X) (solid line) and its approximation (dashed line) given by equation 10, where it is assumed W = 0.6 (The pedestal effect is highlighted.)

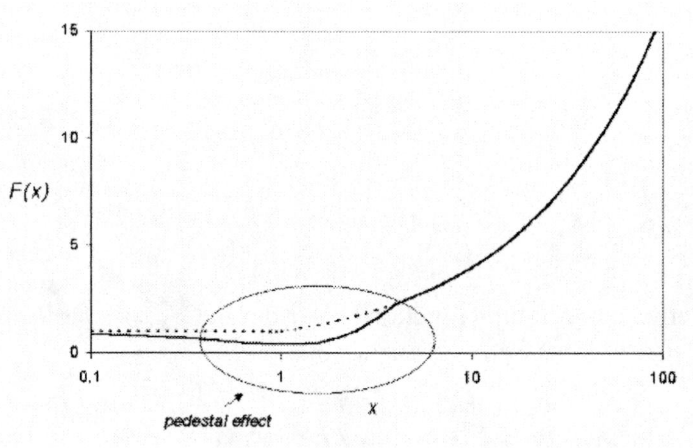

$$JNC_m(f,\theta,w,L_o)=JNC(f,\theta,w,L_o)\cdot \cdot\max\left(1,\left|\frac{C_m(f,\theta,w,L_o)}{JNC(f,\theta,w,L_o)}\right|^W\right) \quad \textbf{(11)}$$

It is important to note that masking only affects the AC components of the image. The effect of the DC coefficient on the threshold is expressed by equation 6, in which the influence of background mean luminance L_o on human vision is taken into account.

Non-Iso-Frequency Masking

When the masking frequency (f_m, θ_m) departs from signal frequency (f, θ) JNC_m increment decreases. A possibility to model *non-iso-frequency masking* consists in introducing in equation 11 a weighing function, which takes into account that each frequency component contributes differently to the masking, according to its frequency position. The weighing function can be modelled as Gaussian-like (Comes & Macq, 1990):

$$g(f_m/f,\theta_m-\theta)=\exp\left[-\left(\frac{\log_2^2(f_m/f)}{\sigma_f^2}+\frac{(\theta_m-\theta)^2}{\sigma_\theta^2}\right)\right], \quad \textbf{(12)}$$

where

$$\sigma_f = 1.2 \log_2 B_f,$$
$$\sigma_\theta = 1.2 B_\theta, \tag{13}$$

$$B_f = \sqrt{2},$$
$$B_\theta = 27 - 3\log_2 f. \tag{14}$$

By inserting the weighing function (12) in the JNC_m expression, the value of the *masked just noticeable contrast* is obtained:

$$JNC_m(f,\theta,w,L_o) = JNC(f,\theta,w,L_o)\cdot$$
$$\cdot\max\left(1,\ \left|g(f_m/f,\theta_m-\theta)\frac{C_m(f_m,\theta_m,w,L_m)}{JNC(f_m,\theta_m,w,L_m)}\right|^W\right) \tag{15}$$

where the stimulus at spatial frequency (f, θ) is masked by the stimulus at spatial frequency (f_m, θ_m). Note that the mean luminance's L_o and L_m can be supposed to be identical when both the frequencies f and f_m belong to the same spatial region. Furthermore, when $(f_m, \theta_m) = (f, \theta)$ the weighing function assumes value 1, thus reducing to equation 11.

EXPLOITATION OF HVS CONCEPTS FOR DATA HIDING

It is widely known among watermarking researchers that HVS characteristics have to be carefully considered for developing a watermarking system that minimises the image visual degradation while maximising robustness (Cox & Miller, 1997; Tewfik & Swanson, 1997). Let us, thus, see how the concepts deriving from the analysis of the models of human perception can be exploited for better hiding data into images.

Basically, we distinguish two different approaches for considering HVS concepts during the data embedding process. The former approach considers the selection of appropriate features that are most suitable to be modified, without dramatically affecting perceptual image quality. Basing on the characteristics that control the HVS (i.e., the dependence of the *contrast sensitivity* on frequency and luminance, and the *masking effect*), the idea is to locate which image features can better mask the embedded data. By following the second approach, the inserted data, embedded into an image without a particular care for the selection of the most suitable features, are adapted to the local image content for better reducing their perceptibility. In other words, by referring to the just noticeable contrast, the maximum amount of data that can be introduced into an image is locally adapted.

Let us consider host feature selection first. By carefully observing the simple basic rules describing the mechanisms underlying the HVS we discussed above, it is readily seen that some of them are more naturally expressed in the spatial domain, whereas others are more easily modelled in the frequency domain. Let us consider, for example, the *CSF* and the masking models described in the previous section. The most suitable domain to describe them is, obviously, the frequency domain. This is not the case, however, when the lower sensitivity to disturbances in bright and dark regions has to be taken into account, a phenomenon that is clearly easier to describe in the spatial domain. Despite their simplicity, these examples point out the difficulty of fully exploiting the characteristics of the HVS by simply choosing the set of features the mark has to be inserted in. Of course, this does not mean that a proper selection of the host feature is of no help in watermark hiding. On the contrary, many systems have been proposed where embedding is performed in a feature domain that is known to be relatively more immune to disturbances. This is the case of frequency domain watermarking algorithms. Let us consider the curves reported in Figures 2 and 4. If we ignore very low frequencies (due to its very small extension the region of very low frequencies is usually not considered), we see how watermark hiding is more easily achieved avoiding marking the low frequency portion of the spectrum where disturbances are more easily perceived by the HSV. By relying on perceptibility considerations only, the frequency portion of the spectrum turns out to be a perfect place to hide information. When considering robustness to attacks, though, a high frequency watermark turns out to be too vulnerable to attacks such as low-pass filtering and JPEG compression, for which a low-pass watermark would be preferable. The most adopted solution consists in trading off between the two requirements, thus embedding the watermark into the medium-high portion of the frequency spectrum.

Similar considerations are valid for hybrid techniques, that is, those techniques embedding the watermark in a domain retaining both spatial and frequency localisation, as it is the case, for example, of wavelet- or block-DCT-based systems. In particular, the situation for block-DCT methods is identical to the frequency domain case; high frequency coefficients are usually preferred for embedding, in order to reduce visibility. The same objective can be reached in the *DWT* (Discrete Wavelet Transform) case by performing embedding in the finest sub-bands. By starting from these considerations, we can conclude that

Figure 6. General scheme for exploiting a masking function in a data hiding system

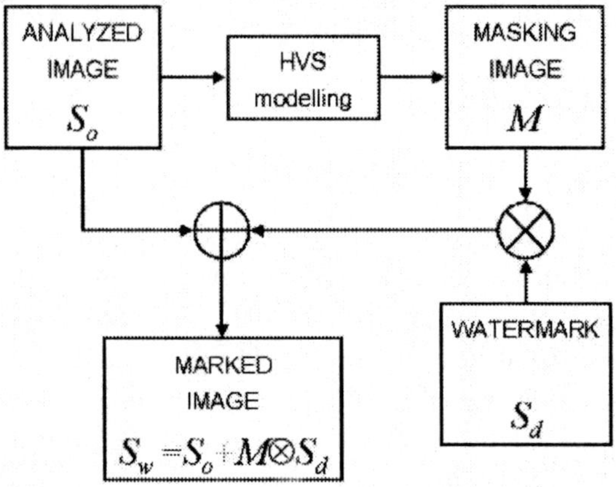

perceptual data hiding through feature selection is not very easy to be performed. In particular, if it is desired that watermark recovery has to be achieved also after image manipulations (attacks), which can make the selected features no longer available or identifiable, the sole possibility is to select the features on a fixed basis. This choice, nevertheless, implies that the embedded data are not always inserted into the most suitable image features.

The second possibility of exploiting the properties of the HVS to effectively hide a message into a host image consists in first designing the watermark in an arbitrary domain without taking HVS considerations into account, and then modifying the disturbance introduced by the watermark by locally adapting it to the image content. To be more specific the watermarked image is obtained by blending the original image, say S_o, and the to-be-inserted signal, here identified by a disturbance image S_d having the same cardinality of S_o, in such a way that the embedded signal is weighed by a function (M). M, which should be calculated by exploiting all the concepts regulating the HVS, gives a point-by-point measure of how insensitive to disturbances the cover image is. The perceptually adapted watermarked image (S'_w) can be thus obtained as follows:

$$S'_w = S_o + M \otimes S_d, \tag{16}$$

where by ⊗ we have indicated the sample-by-sample product, between the masking function M and the watermark image S_d (see Figure 6).

The inserted watermark S_d can be obtained as the difference between the image S_w watermarked without taking care about perceptibility issues (e.g., uniformly) and the original image S_o:

$$S_d = S_w - S_o. \tag{17}$$

Regardless of the domain where watermark embedding has been performed, and on the embedding rule, this difference always models the signal added to the original image for carrying the hidden information.

Whereas the general shape of M is easily found (e.g., lower values are expected in flat areas, whereas textured areas should be characterised by higher values of M), the exact definition of M is a complicated task, possibly involving a complex manual tuning phase. Let us suppose, for example, that M takes values in the [0,1] interval; that is, the effect of the blending mask is only to reduce the watermark strength in the most perceptually sensitive regions. In this case S_w should be tuned so that the hidden signal is just below the visibility threshold in very textured regions (where M is likely to take values close to 1) and well visible in all the other image areas. The mask, if properly designed, will reduce watermark strength on the other image regions in such a way to make it imperceptible everywhere. This procedure requires a manual tuning of the watermark strength during the embedding process to achieve S_w and this limits its efficacy when a large amount of images need to be watermarked.

A different possibility is that mask values indicate directly the maximum amount of the watermark strength that can be used for each region of the image at hand: in this case mask values are not normalised between [0,1], and the image can be watermarked to achieve S_w without tuning the watermark strength in advance.

In the following sections we will describe how this second approach can be implemented by relying on the HVS model introduced previously. Before going into the details of mask building, however, some limitations of classical HVS models will be pointed out and some innovative solutions outlined.

LIMITS OF CLASSICAL HVS MODELS AND A NEW APPROACH

Having described (in the second section) the main phenomena regulating the HVS, we now consider how these factors can be modelled to be used during a data hiding process. Let us recall the two concepts that mainly influence the human perception: the *contrast sensitivity* and the *masking effect*. The strict dependence of these factors on both frequency and luminance of the considered stimuli imposes the need to achieve good models that simultaneously take into account the two parameters.

Several HVS models have been proposed so far; without going into a description of related literature, we will point out some important limits of classical approaches, and describe some possible solutions to cope with these

Figure 7. Block-based DCT analysis of the image permits trading off between spatial and frequency localisation

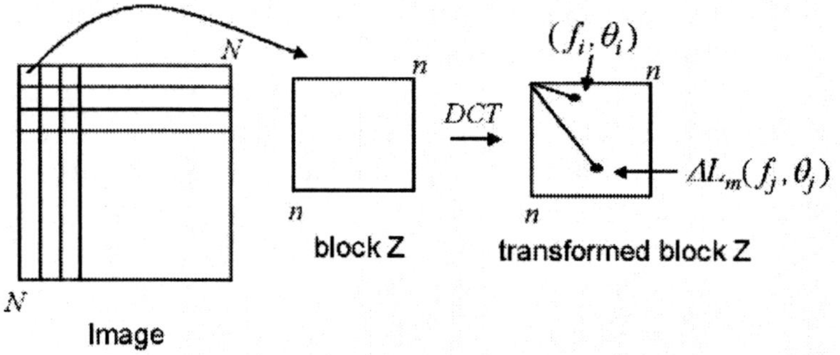

problems. More specifically, we will detail a new approach for HVS modelling, which will be exploited in the next section for building a blending mask.

The first problem in the models proposed so far is the lack of simultaneous spatial and frequency localisation. Classical models usually work either in the spatial domain, thus achieving a good spatial localisation, or in the frequency domain, thus achieving a good frequency localisation, but a simultaneous spatial and frequency localisation is not satisfactorily obtained.

To consider frequency localisation, a possibility for theoretical models operating in the spatial domain is to apply a multiple channel filtering. Such an approach, however, presents the drawback of artificially introducing a partitioning of the frequency plane, which separates the effects of close frequencies (that actually influence each other) when they belong to different channels. On the other hand, the main problem with classical HVS masking models operating in the frequency domain is that sinusoidal stimuli (e.g., a watermark embedded in the frequency domain) are spread all over the image, and since images are usually non-stationary, the possible presence of a masking signal is a spatially varying property, and, as such, is difficult to be handled in the frequency domain.

A possibility to trade off between spatial and frequency localisation consists in splitting the analysed $N \times N$ image into $n \times n$ blocks. Each block is, then, *DCT* transformed (see Figure 7). Block-based analysis permits considering the image properties localised spatially, by taking into account all the sinusoidal masking stimuli present only in the block itself.

A second problem comes out when the masking effect is considered. Most masking models only account for the presence of a single sinusoidal mask by considering the iso-frequency case. This is not the case in practical applications where the masking signal, namely the host image, is nothing but a sinusoid.

To take into account the non-sinusoidal nature of the masking signal (the host image), for each *i*-th position in each block *Z*, the contributions of all the surrounding frequencies (f_j , θ_j) of the same block must be considered. By starting from the *non- iso-frequency masking* (equation 15), a sum of the weighed masking contributions on the whole block must be introduced.

Swanson et al. (1998) propose a summation rule of the form:

$$JNC_m(f_i,\theta_i,w,L_Z)=\left\{\sum_{j\in Z}\left[JNC(f_i,\theta_i,w,L_Z)\cdot\right.\right.$$

$$\left.\left.\cdot\max\left\{1,\left|g(f_j/f_i,\theta_j-\theta_i)\frac{C_m(f_j,\theta_j,w,L_Z)}{JNC(f_j,\theta_j,w,L_Z)}\right|^W\right\}\right]^2\right\}^{1/2}. \quad \textbf{(18)}$$

Such a rule presents some limits, which will be evidenced in a while, thus calling for a different summation rule:

$$JNC_m(f_i,\theta_i,w,L_Z)=JNC(f_i,\theta_i,w,L_Z)\cdot$$

$$\cdot\max\left\{1,\left[\sum_{j\in Z}\left|g(f_j/f_i,\theta_j-\theta_i)\frac{C_m(f_j,\theta_j,w,L_Z)}{JNC(f_j,\theta_j,w,L_Z)}\right|\right]^W\right\}. \quad \textbf{(19)}$$

Let us note that the contrast of the masking component C_m is given by:

$$C_m(f_j,\theta_j,w,L_Z)=\frac{\Delta L_m(f_j,\theta_j,w)}{L_Z}, \quad \textbf{(20)}$$

where $\Delta L_m(f_j, \theta_j)$ is the amplitude of the sinusoidal masking component at frequency (f_j, θ_j). Furthermore, for each block Z the mean luminance L_z is measured based on the value of the corresponding DC coefficient.

By comparing equations 18 and 19, it is evident that the novelty of equation 19 is the introduction of the Σ operator inside the max operator. In particular, we consider the sum of all the weighed masking contributions in the block and then apply the formula proposed by Watson for the masked JNC to the sum, by considering it as a single contribution (this justifies the position of the exponent W outside the Σ operator). The validity of the proposed expression can be verified by considering that if all masking frequency components are null, equation 19 must reduce to the non-masked JNC (equation 11). Moreover, if only two close frequencies contribute to masking and, as an extreme case, these two frequencies coincide, the masking effect of these two components must be added as a single sinusoidal mask.

Such conditions are not satisfied by equation 18. It can be observed, in fact, that if no masking frequency is present in *Z*, the masked JNC differs from the non-masked JNC by a factor $(N_z)^{1/2}$, where N_z indicates the number of frequency components contained in Z. In other words, contributions of masking components are always considered even when such components are null. From experimental results we evidenced that this situation occurs with a probability of around 50%. In addition, if equation 18 is adopted, when two coincident frequencies contribute to the masking, their masking effects cannot be added as a single sinusoidal mask.

As a third consideration it appears that all the techniques described so far produce masking functions that depend only on the image characteristics, that is, on the characteristics of the masking signal, but not on the characteristics of the disturbing signal. On the contrary, to estimate the maximum amount of disturbing signal that can be inserted into an image by preserving its perceptual quality, it should be considered how the modifications caused by watermark insertion influence each other. For example, we consider two contiguous coefficients of a full-frame transform $X_1(f_1)$ and $X_2(f_2)$: the modifications imposed separately to X_1 and X_2 both contribute to the disturbance of both the corresponding frequencies f_1 and f_2. Instead, usual models do not consider this effect, by simply limiting the amount of modification of each coefficient in dependence on the masking capability of its neighbourhood, but without considering the disturbance of neighbouring coefficients.

A different approach must then be valued: instead of considering the single disturbing components separately, we adopt a new formula for expressing the disturb contrast for each position of the image, which we call the *Equivalent Disturb Contrast* C_{deq}. Such a formula takes into account all the considerations expressed until now. In particular, to trade off between spatial and frequency localisation of noise, a *block-based DCT* decomposition is applied to the disturbing image. Furthermore, to take into account the non-sinusoidal characteristics of the noise signal, for each *i*-th position of block *Z* all the disturbing components belonging to the same block are added by using the weighing function *g* (equation 12). The equivalent disturb contrast C_{deq} is then written as:

$$C_{d_{eq}}(f_i,\theta_i,w,L_Z)=\sum_{j\in Z}\left|g(f_j/f_i,\theta_j-\theta_i)C_d(f_i,\theta_i,w,L_Z)\right| \quad \textbf{(21)}$$

where C_d is the contrast of the disturb component defined as:

$$C_d(f_j,\theta_j,w,L_Z)=\frac{\Delta L_d(f_j,\theta_j,w)}{L_Z}, \quad \textbf{(22)}$$

with $\Delta L_d(f_j, \theta_j, w)$ being the amplitude of the sinusoidal noise signal at frequency (f_j, θ_j).

In conclusion, in order to guarantee the invisibility of a disturbance (i.e., the watermark) in a given image, for each frequency of each block Z, the equivalent disturb contrast C_{deq} computed by equation 21 must be smaller than the value of the masked just noticeable contrast JNC_m obtained by equation 19, which is:

$$C_{d_{eq}}(f_i, \theta_i, w, L_Z) \leq JNC_m(f_i, \theta_i, w, L_Z) \quad \forall i \in Z, \forall Z \qquad \textbf{(23)}$$

IMPROVED MASK BUILDING FOR DATA HIDING

The goal of this section is to present a method for building a mask that indicates, for each region of a given image, the maximum allowable energy of the watermark, under the constraint of image quality preservation. Such an approach will be based on the enhanced HVS model presented in the previous section, and it will provide a masking function for improving watermark invisibility and strength.

Before going on, it is worth noting that, so far, the behaviour of the HVS has been described in terms of luminance; however, digital images are usually stored as grey-level values, and a watermarking system will directly affect grey-level values. It is the goal of the next section to describe how grey-level values are related to the luminance perceived by the eye.

Luminance vs. Grey-Level Pixel Values

The luminance perceived by the eye does not depend solely on the grey level of the pixels forming the image. On the contrary, several other factors must be taken into account, including: the environment lighting conditions, the shape of the filter modelling the low pass behaviour of the eye, and of course the way the image is reproduced. In this framework we will concentrate on the case of pictures reproduced by a cathode ray tube (CRT), for which the dependence between grey-level values and luminance is better known and more easily modelled.

It is known that the relation between the grey level I of an image pixel and the luminance L of the light emitted by the corresponding CRT element is a non-linear one. More specifically, such a relation as is usually modelled by the expression (20):

$$L = L(I) = q + (mI)^{\gamma}, \qquad \textbf{(24)}$$

with q defining luminance corresponding to a black image, m defines the contrast and γ accounts for the intrinsic non-linearity of the CRT emitting elements (the phosphors). While γ is a characteristic parameter of any given CRT, q and m depend on "brightness" and "contrast" regulations usually accessible to the user through the CRT electronics.

A first possibility to map HVS concepts from luminance to grey-level domain consists in mapping grey-level values through (24), thus obtaining a luminance image, operating on this image according to the proposed model, and finally going back to grey-level domain through the inverse of (24). Alternatively, we can try to directly write the just noticeable contrast as a function of grey-level values. In analogy to equation 8, this can be done by considering a generic grey-level image composed of a uniform background I_o, a masking sinusoidal signal of amplitude ΔI_m and a disturbing sinusoidal stimulus of amplitude ΔI:

$$\begin{aligned} I(x,y) = I_o + \Delta I_m \cos(2\pi f_m (x\cos\theta_m + y sin\theta_m)) + \\ + \Delta I \cos(2\pi f (x\cos\theta + y sin\theta)), \end{aligned} \quad (25)$$

which is mapped to a luminance pattern through equation 24:

$$\begin{aligned} L(x,y) = L(I(x,y)) \approx L(I_o) + \\ L'(I_o)\Delta I_m \cos(2\pi f_m (x\cos\theta_m + y sin\theta_m)) + \\ L'(I_o)\Delta I \cos(2\pi f (x\cos\theta + y sin\theta)), \end{aligned} \quad (26)$$

where $L'(I_o)$ is the derivative of the luminance mapping function given in (24) and where a linear approximation of $L(x,y)$ is adopted. By comparing (26) with (8) we have that, as a first approximation, $\Delta L_m = L'(I_o)\,\Delta I_m$ and $\Delta L = L'(I_o)\,\Delta I$. The just noticeable contrast in the grey-level domain can thus be expressed by the formula:

$$\begin{aligned} JNC_I(f_i,\theta_i,w,I_o) &= \frac{\Delta I_{jn}(f_i,\theta_i,w)}{I_o} \approx \frac{\Delta L_{jn}(f_i,\theta_i,w)}{I_o L'(I_o)} = \\ &= \frac{JNC(f_i,\theta_i,w,L_o)L_o}{I_o L'(I_o)} \approx \\ &\approx \frac{L(I_o)}{I_o L'(I_o)} JNC(f_i,\theta_i,w,L(I_o)). \end{aligned} \quad (27)$$

Figure 8. Plot of the just noticeable grey-level stimulus vs. image background grey-level, for a frequency of five cycles/degree (The amplitude of the just noticeable disturbance increases for low and high background grey-level values.)

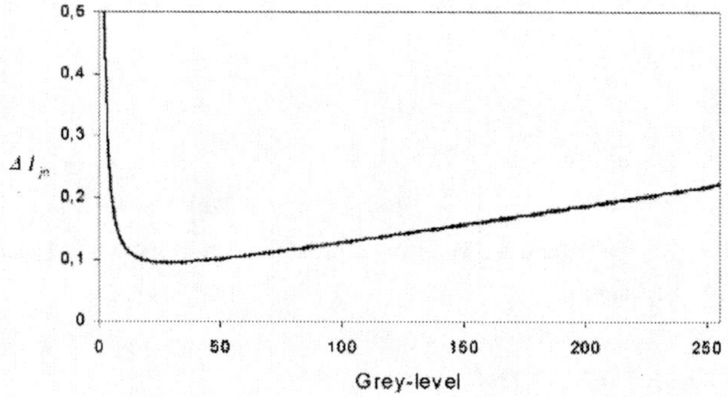

Once q, m, and γ are known, the above equations permit operating directly on grey-level images. In Figure 8 the just noticeable grey-level visibility threshold ($\Delta I_{jn} = I \cdot JNC_I$) is reported with respect to grey-level values for an angular frequency of 5 cycles/degree: the values of the parameters describing the CRT response have been set to $q = 0.04$, $m = 0.03$ and $\gamma = 2.2$ and have been estimated on a Philips CRT monitor. It is evident how this plot is in agreement with the fact that more noise can be tolerated in the dark and bright regions of the image.

By using the previous relation for JNC_I, both the masked just noticeable contrast and the equivalent disturb contrast can be expressed directly in the grey-level domain. By referring to equation 19 and 21, we obtain:

$$JNC_{Im}(f_i,\theta_i,w,I_Z) \approx JNC_I(f_i,\theta_i,w,I_Z) \cdot$$
$$\cdot \max\left\{1, \left[\sum_{j\in Z}\left| g(f_j/f_i,\theta_j-\theta_i)\frac{C_{Im}(f_j,\theta_j,w,I_z)}{JNC_I(f_j,\theta_j,w,I_z)}\right|\right]^W\right\}, \quad \textbf{(28)}$$

and:

$$C_{I_{d_{eq}}}(f_i,\theta_i,w,I_z) = \sum_{j\in Z}\left| g(f_j/f_i,\theta_j-\theta_i) C_{I_d}(f_j,\theta_j,w,I_z)\right|, \quad \textbf{(29)}$$

where the contrast values JNC_I, C_{Im}, C_{Id} are computed by referring to equation 27, whereby any contrast C_{Id} can be given the form:

$$C_l(f_i,\theta_i,w,I_0)=\frac{\Delta I(f_i,\theta_i,w)}{I_0}\approx\frac{L(I_0)}{I_0L'(I_0)}C(f_i,\theta_i,w,L(I_0)). \quad (30)$$

By expressing equation 23 in the grey-level domain, we finally find the relation assuring the invisibility of the watermark, by processing directly grey-level images:

$$C_{I_{d_{eq}}}(f_i,\theta_i,w,I_Z)\leq JNC_{I_m}(f_i,\theta_i,w,I_Z),\ \forall i\in Z,\forall Z. \quad (31)$$

By relying on this formula we will now present an approach for building an improved masking function.

Improved Mask Building

Let us consider an original signal (i.e., an image) S_o and its marked version S_w. The difference between S_w and S_o, that is, the inserted watermark S_d, represents the disturbing signal, while S_o represents the masking signal. Now, by applying the approach detailed in the previous section, it is possible to determine the maximum allowable energy of the watermark in order to preserve image quality. In particular, a *block-based DCT* analysis is applied to both S_o and S_d in order to obtain for each coefficient of each block the masked just noticeable contrast and the equivalent disturb contrast expressions.

The host image S_o is divided into blocks of size $n\times n$. Let us indicate them by $B_o^Z(i, k)$. Then each block is *DCT*-transformed into $b_o^Z(u, v)$. This transform allows us to decompose each image block as the sum of a set of sinusoidal stimuli. In particular, for each block Z the mean grey-level is given by $I_z = b'^Z_o(0, 0) = b_o^Z(0,0)/2n$. Furthermore, each coefficient at frequency (u, v) gives birth to two sinusoidal stimuli, having the same amplitude, the same frequency f_{uv}, but opposite orientations $\pm\theta_{uv}$. The amplitude is generally given by $b'^Z_o(u, v) = b_o^Z(u, v)/2n$, except when $\theta_{uv}\in\{0, \pi\}$ then it results $b'^Z_o(u, v) = b_o^Z(u, v)/\sqrt{2}\,n$.

By relying on equation 28, for a *DCT* coefficient at spatial frequency (u, v) the contributions of all the surrounding frequencies of the same block Z are considered and the value of the masked just noticeable contrast is obtained through the following expression:

$$JNC_{I_m}(u,v,w,b_o^Z(0,0))=JNC_I(u,v,w,b_o^Z(0,0))\cdot$$
$$\cdot\max\left\{1,\left[\sum_{u'=0,v'=0}^{n-1,n-1}\left|g'(u,u',v,v')\frac{b_o'^Z(u',v')/b_o'^Z(0,0)}{JNC_I(u',v',w,b_o'^Z(0,0))}\right|\right]^W\right\}, \quad (32)$$

where $JNC_I(u,v,w,b'^{Z}_{o}(0,0))$ is the non-masked just noticeable contrast for the coefficient at frequency (u, v), $b'^{Z}_{o}(u', v')/b'^{Z}_{o}(0,0)$ is the contrast of the masking coefficient, and $g'(u, u', v, v')$ is the weighing function that can be obtained by equation 12 as:

$$g'(u,u',v,v') = \exp\left[-\left(\frac{\log_2^2(f_{u'v'}/f_{uv})}{\sigma_f^2}\right)\right] \cdot \exp\left[-\left(\frac{(\theta_{u'v'}-\theta_{uv})^2 + (-\theta_{u'v'}-\theta_{uv})^2}{\sigma_\theta^2}\right)\right], \quad (33)$$

where the fact that each *DCT* coefficient accounts for two sinusoidal components with the same spatial frequencies but opposite orientations, and that the just noticeable contrast has the same value for stimuli having opposite orientations, has been considered.

In order to guarantee the invisibility of a sinusoidal disturbance in a given block, the contrast of the component of the disturbance at a given frequency (u, v) must be smaller than the value of the JNC_{Im} obtained by equation 32. A *block based DCT* is also applied to the disturbing signal S_d, computed as the difference between the watermarked signal S_w and the original signal S_o. Each block Z of S_d (i.e., $B_d^Z(i, k)$) is decomposed as a sum of sinusoidal stimuli (i.e., $b_d^Z(u, v)$).

What we want to get is a threshold on the maximum allowable modification that each coefficient can sustain. We have to consider that nearby watermarking coefficients will reinforce each other; thus, by relying on equation 29, we can rewrite the equivalent disturb contrast at coefficient (u, v) in block Z as:

$$C_{I_{d_{eq}}}\left(u,v,w,b_o'^{Z}(0,0)\right) = \sum_{u'=0,v'=0}^{n-1,n-1} \left| g'(u,u',v,v') \cdot \frac{c(u')c(v')}{n} \frac{b_d'^{Z}(u',v')}{b_o'^{Z}(0,0)} \right|, \quad (34)$$

where $b'^{Z}_{d}(u',v')/b'^{Z}_{o}(0,0)$ is the contrast of the disturbing signal, and where we have assumed that the same weighing function can be used for modelling the reinforcing effect of neighbouring disturbances. By relying on equation 31, the invisibility constraint results to be:

$$C_{I_{d_{eq}}}\left(u,v,w,b_o'^{Z}(0,0)\right) \le JNC_{I_m}\left(u,v,w,b_o'^{Z}(0,0)\right), \ \forall (u,v) \in Z. \quad (35)$$

Based on this approach, it is possible to build a masking function for spatially shaping any kind of watermark. By referring to equation 16, let us suppose that the mask M is block-wise constant, and let us indicate with M_Z the value assumed by the mask in block Z. By exploiting the linearity property of the *DCT* transform, it is easy to verify that for satisfying the invisibility constraint we must have:

$$M_Z \cdot C_{I_{deq}}\left(u,v,w,b_o^{'Z}(0,0)\right) \le JNC_{I_m}\left(u,v,w,b_o^{'Z}(0,0)\right), \quad \forall (u,v) \in Z, \tag{36}$$

thus boiling down to:

$$M_Z = \min_{(u,v)} \frac{JNC_{I_m}\left(u,v,w,b_o^{'Z}(0,0)\right)}{C_{I_{deq}}\left(u,v,w,b_o^{'Z}(0,0)\right)}, \quad \forall (u,v) \in Z. \tag{37}$$

In Figures 9 to12 the resulting masking functions are shown for some standard images, namely *Lena*, *harbor*, *boat* and *airplane.* These masks produce reliable results, especially on textured areas. This is mainly due to the fact that the disturbing signal frequency content is also considered for building the mask. Moreover, this method allows the maximum amount of watermarking energy that each image can tolerate to be automatically obtained, without resorting to manual tuning.

Figure 9. Mask obtained for the Lena image by means of the block-based DCT perceptual model

Figure 10. Mask obtained for the Harbor image by means of the block-based DCT perceptual model

Figure 11. Mask obtained for the Boat image by means of the block-based DCT perceptual model

Figure 12. Mask obtained for the Airplane image by means of the block-based DCT perceptual model

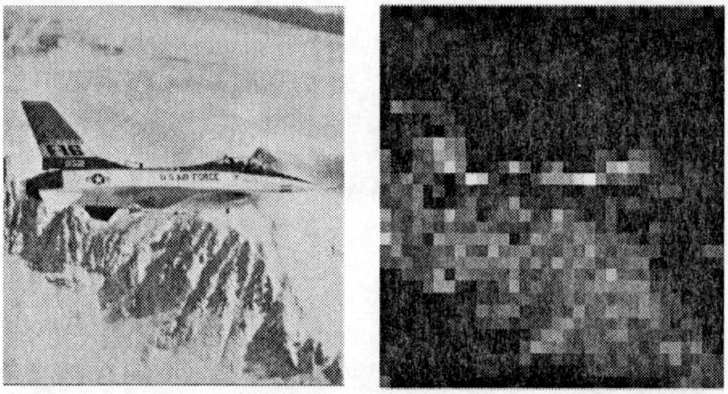

CONCLUSIONS

Two of the main requirements a data-hiding scheme must satisfy regard invisibility and robustness. The watermark must be invisible so that its presence does not affect the quality of the to-be-protected data; on the other hand, it must be resistant against the most common image manipulations, calling for the necessity of embedding a watermark with as high a strength as possible. The availability of accurate models describing the phenomena regulating human vision can give great advantage to satisfy the above requirements.

By starting from the analysis of the main important HVS concepts, we have explored how these factors can be exploited during the data-hiding process. Some important limits of the classical approaches have been pointed out, as well as possible solutions to cope with them. Finally, we have detailed a new possible approach for HVS modelling and its exploitation for building a sensitivity mask.

Due to the space constraints, we limited our analysis to mask building algorithms directly derived from the HVS model. For a couple of alternative (more heuristic) approaches to mask building, readers are referred to Bartolini et al. (1998) and Pereira, Voloshynovskiy and Pun (2001). We also ignored visual masking in domains other than the DFT and DCT ones. A detailed description of an HVS-based data-hiding system operating in the wavelet domain, may be found in Barni, Bartolini and Piva (2001). To further explore the importance and the role of perceptual considerations in a data hiding system, readers may also refer to Wolfgang et al. (1999) and Podilchuk and Zeng (1998).

We purposely limited our analysis to the case of grey-level images, since in many cases the watermark is inserted in the luminance component of the host image. It has to be said, though, that advantages in terms of both robustness and imperceptibility are likely to be got by considering the way the HVS handles colours.

REFERENCES

Ahumada, A.J., Jr., & Beard, B.L. (1996, February). Object detection in a noisy scene. *Proceedings of SPIE: Vol. 2657. Human Vision, Visual Processing, and Digital Display VII* (pp. 190-199). Bellingham, WA.

Barni, M., Bartolini, F., & Piva, A. (2001, May). Improved wavelet-based watermarking through pixel-wise masking. *IEEE Transactions on Image Processing, 10*(5), 783-791.

Barten, P.G. (1990, October). Evaluation of subjective image quality with the square-root integral method. *Journal of Optical Society of America, 7*(10), 2024-2031.

Bartolini, F., Barni, M., Cappellini, V., & Piva, A. (1998, October). Mask building for perceptually hiding frequency embedded watermarks. *Proceedings of*

IEEE International Conference of Image Processing '98, (vol. 1, pp. 450-454). Chicago, IL.

Comes, S., & Macq, B. (1990, October). Human visual quality criterion. *Proceedings of SPIE: Vol. 1360. Visual Communications and Image Processing* (pp. 2-13). Lausanne, CH.

Cox, I., & Miller, M.L. (1997, February). A review of watermarking and the importance of perceptual modeling. *Proceedings of SPIE: Vol. 3016. Human Vision and Electronic Imaging II* (pp. 92-99). Bellingham, WA.

Damera-Venkata, N., Kite, T.D., Geisler, W.S., Evans, B.L., & Bovik, A.C. (2000, April). Image quality assessment based on a degradation model. *IEEE Transactions on Image Processing, 9*(4), 636-650.

Delaigle, J.F., De Vleeschouwer, C., & Macq, B. (1998, May). Watermarking algorithm based on a human visual model. *Signal Processing, 66*(3), 319-336.

Eckert, M.P., & Bradley, A.P. (1998). Perceptual quality metrics applied to still image compression. *Signal Processing, 70,* 177-200.

Foley, J.M., & Legge, G.E. (1981). Contrast detection and near-threshold discrimination. *Vision Research, 21,* 1041-1053.

Kundur, D., & Hatzinakos, D. (1997, October). A robust digital watermarking method using wavelet-based fusion. *Proceedings of IEEE International Conference of Image Processing '97: Vol. 1* (pp. 544-547). Santa Barbara, CA.

Legge, G.E., & Foley, J.M. (1980, December). Contrast masking in human vision. *Journal of Optical Society of America, 70*(12), 1458-1471.

Pereira, S., Voloshynovskiy, S., & Pun, T. (2001, June). Optimal transform domain watermark embedding via linear programming. *Signal Processing, 81*(6), 1251-1260.

Petitcolas, F.A., Anderson, R.J., & Kuhn, M.G. (1999, July). Information hiding: A survey. *Proceedings of IEEE, 87*(7), 1062-1078.

Podilchuk, C.I., & Zeng, W. (1998, May). Image-adaptive watermarking using visual models. *IEEE Journal on Selected Areas in Communications, 16*(4), 525-539.

Swanson, M.D., Zhu, B., & Tewfik, A.H. (1998, May). Multiresolution scene-based video watermarking using perceptual models. *IEEE Journal on Selected Areas in Communications, 16*(4), 540-550.

Tewfik, A.H., & Swanson, M. (1997, July). Data hiding for multimedia personalization, interaction, and protection. *IEEE Signal Processing Magazine, 14*(4), 41-44.

Van Schyndel, R.G., Tirkel, A.Z., & Osborne, C.F. (1994, November). A digital watermark. *Proceedings of IEEE International Conference of Image Processing '94: Vol. 2* (pp. 86-90). Austin, TX.

Voloshynovskiy, S., Pereira, S., Iquise, V., & Pun, T. (2001, June). Attack modelling: Towards a second generation watermarking benchmark. *Signal Processing, 81*(6), 1177-1214.

Watson, A.B. (1987, December). Efficiency of an image code based on human vision. *Journal of Optical Society of America, 4*(12), 2401-2417.

Watson, A.B. (1993, February). Dct quantization matrices visually optimized for individual images. *Proceedings of SPIE: Vol. 1913. Human Vision, Visual Processing and Digital Display IV* (pp. 202-216). Bellingham, WA.

Wolfgang, R.B., Podilchuk, C.I., & Delp, E.J. (1999, July). Perceptual watermarks for digital images and video. *Proceedings of IEEE, 87*(7), 1108-1126.

Chapter III

Audio Watermarking: Properties, Techniques and Evaluation

Andrés Garay Acevedo, Georgetown University, USA

ABSTRACT

The recent explosion of the Internet as a collaborative medium has opened the door for people who want to share their work. Nonetheless, the advantages of such an open medium can pose very serious problems for authors who do not want their works to be distributed without their consent. As new methods for copyright protection are devised, expectations around them are formed and sometimes improvable claims are made. This chapter covers one such technology: audio watermarking. First, the field is introduced, and its properties and applications are discussed. Then, the most common techniques for audio watermarking are reviewed, and the framework is set for the objective measurement of such techniques. The last part of the chapter proposes a novel test and a set of metrics for thorough benchmarking of audio watermarking schemes. The development of such a benchmark constitutes a first step towards the standardization of the requirements and properties that such systems should display.

INTRODUCTION

The recent explosion of the Internet as a collaborative medium has opened the door for people who want to share their work. Nonetheless, the advantages of such an open medium can pose very serious problems for authors who do not want their works to be distributed without their consent. The digital nature of the information that traverses through modern networks calls for new and improved methods for copyright protection[1].

In particular, the music industry is facing several challenges (as well as opportunities) as it tries to adapt its business to the new medium. Content protection is a key factor towards a comprehensive information commerce infrastructure (Yeung, 1998), and the industry expects new technologies will help them protect against the misappropriation of musical content.

One such technology, digital watermarking, has recently brought a tide of publicity and controversy. It is an emerging discipline, derived from an older science: steganography, or the hiding of a secret message within a seemingly innocuous cover message. In fact, some authors treat watermarking and steganography as equal concepts, differentiated only by their final purpose (Johnson, Duric, & Jajodia, 2001).

As techniques for digital watermarking are developed, claims about their performance are made public. However, different metrics are typically used to measure performance, making it difficult to compare both techniques and claims. Indeed, there are no standard metrics for measuring the performance of watermarks for digital audio. Robustness does not correspond to the same criteria among developers (Kutter & Petitcolas, 1999). Such metrics are needed before we can expect to see a commercial application of audio watermarking products with a provable performance.

The objective of this chapter is to propose a methodology, including performance metrics, for evaluating and comparing the performance of digital audio watermarking schemes. In order to do this, it is necessary first to provide a clear definition of what constitutes a watermark and a watermarking system in the context of digital audio. This is the topic of the second section, which will prove valuable later in the chapter, as it sets a framework for the development of the proposed test.

After a clear definition of a digital watermark has been presented, a set of key properties and applications of digital watermarks can be defined and discussed. This is done in the third section, along with a classification of audio watermarking schemes according to the properties presented. The importance of these properties will be reflected on the proposed tests, discussed later in the chapter. The survey of different applications of watermarking techniques gives a practical view of how the technology can be used in a commercial and legal environment. The specific application of the watermarking scheme will also determine the actual test to be performed to the system.

The fourth section presents a survey of specific audio watermarking techniques developed. Five general approaches are described: amplitude modification, dither watermarking, echo watermarking, phase distortion, and spread spectrum watermarking. Specific implementations of watermarking algorithms (i.e., test subjects) will be evaluated in terms of these categories[2].

The next three sections describe how to evaluate audio watermarking technologies based on three different parameters: fidelity, robustness, and imperceptibility. Each one of these parameters will be precisely defined and discussed in its respective section, as they directly reflect the interests of the three main actors involved in the communication process[3]: sender, attacker, and receiver, respectively.

Finally, the last section provides an account on how to combine the three parameters described above into a single performance measure of quality. It must be stated, however, that this measure should be dependant upon the desired application of the watermarking algorithm (Petitcolas, 2000).

The topics discussed in this chapter come not only from printed sources but also from very productive discussions with some of the active researchers in the field. These discussions have been conducted via e-mail, and constitute a rich complement to the still low number of printed sources about this topic. Even though the annual number of papers published on watermarking has been nearly doubling every year in the last years (Cox, Miller, & Bloom, 2002), it is still low. Thus it was necessary to augment the literature review with personal interviews.

WATERMARKING: A DEFINITION

Different definitions have been given for the term *watermarking* in the context of digital content. However, a very general definition is given by Cox et al. (2002), which can be seen as application independent: "We define watermarking as the practice of imperceptibly altering a Work to embed a message about that Work". In this definition, the word *work* refers to a specific song, video or picture[4].

A crucial point is inferred by this definition, namely that the information hidden within the work, the watermark itself, contains information about the work where it is embedded. This characteristic sets a basic requirement for a watermarking system that makes it different from a general steganographic tool. Moreover, by distinguishing between embedded data that relate to the cover work and hidden data that do not, we can derive some of the applications and requirements of the specific method. This is exactly what will be done later.

Another difference that is made between watermarking and steganography is that the former has the additional notion of robustness against attacks (Kutter & Hartung, 2000). This fact also has some implications that will be covered later on.

Finally, if we apply Cox's definition of watermarking into the field of audio signal processing, a more precise definition, this time for audio watermarking, can be stated. Digital audio watermarking is defined as the process of "embedding a user specified bitsream in digital audio such that the addition of the watermark (bitstream) is perceptually insignificant" (Czerwinski, Fromm, & Hodes, 1999).

This definition should be complemented with the previous one, so that we do not forget the watermark information refers to the digital audio file.

Elements of an Audio Watermarking System

Embedded watermarks are recovered by running the inverse process that was used to embed them in the cover work, that is, the original work. This means that all watermarking systems consist of at least two generic building blocks: a watermark embedding system and a watermark recovery system.

Figure 1 shows a basic watermarking scheme, in which a watermark is both embedded and recovered in an audio file. As can be seen, this process might also involve the use of a secret key. In general terms, given the audio file *A,* the watermark *W* and the key *K,* the embedding process is a mapping of the form $A \times K \times W \rightarrow A'$

Conversely, the recovery or extraction process receives a tentatively watermarked audio file A', and a recovery key K' (which might be equal to *K*), and it outputs either the watermark *W* or a confidence measure about the existence of *W* (Petitcolas, Anderson, & G., 1999).

At this point it is useful to attempt a formal definition of a watermarking system, based on that of Katzenbeisser (2000), and which takes into account the architecture of the system. The quintuple $\xi = \langle C, W, K, D_k, E_k \rangle$, where *C* is the set of possible audio *covers*[5], *W* the set of *watermarks* with $|C| \geq |W|$, *K* the set of secret *keys,* E_k: $C \times K \times W \rightarrow C$ the embedding function and D_k: $C \times K \rightarrow W$ the extraction function, with the property that $D_k(E_k(c, k, w)\, k) = w$ for all $w \in W$, $c \in C$ and $k \in K$ is called a *secure audio watermarking system.*

This definition is almost complete, but it fails to cover some special cases. Some differences might arise between a real world system, and the one just defined; for example, some detectors may not output the watermark *W* directly but rather report the existence of it. Nonetheless, it constitutes a good approximation towards a widely accepted definition of an audio watermarking system.

If one takes into account the small changes that a marking scheme can have, a detailed classification of watermarking schemes is possible. In this classification, the different schemes fall into three categories, depending on the set of

Figure 1. Basic watermarking system

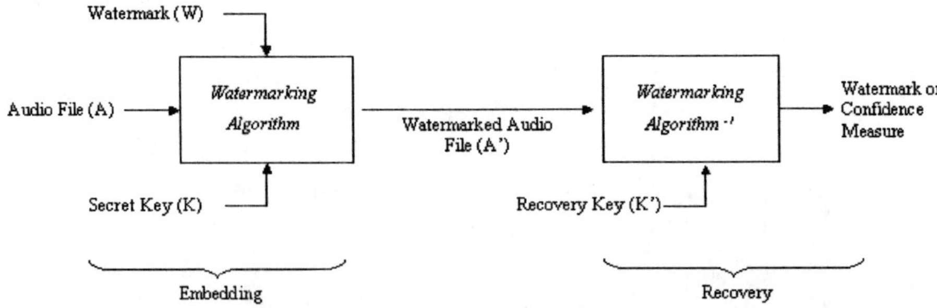

inputs and outputs (Kutter & Hartung, 2000). Furthermore, a specific and formal definition for each scheme can be easily given by adapting the definition just given for an audio watermarking system.

Private watermarking systems require the original audio A file in order to attempt recovery of the watermark W. They may also require a copy of the embedded watermark and just yield a yes or no answer to the question: does A' contain W?

Semi-private watermarking schemes do not use the original audio file for detection, but they also answer the yes/no question shown above. This could be described by the relation $A' \times K \times W \rightarrow \{$"Yes", "No"$\}$.

Public watermarking (also known as *blind* or *oblivious* watermarking) requires neither the original file A, nor the embedded watermark W. These systems just extract n bits of information from the watermarked audio file. As can be seen, if a key is used then this corresponds to the definition given for a *secure watermarking system.*

Watermark as a Communication Process

A watermarking process can be modeled as a communication process. In fact, this assumption is used throughout this chapter. This will prove to be beneficial in the next chapter when we differentiate between the requirements of the content owner and consumer. A more detailed description of this model can be found in Cox et al. (2002).

In this framework, the watermarking process is viewed as a transmission channel through which the watermark message is communicated. Here the cover work is just part of the channel. This is depicted in Figure 2, based on that from Cox et al. (2002).

In general terms, the embedding process consists of two steps. First, the watermark message m is mapped into an added pattern[6] W_a, of the same type and dimension as the cover work A. When watermarking audio, the watermark encoder produces an audio signal. This mapping may be done with a watermark key K. Next, W_a is embedded into the cover work in order to produce the watermarked audio file A'.

Figure 2. Watermark communication process

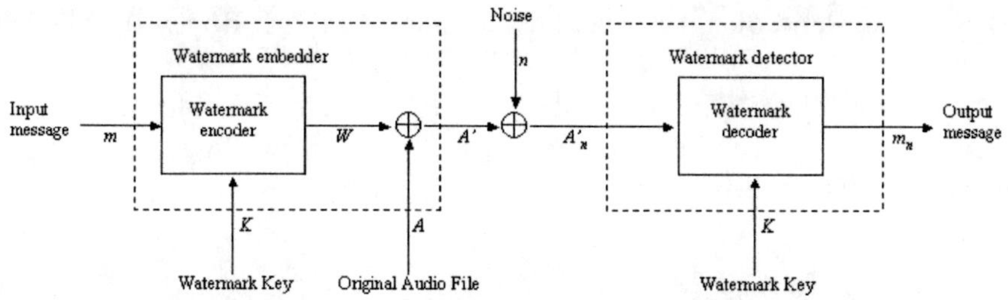

After the pattern is embedded, the audio file is processed in some way. This is modeled as the addition of noise to the signal, which yields a noisy work A'_n. The types of processing performed on the work will be discussed later, as they are of no importance at this moment. However, it is important to state the presence of noise, as any transmission medium will certainly induce it.

The watermark detector performs a process that is dependant on the type of watermarking scheme. If the decoder is a *blind or public decoder,* then the original audio file A is not needed during the recovery process, and only the key K is used in order to decode a watermark message m_n. This is the case depicted in Figure 2, as it is the one of most interest to us.

Another possibility is for the detector to be *informed.* In this case, the original audio cover A must be extracted from A'_n in order to yield W_n, prior to running the decoding process. In addition, a confidence measure can be the output of the system, rather than the watermark message.

PROPERTIES, CLASSIFICATION AND APPLICATIONS

After a proper definition of a watermarking scheme, it is possible now to take a look at the fundamental properties that comprise a watermark. It can be stated that an ideal watermarking scheme will present all of the characteristics here detailed, and this ideal type will be useful for developing a quality test.

However, in practice there exists a fundamental trade-off that restricts watermark designers. This fundamental trade-off exists between three key variables: robustness, payload and perceptibility (Cox, Miller, Linnartz, & Kalker, 1999; Czerwinski et al., 1999; Johnson et al., 2001; Kutter & Petitcolas, 1999; Zhao, Koch, & Luo, 1998). The relative importance given to each of these variables in a watermarking implementation depends on the desired application of the system.

Fundamental Properties

A review of the literature quickly points out the properties that an ideal watermarking scheme should possess (Arnold, 2000; Boney, Tewfik & Hamdy, 1996; Cox, Miller, & Bloom, 2000; Cox et al., 1999, 2002; Kutter & Hartung, 2000; Kutter & Petitcolas, 1999; Swanson, Zhu, Tewfik, & Boney, 1998). These are now discussed.

Imperceptibility. "The watermark should not be noticeable … nor should [it] degrade the quality of the content" (Cox et al., 1999). In general, the term refers to a similarity between the original and watermarked versions of the cover work.

In the case of audio, the term *audibility* would be more appropriate; however, this could create some confusion, as the majority of the literature uses *perceptibility*. This is the same reason why the term *fidelity* is not used at this point, even though Cox et al. (1999) point out that if a watermark is truly imperceptible, then it can be removed by perceptually-based lossy compression algorithms. In fact, this statement will prove to be a problem later when trying to design a measure of watermark perceptibility. Cox's statement implies that some sort of perceptibility criterion must be used not only to design the watermark, but to quantify the distortion as well. Moreover, it implies that this distortion must be measured at the point where the audio file is being presented to the consumer/receiver.

If the distortion is measured at the receiver's end, it should also be measured at the sender's. That is, the distortion induced by a watermark must also be measured before any transmission process. We will refer to this characteristic at the sending end by using the term *fidelity*.

This distinction between the terms *fidelity* and *imperceptibility* is not common in the literature, but will be beneficial at a later stage. Differentiating between the amount and characteristics of the noise or distortion that a watermark introduces in a signal before and after the transmission process takes into account the different expectations that content owners and consumers have from the technology. However, this also implies that the metric used to evaluate this effect must be different at these points. This is exactly what will be done later on this chapter.

Artifacts introduced through a watermarking process are not only annoying and undesirable, but may also reduce or destroy the commercial value of the watermarked data (Kutter & Hartung, 2000). Nonetheless, the perceptibility of the watermark can increase when certain operations are performed on the cover signal.

Robustness refers to the ability to detect the watermark after common signal processing operations and hostile attacks. Examples of common operations performed on audio files include noise reduction, volume adjustment or normalization, digital to analog conversion, and so forth. On the other hand, a hostile attack is a process specifically designed to remove the watermark.

Not all watermarking applications require robustness against all possible signal processing operations. Only those operations likely to occur between the embedding of the mark and the decoding of it should be addressed. However, the number and complexity of attack techniques is increasing (Pereira, Voloshynovskiy, Madueño, Marchand-Maillet, & Pun, 2001; Voloshynovskiy, Pereira, Pun, Eggers, & Su, 2001), which means that more scenarios have to be taken into account when designing a system. A more detailed description of these attacks is given in the sixth section.

Robustness deals with two different issues; namely the presence and detection of the watermark after some processing operation. It is not necessary to remove a watermark to render it useless; if the detector cannot report the presence of the mark then the attack can be considered successful. This means that a watermarking scheme is robust when it is able to withstand a series of attacks that try to degrade the quality of the embedded watermark, up to the point where it's removed, or its recovery process is unsuccessful. "No such perfect method has been proposed so far, and it is not clear yet whether an absolutely secure watermarking method exists at all" (Kutter & Hartung, 2000).

Some authors prefer to talk about *tamper resistance* or even *security* when referring to hostile attacks; however, most of the literature encompasses this case under the term *robustness.*

The *effectiveness* of a watermarking system refers to the probability that the output of the embedder will be watermarked. In other words, it is the probability that a watermark detector will recognize the watermark immediately after inserting it in the cover work. What is most amazing about this definition is the implication that a watermarking system might have an effectiveness of less than 100%. That is, it is possible for a system to generate marks that are not fully recoverable even if no processing is done to the cover signal. This happens because perfect effectiveness comes at a very high cost with respect to other properties, such as perceptibility (Cox et al., 2002). When a known watermark is not successfully recovered by a detector it is said that a false negative, or type-II error, has occurred (Katzenbeisser, 2000).

Depending on the application, one might be willing to sacrifice some performance in exchange for other characteristics. For example, if extremely high fidelity is to be achieved, one might not be able to successfully watermark certain type of works without generating some kind of distortion. In some cases, the effectiveness can be determined analytically, but most of the time it has to be estimated by embedding a large set of works with a given watermark and then trying to extract that mark. However, the statistical characteristics of the test set must be similar to those of the works that will be marked in the real world using the algorithm.

Data payload. In audio watermarking this term refers to the number of embedded bits per second that are transmitted. A watermark that encodes N bits is referred to as an N-bit watermark, and can be used to embed 2^N different messages. It must be said that there is a difference between the encoded message m, and the actual bitstream that is embedded in the audio cover work. The latter is normally referred to as a *pseudorandom* (PN) *sequence.*

Many systems have been proposed where only one possible watermark can be embedded. The detector then just determines whether the watermark is present or not. These systems are referred to as *one-bit watermarks,* as only two different values can be encoded inside the watermark message. In discussing the data payload of a watermarking method, it is also important to distinguish between the number of distinct watermarks that may be inserted, and the number of watermarks that may be detected by a single iteration with a given watermark detector. In many watermarking applications, each detector need not test for all the watermarks that might possibly be present (Cox et al., 1999). For example, one might insert two different watermarks into the same audio file, but only be interested in recovering the last one to be embedded.

Other Properties

Some of the properties reviewed in the literature are not crucial for testing purposes; however they must be mentioned in order to make a thorough description of watermarking systems.

- *False positive rate.* A false positive or type-I error is the detection of a watermark in a work that does not actually contain one. Thus a false positive rate is the expected number of false positives in a given number of runs of the watermark detector. Equivalently, one can detect the probability that a false positive will occur in a given detector run.
  In some applications a false positive can be catastrophic. For example, imagine a DVD player that incorrectly determines that a legal copy of a disk (for example a homemade movie) is a non-factory-recorded disk and refuses to play it. If such an error is common, then the reputation of DVD players and consequently their market can be seriously damaged.
- *Statistical invisibility.* This is needed in order to prevent unauthorized detection and/or removal. Performing statistical tests on a set of watermarked files should not reveal any information about the nature of the embedded information, nor about the technique used for watermarking (Swanson et al., 1998). Johnson et al. (2001) provide a detailed description of known signatures that are created by popular information hiding tools. Their techniques can be also extended for use in some watermarking systems.
- *Redundancy.* To ensure robustness, the watermark information is embedded in multiple places on the audio file. This means that the watermark can usually be recovered from just a small portion of the watermarked file.
- *Compression ratio,* or similar compression characteristics as the original file. Audio files are usually compressed using different schemes, such as MPEG-Layer 3 audio compression. An audio file with an embedded watermark should yield a similar compression ratio as its unmarked counterpart, so that its value is not degraded. Moreover, the compression process should not remove the watermark.
- *Multiple watermarks.* Multiple users should be able to embed a watermark into an audio file. This means that a user has to ideally be able to embed a

watermark without destroying any preexisting ones that might be already residing in the file. This must hold true even if the watermarking algorithms are different.

- *Secret keys.* In general, watermarking systems should use one or more cryptographically secure keys to ensure that the watermark cannot be manipulated or erased. This is important because once a watermark can be read by someone, this same person might alter it since both the location and embedding algorithm of the mark will be known (Kutter & Hartung, 2000). It is not safe to assume that the embedding algorithm is unknown to the attacker.
  As the security of the watermarking system relies in part on the use of secret keys, the *keyspace* must be large, so that a brute force attack is impractical. In most watermarking systems the key is the PN-pattern itself, or at least is used as a seed in order to create it. Moreover, the watermark message is usually encrypted first using a cipher key, before it is embedded using the watermark key. This practice adds security at two different levels. In the highest level of secrecy, the user cannot read or decode the watermark, or even detect its presence. The second level of secrecy permits any user to detect the presence of the watermark, but the data cannot be decoded without the proper key.
  Watermarking systems in which the key is known to various detectors are referred to as *unrestricted-key* watermarks. Thus, algorithms for use as unrestricted-key systems must employ the same key for every piece of data (Cox et al., 1999). Those systems that use a different key for each watermark (and thus the key is shared by only a few detectors) are known as restricted-key watermarks.
- *Computational cost.* The time that it takes for a watermark to be embedded and detected can be a crucial factor in a watermarking system. Some applications, such as broadcast monitoring, require real time watermark processing and thus delays are not acceptable under any circumstances. On the other hand, for court disputes (which are rare), a detection algorithm that takes hours is perfectly acceptable as long as the effectiveness is high.

Additionally, the number of embedders and detectors varies according to the application. This fact will have an effect on the *cost* of the watermarking system. Applications such as DVD copy control need few embedders but a detector on each DVD player; thus the cost of recovering should be very low, while that of embedding could be a little higher[7]. Whether the algorithms are implemented as plug-ins or dedicated hardware will also affect the economics of deploying a system.

Different Types of Watermarks

Even though this chapter does not relate to all kinds of watermarks that will be defined, it is important to state their existence in order to later derive some of the possible applications of watermarking systems.

- *Robust watermarks* are simply watermarks that are robust against attacks. Even if the existence of the watermark is known, it should be difficult for an attacker to destroy the embedded information without the knowledge of the key[8]. An implication of this fact is that the amount of data that can be embedded (also known as the *payload*) is usually smaller than in the case of steganographic methods. It is important to say that watermarking and steganographic methods are more complementary than competitive.
- *Fragile watermarks* are marks that have only very limited robustness (Kutter & Hartung, 2000). They are used to detect modifications of the cover data, rather than convey inerasable information, and usually become invalid after the slightest modification of a work. Fragility can be an advantage for authentication purposes. If a very fragile mark is detected intact in a work, we can infer that the work has probably not been altered since the watermark was embedded (Cox et al., 2002). Furthermore, even *semi-fragile* watermarks can help localize the exact location where the tampering of the cover work occurred.
- *Perceptible watermarks,* as the name states, are those that are easily perceived by the user. Although they are usually applied to images (as visual patterns or logos), it is not uncommon to have an audible signal overlaid on top of a musical work, in order to discourage illegal copying. As an example, the IBM Digital Libraries project (Memon & Wong, 1998; Mintzer, Magerlein, & Braudaway, 1996) has developed a visible watermark that modifies the brightness of an image based on the watermark data and a secret key. Even though perceptible watermarks are important for some special applications, the rest of this chapter focuses on imperceptible watermarks, as they are the most common.
- *Bitstream watermarks* are marks embedded directly into compressed audio (or video) material. This can be advantageous in environments where compressed bitstreams are stored in order to save disk space, like Internet music providers.
- *Fingerprinting* and *labeling* denote special applications of watermarks. They relate to watermarking applications where information such as the creator or recipient of the data is used to form the watermark. In the case of fingerprinting, this information consists of a unique code that uniquely identifies the recipient, and that can help to locate the source of a leak in confidential information. In the case of labeling, the information embedded

is a unique data identifier, of interest for purposes such as library retrieving. A more thorough discussion is presented in the next section.

Watermark Applications

In this section the seven most common application for watermarking systems are presented. What is more important, all of them relate to the field of audio watermarking. It must be kept in mind that each of these applications will require different priorities regarding the watermark's properties that have just been reviewed.

- *Broadcast monitoring.* Different individuals are interested in broadcast verification. Advertisers want to be sure that the ads they pay for are being transmitted; musicians want to ensure that they receive royalty payments for the air time spent on their works.
  While one can think about putting human observers to record what they see or hear on a broadcast, this method becomes costly and error prone. Thus it is desirable to replace it with an automated version, and digital watermarks can provide a solution. By embedding a unique identifier for each work, one can monitor the broadcast signal searching for the embedded mark and thus compute the air time. Other solutions can be designed, but watermarking has the advantage of being compatible with the installed broadcast equipment, since the mark is included within the signal and does not occupy extra resources such as other frequencies or header files. Nevertheless, it is harder to embed a mark than to put it on an extra header, and content quality degradation can be a concern.
- *Copyright owner identification.* Under U.S. law, the creator of an original work holds copyright to it the instant the work is recorded in some physical form (Cox et al., 2002). Even though it is not necessary to place a copyright notice in distributed copies of work, it is considered a good practice, since a court can award more damages to the owner in the case of a dispute.
  However, textual copyright notices[9] are easy to remove, even without intention. For example, an image may be cropped prior to publishing. In the case of digital audio the problem is even worse, as the copyright notice is not visible at all times.
  Watermarks are ideal for including copyright notices into works, as they can be both imperceptible and inseparable from the cover that contains them (Mintzer, Braudaway, & Bell, 1998). This is probably the reason why copyright protection is the most prominent application of watermarking today (Kutter & Hartung, 2000). The watermarks are used to resolve rightful ownership, and thus require a very high level of robustness (Arnold, 2000). Furthermore, additional issues must be considered; for example, the marks must be unambiguous, as other parties can try to embed counterfeit

copyright notices. Nonetheless, it must be stated that the legal impact of watermark copyright notices has not yet been tested in court.

- *Proof of ownership.* Multimedia owners may want to use watermarks not just to identify copyright ownership, but also to actually prove ownership. This is something that a textual notice cannot easily do, since it can be forged.
  One way to resolve an ownership dispute is by using a central repository, where the author registers the work prior to distribution. However, this can be too costly[10] for many content creators. Moreover, there might be lack of evidence (such as sketch or film negatives) to be presented at court, or such evidence can even be fabricated.
  Watermarks can provide a way for authenticating ownership of a work. However, to achieve the level of security required for proof of ownership, it is probably necessary to restrict the availability of the watermark detector (Cox et al., 2002). This is thus not a trivial task.
- *Content authentication.* In authentication applications the objective is to detect modifications of the data (Arnold, 2000). This can be achieved with fragile watermarks that have low robustness to certain modifications. This proves to be very useful, as it is becoming easier to tamper with digital works in ways that are difficult to detect by a human observer.
  The problem of authenticating messages has been well studied in cryptography; however, watermarks are a powerful alternative as the signature is embedded directly into the work. This eliminates the problem of making sure the signature stays with the work. Nevertheless, the act of embedding the watermark must not change the work enough to make it appear invalid when compared with the signature. This can be accomplished by separating the cover work in two parts: one for which the signature is computed, and the other where it is embedded.
  Another advantage of watermarks is that they are modified along with the work. This means that in certain cases the location and nature of the processing within the audio cover can be determined and thus inverted. For example, one could determine if a lossy compression algorithm has been applied to an audio file[11].
- *Transactional watermarks.* This is an application where the objective is to convey information about the legal recipient of digital data, rather than the source of it. This is done mainly to identify single distributed copies of data, and thus monitor or trace back illegally produced copies of data that may circulate[12].
  The idea is to embed a unique watermark in each distributed copy of a work, in the process we have defined as fingerprinting. In these systems, the watermarks must be secure against a collusion attack, which is explained in the sixth section, and sometimes have to be extracted easily, as in the case of automatic Web crawlers that search for pirated copies of works.

- *Copy control/device control.* Transactional watermarks as well as watermarks for monitoring, identification, and proof of ownership do not *prevent* illegal copying (Cox et al., 2000). Copy protection is difficult to achieve in open systems, but might be desirable in proprietary ones. In such systems it is possible to use watermarks to indicate if the data can be copied or not (Mintzer et al., 1998).

  The first and strongest line of defense against illegal copying is encryption, as only those who possess the decryption key can access the content. With watermarking, one could do a very different process: allow the media to be perceived, yet still prevent it from being recorded. If this is the case, a watermark detector must be included on every manufactured recorder, preferably in a tamper resistant device. This constitutes a serious nontechnical problem, as there is no natural incentive for recording equipment manufacturers to include such a detector on their machines. This is due to the fact that the value of the recorder is reduced from the point of view of the consumer.

  Similarly, one could implement *play control,* so that illegal copies can be made but not played back by compliant equipment. This can be done by checking a media signature, or if the work is properly encrypted for example. By mixing these two concepts, a buyer will be left facing two possibilities: buying a compliant device that cannot play pirated content, or a noncompliant one that can play pirated works but not legal ones.

  In a similar way, one could control a playback device by using embedded information in the media they reproduce. This is known as device control. For example, one could signal how a digital audio stream should be equalized, or even extra information about the artist. A more extreme case can be to send information in order to update the firmware of the playback device while it is playing content, or to order it to shut down at a certain time. This method is practical, as the need for a signaling channel can be eliminated.
- *Covert communication.* Even though it contradicts the definition of watermark given before, some people may use watermarking systems in order to hide data and communicate secretly. This is actually the realm of steganography rather than watermarking, but many times the boundaries between these two disciplines have been blurred. Nonetheless, in the context of this chapter, the hidden message is not a watermark but rather a robust covert communication.

  The use of watermarks for hidden annotation (Zhao et al., 1998), or labeling, constitutes a different case, where watermarks are used to create hidden labels and annotations in content such as medical imagery or geographic maps, and indexes in multimedia content for retrieval purposes. In these cases, the watermark requirements are specific to the actual media where the watermark will be embedded. Using a watermark that distorts a patient's radiography can have serious legal consequences, while the recovery speed is crucial in multimedia retrieval.

AUDIO WATERMARKING TECHNIQUES

In this section the five most popular techniques for digital audio watermarking are reviewed. Specifically, the different techniques correspond to the methods for merging (or inserting) the cover data and the watermark pattern into a single signal, as was outlined in the communication model of the second section.

There are two critical parameters to most digital audio representations: sample quantization method and temporal sampling rate. Data hiding in audio signals is especially challenging, because the human auditory system (HAS) operates over a wide dynamic range. Sensitivity to additive random noise is acute. However, there are some "holes" available. While the HAS has a large dynamic range, it has a fairly small differential range (Bender, Gruhl, Morimoto, & Lu, 1996). As a result, loud sounds tend to mask out quiet sounds. This effect is known as *masking,* and will be fully exploited in some of the techniques presented here (Swanson et al., 1998).

These techniques do not correspond to the actual implementation of commercial products that are available, but rather constitute the basis for some of them. Moreover, most real world applications can be considered a particular case of the general methods described below.

Finally, it must be stated that the methods explained are specific to the domain of audio watermarking. Several other techniques that are very popular for hiding marks in other types of media, such as discrete cosine transform (DCT) coefficient quantization in the case of digital images, are not discussed. This is done because the test described in the following sections is related only to watermarking of digital audio.

Amplitude Modification

This method, also known as *least significant bit (LSB) substitution,* is both common and easy to apply in both steganography and watermarking (Johnson & Katzenbeisser, 2000), as it takes advantage of the quantization error that usually derives from the task of digitizing the audio signal.

As the name states, the information is encoded into the least significant bits of the audio data. There are two basic ways of doing this: the lower order bits of the digital audio signal can be fully substituted with a pseudorandom (PN) sequence that contains the watermark message *m,* or the PN-sequence can be embedded into the lower order bitstream using the output of a function that generates the sequence based on both the nth bit of the watermark message and the nth sample of the audio file (Bassia & Pitas, 1998; Dugelay & Roche, 2000).

Ideally, the embedding capacity of an audio file with this method is 1 kbps per 1 kHz of sampled data. That is, if a file is sampled at 44 kHz then it is possible to embed 44 kilobits on each second of audio. In return for this large channel capacity, audible noise is introduced. The impact of this noise is a direct function of the content of the host signal. For example, crowd noise during a rock concert would mask some of the noise that would be audible in a string quartet performance. Adaptive data attenuation has been used to compensate for this variation in content (Bender et al., 1996). Another option is to shape the PN-sequence itself so that it matches the audio masking characteristics of the cover signal (Czerwinski et al., 1999).

The major disadvantage of this method is its poor immunity to manipulation. Encoded information can be destroyed by channel noise, resampling, and so forth, unless it is encoded using redundancy techniques. In order to be robust, these techniques reduce the data rate, often by one to two orders of magnitude. Furthermore, in order to make the watermark more robust against localized filtering, a pseudorandom number generator can be used to spread the message over the cover in a random manner. Thus, the distance between two embedded bits is determined by a secret key (Johnson & Katzenbeisser, 2000). Finally, in some implementations the PN-sequence is used to retrieve the watermark from the audio file. In this way, the watermark acts at the same time as the key to the system.

Recently proposed systems use amplitude modification techniques in a transform space rather than in the time (or spatial) domain. That is, a transformation is applied to the signal, and then the least significant bits of the coefficients representing the audio signal *A* on the transform domain are modified in order to embed the watermark *W*. After the embedding, the inverse transformation is performed in order to obtain the watermarked audio file *A'*. In this case, the technique is also known as *coefficient quantization.* Some of the transformations used for watermarking are the discrete Fourier transform (DFT), discrete cosine transform (DCT), Mellin-Fourier transform, and wavelet transform (Dugelay & Roche, 2000). However, their use is more popular in the field of image and video watermarking.

Dither Watermarking

Dither is a noise signal that is added to the input audio signal to provide better sampling of that input when digitizing the signal (Czerwinski et al., 1999). As a result, distortion is practically eliminated, at the cost of an increased noise floor.

To implement dithering, a noise signal is added to the input audio signal with a known probability distribution, such as Gaussian or triangular. In the particular case of dithering for watermark embedding, the watermark is used to modulate the dither signal. The host signal (or original audio file) is quantized using an associated dither quantizer (RLE, 1999). This technique is known as *quantization index modulation* (QIM) (Chen & Wornell, 2000).

For example, if one wishes to embed one bit (m=1 or m=2) in the host audio signal A then one would use two different quantizers, each one representing a possible value for m. If the two quantizers are shifted versions of each other, then they are called *dither quantizers,* and the process is that of *dither modulation.* Thus, QIM refers to embedding information by first modulating an index or sequence of indices with the embedded information and then quantizing the host signal with the associated quantizer or sequence of quantizers (Chen & Wornell, 1999).

A graphical view of this technique is shown in Figure 3, taken from Chen (2000). Here, the points marked with X's and O's belong to two different quantizers, each with an associated index; that is, each one embedding a different value. The distance d_{min} can be used as an informal measure of robustness, while the size of the quantization cells (one is shown in the figure) measures the distortion on the audio file. If the watermark message m=1, then the audio signal is quantized to the nearest X. If m=2 then it is quantized to the nearest O.

The two quantizers must not intersect, as can be seen in the figure. Furthermore, they have a discontinuous nature. If one moves from the interior of the cell to its exterior, then the corresponding value of the quantization function jumps from an X in the cell's interior to one X on its exterior. Finally, as noted above, the number of quantizers in the ensemble determines the information-embedding rate (Chen & Wornell, 2000).

As was said above, in the case of dither modulation, the quantization cells of any quantizer in the ensemble are shifted versions of the cells of any other quantizer being used as well. The shifts traditionally correspond to pseudorandom vectors called the *dither* vectors. For the task of watermarking, these vectors are modulated with the watermark, which means that each possible

Figure 3. A graphical view of the QIM technique

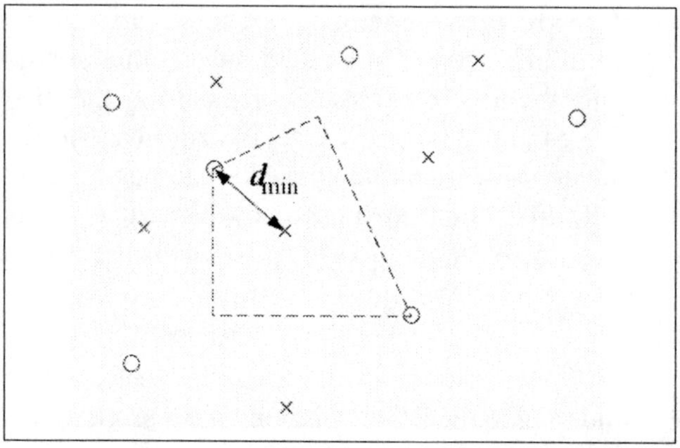

embedded signal maps uniquely to a different dither vector. The host signal A is then quantized with the resulting dithered quantizer in order to crate the watermarked audio signal A'.

Echo Watermarking

Echo watermarking attempts to embed information on the original discrete audio signal $A(t)$ by introducing a repeated version of a component of the audio signal with small enough offset (or delay), initial amplitude and decay rate $\alpha A(t - \Delta t)$ to make it imperceptible. The resulting signal can be then expressed as $A'(t) = A(t) + \alpha A(t - \Delta t)$.

In the most basic echo watermarking scheme, the information is encoded in the signal by modifying the delay between the signal and the echo. This means that two different values Δt and $\Delta t'$ are used in order to encode either a zero or a one. Both offset values have to be carefully chosen in a way that makes the watermark both inaudible and recoverable (Johnson & Katzenbeisser, 2000).

As the offset between the original and the echo decreases, the two signals blend. At a certain point, the human ear cannot distinguish between the two signals. The echo is perceived as added resonance (Bender et al., 1996). This point is hard to determine exactly, as it depends on many factors such as the quality of the original recording, the type of sound being echoed, and the listener. However, in general one can expect the value of the offset Δt to be around one millisecond.

Since this scheme can only embed one bit in a signal, a practical approach consists of dividing the audio file into various blocks prior to the encoding process. Then each block is used to encode a bit, with the method described above. Moreover, if consecutive blocks are separated by a random number of unused samples, the detection and removal of the watermark becomes more difficult (Johnson & Katzenbeisser, 2000). Finally, all the blocks are concatenated back, and the watermarked audio file A' is created. This technique results in an embedding rate of around 16 bits per second without any degradation of the signal. Moreover, in some cases the resonance can even create a richer sound.

For watermark recovery, a technique known as *cepstrum autocorrelation* is used (Czerwinski et al., 1999). This technique produces a signal with two pronounced amplitude humps or *spikes*. By measuring the distance between these two spikes, one can determine if a one or a zero was initially encoded in the signal. This recovery process has the benefit that the original audio file A is not needed. However, this benefit also becomes a drawback in that the scheme presented here is susceptible to attack. This will be further explained in the sixth section.

Phase Coding

It is known that the human auditory system is less sensitive to the phase components of sound than to the noise components, a property that is exploited by some audio compression schemes. Phase coding (or phase distortion) makes use of this characteristic as well (Bender et al., 1996; Johnson & Katzenbeisser, 2000).

The method works by substituting the phase of the original audio signal *A* with one of two reference phases, each one encoding a bit of information. That is, the watermark data *W* is represented by a phase shift in the phase of *A*.

The original signal *A* is split into a series of short sequences A_i, each one of length *l*. Then a discrete Fourier transform (DFT) is applied to each one of the resulting segments. This transforms the signal representation from the time domain to the frequency domain, thus generating a matrix of phases Φ and a matrix of Fourier transform magnitudes.

The phase shifts between consecutive signal segments must be preserved in the watermarked file *A'*. This is necessary because the human auditory system is very sensitive to relative phase differences, but not to absolute phase changes. In other words, the phase coding method works by substituting the phase of the initial audio segment with a reference phase that represents the data. After this, the phase of subsequent segments is adjusted in order to preserve the relative phases between them (Bender et al., 1996).

Given this, the embedding process inserts the watermark information in the phase vector of the first segment of *A*, namely $\vec{\Phi}_0$. Then it creates a new phase matrix Φ', using the original phase differences found in Φ.

After this step, the original matrix of Fourier transform magnitudes is used alongside the new phase matrix Φ' to construct the watermarked audio signal *A'*, by applying the inverse Fourier transform (that is, converting the signal back to the time domain). At this point, the absolute phases of the signal have been modified, but their relative differences are preserved. Throughout the process, the matrix of Fourier amplitudes remains constant. Any modifications to it could generate intolerable degradation (Dugelay & Roche, 2000).

In order to recover the watermark, the length of the segments, the DFT points, and the data interval must be known at the receiver. When the signal is divided into the same segments that were used for the embedding process, the following step is to calculate the DFT for each one of these segments. Once the transformation has been applied, the recovery process can measure the value of vector $\vec{\Phi}_0$ and thereby restore the originally encoded value for *W*.

With phase coding, an embedding rate between eight and 32 bits per second is possible, depending on the audio context. The higher rates are usually achieved when there is a noisy background in the audio signal. A higher embedding rate can result in phase dispersion, a distortion[13] caused by a break in the relationship of the phases between each of the frequency components (Bender et al., 1996).

Spread Spectrum Watermarking

Spread spectrum techniques for watermarking borrow most of the theory from the communications community (Czerwinski et al., 1999). The main idea is to embed a narrow-band signal (the watermark) into a wide-band channel (the audio file). The characteristics of both *A* and *W* seems to suit this model perfectly. In addition, spread spectrum techniques offer the possibility of protecting the watermark privacy by using a secret key to control the pseudorandom sequence generator that is needed in the process.

Generally, the message used as the watermark is a narrow band signal compared to the wide band of the cover (Dugelay & Roche, 2000; Kirovski & Malvar, 2001). Spread spectrum techniques allow the frequency bands to be matched before embedding the message. Furthermore, high frequencies are relevant for the invisibility of the watermark but are inefficient as far as robustness is concerned, whereas low frequencies have the opposite characteristics. If a low energy signal is embedded on each of the frequency bands, this conflict is partially solved. This is why spread spectrum techniques are valuable not only for robust communication but for watermarking as well.

There are two basic approaches to spread spectrum techniques: *direct sequence* and *frequency hopping*. In both of these approaches the idea is to spread the watermark data across a large frequency band, namely the entire audible spectrum.

In the case of direct sequence, the cover signal *A* is modulated by the watermark message *m* and a pseudorandom (PN) noise sequence, which has a wide frequency spectrum. As a consequence, the spectrum of the resulting message m' is spread over the available band. Then, the spread message m' is attenuated in order to obtain the watermark *W*. This watermark is then added to the original file, for example as additive random noise, in order to obtain the watermarked version A'. To keep the noise level down, the attenuation performed to m' should yield a signal with about 0.5% of the dynamic range of the cover file *A* (Bender et al., 1996).

In order to recover the watermark, the watermarked audio signal A' is modulated with the PN-sequence to remove it. The demodulated signal is then *W*. However, some keying mechanisms can be used when embedding the watermark, which means that at the recovery end a detector must also be used. For example, if bi-phase shift keying is used when embedding *W*, then a phase detector must be used at the recovery process (Czerwinski et al., 1999).

In the case of *frequency hopping,* the cover frequency is altered using a random process, thus describing a wide range of frequency values. That is, the frequency-hopping method selects a pseudorandom subset of the data to be watermarked. The watermark *W* is then attenuated and merged with the selected data using one of the methods explained in this chapter, such as coefficient quantization in a transform domain. As a result, the modulated watermark has a wide spectrum.

For the detection process, the pseudorandom generator used to alter the cover frequency is used to recover the parts of the signal where the watermark is hidden. Then the watermark can be recovered by using the detection method that corresponds to the embedding mechanism used.

A crucial factor for the performance of spread spectrum techniques is the synchronization between the watermarked audio signal A' and the PN-sequence (Dugelay & Roche, 2000; Kirovski & Malvar, 2001). This is why the particular PN-sequence used acts as a key to the recovery process. Nonetheless, some attacks can focus on this delicate aspect of the model.

MEASURING FIDELITY

Artists, and digital content owners in general, have many reasons for embedding watermarks in their copyrighted works. These reasons have been stated in the previous sections. However, there is a big risk in performing such an operation, as the quality of the musical content might be degraded to a point where its value is diminished. Fortunately, the opposite is also possible and, if done right, digital watermarks can add value to content (Acken, 1998).

Content owners are generally concerned with the degradation of the cover signal quality, even more than users of the content (Craver, Yeo, & Yeung, 1998). They have access to the unwatermarked content with which to compare their audio files. Moreover, they have to decide between the amount of tolerance in quality degradation from the watermarking process and the level of protection that is achieved by embedding a stronger signal. As a restriction, an embedded watermark has to be detectable in order to be valuable.

Given this situation, it becomes necessary to measure the impact that a marking scheme has on an audio signal. This is done by measuring the fidelity of the watermarked audio signal A', and constitutes the first measure that is defined in this chapter.

As fidelity refers to the similitude between an original and a watermarked signal, a statistical metric must be used. Such a metric will fall in one of two categories: difference metrics or correlation metrics.

Difference metrics, as the name states, measure the difference between the undistorted original audio signal A and the distorted watermarked signal A'. The popularity of these metrics is derived from their simplicity (Kutter & Petitcolas, 1999). In the case of digital audio, the most common difference metric used for quality evaluation of watermarks is the *signal to noise ratio* (SNR). This is usually measured in decibels (dB), so $\text{SNR(dB)} = 10 \log_{10} (\text{SNR})$.

The signal to noise ratio, measured in decibels, is defined by the formula:

$$SNR(dB) = 10\log_{10} \frac{\sum_n A_n{}^2}{\sum_n (A_n - A'_n)^2}$$

where A_n corresponds to the nth sample of the original audio file A, and A'_n to the nth sample of the watermarked signal A'. This is a measure of quality that reflects the quantity of distortion that a watermark imposes on a signal (Gordy & Burton, 2000).

Another common difference metric is the *peak signal to noise ratio* (PSNR), which measures the maximum signal to noise ratio found on an audio signal. The formula for the PSNR, along with some other difference metrics found in the literature are presented in Table 1 (Kutter & Hartung, 2000; Kutter & Petitcolas, 1999).

Although the tolerable amount of noise depends on both the watermarking application and the characteristics of the unwatermarked audio signal, one could expect to have perceptible noise distortion for SNR values of 35dB (Petitcolas & Anderson, 1999).

Correlation metrics measure distortion based on the statistical correlation between the original and modified signals. They are not as popular as the

Table 1. Common difference distortion metrics

Maximum Difference	$MD = \max \mid A_n - A'_n \mid$
Average Absolute Difference	$AD = \frac{1}{N}\sum_n \mid A_n - A'_n \mid$
Normalized Average Absolute Difference	$NAD = \sum_n \mid A_n - A'_n \mid / \sum_n \mid A_n \mid$
Mean Square Error	$MSE = \frac{1}{N}\sum_n (A_n - A'_n)^2$
Normalized Mean Square Error	$NMSE = \sum_n (A_n - A'_n)^2 / \sum_n A_n{}^2$
LP-Norm	$LP = \left(\frac{1}{N}\sum_n \mid A_n - A'_n \mid\right)^{1/p}$
Laplacian Mean Square Error	$LMSE = \sum_n (\nabla^2 A_n - \nabla^2 A'_n)^2 / \sum_n (\nabla^2 A_n)^2$
Signal to Noise Ratio	$SNR = \sum_n A_n{}^2 / \sum_n (A_n - A'_n)^2$
Peak Signal to Noise Ratio	$PSNR = N \max_n A_n^2 / \sum_n (A_n - A'_n)^2$
Audio Fidelity	$AF = 1 - \sum_n (A_n - A'_n)^2 / \sum_n A_n{}^2$

Table 2. Correlation distortion metrics

Normalized Cross-Correlation	$NC = \sum_n A_n \tilde{A}_n / \sum_n A_n^{\,2}$
Correlation Quality	$CQ = \sum_n A_n \tilde{A}_n / \sum_n A_n$

difference distortion metrics, but it is important to state their existence. Table 2 shows the most important of these.

For the purpose of audio watermark benchmarking, the use of the *signal to noise ratio* (SNR) should be used to measure the fidelity of the watermarked signal with respect to the original. This decision follows most of the literature that deals with the topic (Gordy & Burton, 2000; Kutter & Petitcolas, 1999, 2000; Petitcolas & Anderson, 1999). Nonetheless, in this measure the term *noise* refers to statistical noise, or a deviation from the original signal, rather than to perceived noise on the side of the hearer. This result is due to the fact that the SNR is not well correlated with the human auditory system (Kutter & Hartung, 2000). Given this characteristic, the effect of perceptual noise needs to be addressed later.

In addition, when a metric that outputs results in decibels is used, comparisons are difficult to make, as the scale is not linear but rather logarithmic. This means that it is more useful to present the results using a normalized quality rating. The ITU-R Rec. 500 quality rating is perfectly suited for this task, as it gives a quality rating on a scale of 1 to 5 (Arnold, 2000; Piron et al., 1999). Table 3 shows the rating scale, along with the quality level being represented.

This quality rating is computed by using the formula:

$$Quality = F = \frac{5}{1 + N * SNR}$$

where N is a normalization constant and SNR is the measured signal to noise ratio. The resulting value corresponds to the fidelity F of the watermarked signal.

Table 3. ITU-R Rec. 500 quality rating

Rating	Impairment	Quality
5	Imperceptible	Excellent
4	Perceptible, not annoying	Good
3	Slightly annoying	Fair
2	Annoying	Poor
1	Very annoying	Bad

Data Payload

The fidelity of a watermarked signal depends on the amount of embedded information, the strength of the mark, and the characteristics of the host signal. This means that a comparison between different algorithms must be made under equal conditions. That is, while keeping the payload fixed, the fidelity must be measured on the same audio cover signal for all watermarking techniques being evaluated.

However, the process just described constitutes a single measure event and will not be representative of the characteristics of the algorithms being evaluated, as results can be biased depending on the chosen parameters. For this reason, it is important to perform the tests using a variety of audio signals, with changing size and nature (Kutter & Petitcolas, 2000). Moreover, the test should also be repeated using different keys.

The amount of information that should be embedded is not easy to determine, and depends on the application of the watermarking scheme. In Kutter and Petitcolas (2000) a message length of 100 bits is used on their test of image watermarking systems as a representative value. However, some secure watermarking protocols might need a bigger payload value, as the watermark W could include a cryptographic signature for both the audio file A, and the watermark message m in order to be more secure (Katzenbeisser & Veith, 2002). Given this, it is recommended to use a longer watermark bitstream for the test, so that a real world scenario is represented. A watermark size of 128 bits is big enough to include two 56-bit signatures and a unique identification number that identifies the owner.

Speed

Besides fidelity, the content owner might be interested in the time it takes for an algorithm to embed a mark (Gordy & Burton, 2000). Although speed is dependent on the type of implementation (hardware or software), one can suppose that the evaluation will be performed on software versions of the algorithms. In this case, it is a good practice to perform the test on a machine with similar characteristics to the one used by the end user (Petitcolas, 2000). Depending on the application, the value for the time it takes to embed a watermark will be incorporated into the results of the test. This will be done later, when all the measures are combined together.

MEASURING ROBUSTNESS

Watermarks have to be able to withstand a series of signal operations that are performed either intentionally or unintentionally on the cover signal and that can affect the recovery process. Given this, watermark designers try to guarantee a minimum level of robustness against such operations. Nonetheless, the concept of robustness is ambiguous most of the time and thus claims about a watermarking scheme being robust are difficult to prove due to the lack of testing standards (Craver, Perrig, & Petitcolas, 2000).

By defining a standard metric for watermark robustness, one can then assure fairness when comparing different technologies. It becomes necessary to create a detailed and thorough test for measuring the ability that a watermark has to withstand a set of clearly defined signal operations. In this section these signal operations are presented, and a practical measure for robustness is proposed.

How to Measure

Before defining a metric, it must be stated that one does not need to erase a watermark in order to render it useless. It is said that a watermarking scheme is robust when it is able to withstand a series of attacks that try to degrade the quality of the embedded watermark, up to the point where it is removed, or its recovery process is unsuccessful. This means that just by interfering with the detection process a person can create a successful attack over the system, even unintentionally.

However, in some cases one can overcome this characteristic by using error-correcting codes or a stronger detector (Cox et al., 2002). If an error correction code is applied to the watermark message, then it is unnecessary to entirely recover the watermark W in order to successfully retrieve the embedded message m. The use of stronger detectors can also be very helpful in these situations. For example, if a marking scheme has a publicly available detector, then an attacker will try to tamper with the cover signal up to the point where the detector does not recognize the watermark's presence[14]. Nonetheless, the content owner may have another version of the watermark detector, one that can successfully recover the mark after some extra set of signal processing operations. This "special" detector might not be released for public use for economic, efficiency or security reasons. For example, it might only be used in court cases. The only thing that is really important is that it is possible to design a system with different detector strengths.

Given these two facts, it makes sense to use a metric that allows for different levels of robustness, instead of one that only allows for two different states (the watermark is either robust or not). With this characteristic in mind, the basic procedure for measuring robustness is a three-step process, defined as follows:

1. For each audio file in a determined test set embed a random watermark W on the audio signal A, with the maximum strength possible that does not

diminish the *fidelity* of the cover below a specified minimum (Petitcolas & Anderson, 1999).

2. Apply a set of relevant signal processing operations to the watermarked audio signal A'.
3. Finally, for each audio cover, extract the watermark W using the corresponding detector and measure the success of the recovery process.

Some of the early literature considered the recovery process successful only if the whole watermark message m was recovered (Petitcolas, 2000; Petitcolas & Anderson, 1999). This was in fact a binary robustness metric. However, the use of the *bit-error rate* has become common recently (Gordy & Burton, 2000; Kutter & Hartung, 2000; Kutter & Petitcolas, 2000), as it allows for a more detailed scale of values. The *bit-error rate* (BER) is defined as the ratio of incorrect extracted bits to the total number of embedded bits and can be expressed using the formula:

$$BER = \frac{100}{l}\sum_{n=0}^{l-1}\begin{cases}1, & W'_n = W_n \\ 0, & W'_n \neq W_n\end{cases}$$

where l is the watermark length, W_n corresponds to the nth bit of the embedded watermark and W'_n corresponds to the nth bit of the recovered watermark. In other words, this measure of robustness is the certainty of detection of the embedded mark (Arnold, 2000). It is easy to see why this measure makes more sense, and thus should be used as the metric when evaluating the success of the watermark recovery process and therefore the robustness of an audio watermarking scheme.

A final recommendation must be made at this point. The three-step procedure just described should be repeated several times, since the embedded watermark W is randomly generated and the recovery can be successful by chance (Petitcolas, 2000).

Up to this point no details have been given about the signal operations that should be performed in the second step of the robustness test. As a rule of thumb, one should include as a minimum the operations that the audio cover is expected to go through in a real world application. However, this will not provide enough testing, as a malicious attacker will most likely have access to a wide range of tools as well as a broad range of skills. Given this situation, several scenarios should be covered. In the following sections the most common signal operations and attacks that an audio watermark should be able to withstand are presented.

Audio Restoration Attack

Audio restoration techniques have been used for several years now, specifically for restoring old audio recordings that have audible artifacts. In audio restoration the recording is digitized and then analyzed for degradations. After these degradations have been localized, the corresponding samples are eliminated. Finally the recording is reconstructed (that is, the missing samples are recreated) by interpolating the signal using the remaining samples.

One can assume that the audio signal is the product of a stationary autoregressive (AR) process of finite order (Petitcolas & Anderson, 1998). With this assumption in mind, one can use an audio segment to estimate a set of AR parameters and then calculate an approximate value for the missing samples. Both of the estimates are calculated using a least-square minimization technique.

Using the audio restoration method just described one can try to render a watermark undetectable by processing the marked audio signal A'. The process is as follows: First divide the audio signal A' into N blocks of size m samples each. A value of m=1000 samples has been proposed in the literature (Petitcolas & Anderson, 1999). A block of length l is removed from the middle of each block and then restored using the AR audio restoration algorithm. This generates a reconstructed block also of size m. After the N blocks have been processed they are concatenated again, and an audio signal B' is produced. It is expected that B' will be closer to A than to A' and thus the watermark detector will not find any mark in it.

An error free restoration is theoretically possible in some cases, but this is not desired since it would produce a signal identical to A'. What is expected is to create a signal that has an error value big enough to mislead the watermark detector, but small enough to prevent the introduction of audible noise. Adjusting the value of the parameter l controls the magnitude of the error (Petitcolas & Anderson, 1999). In particular, a value of l=80 samples has proven to give good results.

Invertibility Attack

When resolving ownership cases in court, the disputing parties can both claim that they have inserted a valid watermark on the audio file, as it is sometimes possible to embed multiple marks on a single cover signal. Clearly, one mark must have been embedded before the other.

The ownership is resolved when the parties are asked to show the original work to court. If Alice has the original audio file A, which has been kept stored in a safe place, and Mallory has a counterfeit original file $\tilde{A}$, which has been derived from A, then Alice can search for her watermark W in Mallory's file and will most likely find it. The converse will not happen, and the case will be resolved (Craver et al., 2000). However, an attack to this procedure can be created, and is known as an *invertibility attack*.

Normally the content owner adds a watermark W to the audio file A, creating a watermarked audio file $A' = A+W$, where the sign "+" denotes the embedding operation. This file is released to the public, while the original A and the watermark W are stored in a safe place. When a suspicious audio file $\tilde{A}$ appears, the difference $\tilde{W} = \tilde{A} - A$ is computed. This difference should be equal to W if A' and $\tilde{A}$ are equal, and very close to W if $\tilde{A}$ was derived from A'. In general, a correlation function $f(W, \tilde{W})$ is used to determine the similarity between the watermark W and the extracted data $\tilde{W}$. This function will yield a value close to 1, if W and $\tilde{W}$ are similar.

However, Mallory can do the following: she can subtract (rather than add) a second watermark $\hat{w}$ from Alice's watermarked file A', using the inverse of the embedding algorithm. This yields an audio file $\hat{A} = A' - \hat{w} = A + W - \hat{w}$, which Mallory can now claim to be the original audio file, along with $\hat{w}$ as the original watermark (Craver, Memon, Yeo, & Yeung, 1998). Now both Alice and Mallory can claim copyright violation from their counterparts.

When the two originals are compared in court, Alice will find that her watermark is present in Mallory's audio file, since $\hat{A} - A = W - \hat{w}$ is calculated, and $f(W-\hat{w}, W) \approx 1$. However, Mallory can show that when $A - \hat{A} = \hat{w} - W$ is calculated, then $f(\hat{w} - W, \hat{w}) \approx 1$ as well. In other words, Mallory can show that her mark is also present in Alice's work, even though Alice has kept it locked at all times (Craver, Memon, & Yeung, 1996; Craver, Yeo et al., 1998). Given the symmetry of the equations, it is impossible to decide who is the real owner of the original file. A deadlock is thus created (Craver, Yeo et al., 1998; Pereira et al., 2001).

This attack is a clear example of how one can render a mark unusable without having to remove it, by exploiting the invertibility of the watermarking method, which allows an attacker to remove as well as add watermarks. Such an attack can be prevented by using a non-invertible cryptographic signature in the watermark W; that is, using a secure watermarking protocol (Katzenbeisser & Veith, 2002; Voloshynovskiy, Pereira, Pun et al., 2001).

Specific Attack on Echo Watermarking

The echo watermarking technique presented in this chapter can be easily "attacked" simply by detecting the echo and then removing the delayed signal by inverting the convolution formula that was used to embed it. However, the problem consists of detecting the echo without knowing the original signal and the possible delay values. This problem is referred to as *blind echo cancellation,* and is known to be difficult to solve (Petitcolas, Anderson, & G., 1998). Nonetheless, a practical solution to this problem appears to lie in the same function that is used for echo watermarking extraction: *cepstrum autocorrelation.* Cepstrum analysis, along with a brute force search can be used together to find the echo signal in the watermarked audio file A'.

A detailed description of the attack is given by Craver et al. (2000), and the idea is as follows: If we take the power spectrum of $A'(t) = A(t) + \alpha A(t - \Delta t)$, denoted by Φ and then calculate the logarithm of Φ, the amplitude of the delayed signal can be augmented using an autocovariance function[15] over the power spectrum $\Phi'(\ln(\Phi))$. Once the amplitude has been increased, then the "hump" of the signal becomes more visible and the value of the delay Δt can be determined (Petitcolas et al., 1998).

Experiments show that when an artificial echo is added to the signal, this attack works well for values of Δt between 0.5 and three milliseconds (Craver et al., 2000). Given that the watermark is usually embedded with a delay value that ranges from 0.5 to two milliseconds, this attack seems to be well suited for the technique and thus very likely to be successful (Petitcolas et al., 1999).

Collusion Attack

A collusion attack, also known as *averaging,* is especially effective against basic fingerprinting schemes. The basic idea is to take a large number of watermarked copies of the same audio file, and average them in order to produce an audio signal without a detectable mark (Craver et al., 2000; Kirovski & Malvar, 2001).

Another possible scenario is to have copies of multiple works that have been embedded with the same watermark. By averaging the sample values of the audio signals, one could estimate the value of the embedded mark, and then try to subtract it from any of the watermarked works. It has been shown that a small number (around 10) of different copies are needed in order to perform a successful collusion attack (Voloshynovskiy, Pereira, Pun et al., 2001). An obvious countermeasure to this attack is to embed more than one mark on each audio cover, and to make the marks dependant on the characteristics of the audio file itself (Craver et al., 2000).

Signal Diminishment Attacks and Common Processing Operations

Watermarks must be able to survive a series of signal processing operations that are commonly performed on the audio cover work, either intentionally or unintentionally. Any manipulation of an audio signal can result in a successful removal of the embedded mark. Furthermore, the availability of advanced audio editing tools on the Internet, such as Audacity (Dannenberg & Mazzoni, 2002), implies that these operations can be performed without an extensive knowledge of digital signal processing techniques. The removal of a watermark by performing one of these operations is known as a signal diminishment attack, and probably constitutes the most common attack performed on digital watermarks (Meerwald & Pereira, 2002).

Given this, a set of the most common signal operations must be specified, and watermark resistance to these must be evaluated. Even though an audio file will most likely not be subject to all the possible operations, a thorough list is necessary. Defining which subset of these operations is relevant for a particular watermarking scheme is a task that needs to be done; however, this will be addressed later in the chapter.

The signal processing operations presented here are classified into eight different groups, according to the presentation made in Petitcolas et al. (2001). These are:

- *Dynamics.* These operations change the loudness profile of the audio signal. The most basic way of performing this consists of increasing or decreasing the loudness directly. More complicated operations include limiting, expansion and compression, as they constitute nonlinear operations that are dependant on the audio cover.
- *Filter.* Filters cut off or increase a selected part of the audio spectrum. Equalizers can be seen as filters, as they increase some parts of the spectrum, while decreasing others. More specialized filters include low-pass, high-pass, all-pass, FIR, and so forth.
- *Ambience.* These operations try to simulate the effect of listening to an audio signal in a room. Reverb and delay filters are used for this purpose, as they can be adjusted in order to simulate the different sizes and characteristics that a room can have.
- *Conversion.* Digital audio files are nowadays subject to format changes. For example, old monophonic signals might be converted to stereo format for broadcast transmission. Changes from digital to analog representation and back are also common, and might induce significant quantization noise, as no conversion is perfect.
- *Lossy compression* algorithms are becoming popular, as they reduce the amount of data needed to represent an audio signal. This means that less bandwidth is needed to transmit the signal, and that less space is needed for its storage. These compression algorithms are based on psychoacoustic models and, although different implementations exist, most of them rely on deleting information that is not perceived by the listener. This can pose a serious problem to some watermarking schemes, as they sometimes will hide the watermark exactly in these imperceptible regions. If the watermarking algorithm selects these regions using the same method as the compression algorithm, then one just needs to apply the lossy compression algorithm to the watermarked signal in order to remove the watermark.
- *Noise* can be added in order to remove a watermark. This noise can even be imperceptible, if it is shaped to match the properties of the cover signal. Fragile watermarks are especially vulnerable to this attack. Sometimes

noise will appear as the product of other signal operations, rather than intentionally.

- *Modulation* effects like vibrato, chorus, amplitude modulation and flanging are not common post-production operations. However, they are included in most of the audio editing software packages and thus can be easily used in order to remove a watermark.
- *Time stretch* and *pitch shift.* These operations either change the length of an audio passage without changing its pitch, or change the pitch without changing its length in time. The use of time stretch techniques has become common in radio broadcasts, where stations have been able to increase the number of advertisements without devoting more air time to these (Kuczynski, 2000).
- *Sample permutations.* This group consists of specialized algorithms for audio manipulation, such as the attack on echo hiding just presented. Dropping of some samples in order to misalign the watermark decoder is also a common attack to spread-spectrum watermarking techniques.

It is not always clear how much processing a watermark should be able to withstand. That is, the specific parameters of the diverse filtering operations that can be performed on the cover signal are not easy to determine. In general terms one could expect a marking scheme to be able to survive several processing operations up to the point where they introduce annoying audible effects on the audio work. However, this rule of thumb is still too vague.

Fortunately, guidelines and minimum requirements for audio watermarking schemes have been proposed by different organizations such as the Secure Digital Music Initiative (SDMI), International Federation of the Phonographic Industry (IFPI), and the Japanese Society for Rights of Authors, Composers and Publishers (JASRAC). These guidelines constitute the baseline for any robustness test. In other words, they describe the minimum processing that an audio watermark should be able to resist, regardless of its intended application. Table 4 summarizes these requirements (JASRAC, 2001; SDMI, 2000).

False Positives

When testing for false positives, two different scenarios must be evaluated. The first one occurs when the watermark detector signals the presence of a mark on an unmarked audio file. The second case corresponds to the detector successfully finding a watermark *W'* on an audio file that has been marked with a watermark *W* (Cox et al., 2002; Kutter & Hartung, 2000; Petitcolas et al., 2001).

The testing procedure for both types of false positives is simple. In the first case one just needs to run the detector on a set of unwatermarked works. For the second case, one can embed a watermark *W* using a given key *K,* and then

Table 4. Summary of SDMI, STEP and IFPI requirements

Processing Operation	Requirements
Digital to analog conversion	Two consecutive digital to analog and analog to digital conversions.
Equalization	10 band graphic equalizer with the following characteristics: Freq. (Hz) 31 62 125 250 500 1k 2k 4k 8k 16k Gain (db) -6 +6 -6 +3 -6 +6 -6 +6 -6 +6
Band-pass filtering	100 Hz – 6 kHz, 12dB/oct.
Time stretch and pitch change	+/- 10% compression and decompression.
Codecs (at typically used data rates)	AAC, MPEG-4 AAC with perceptual noise substitution, MPEG-1 Audio Layer 3, Q-Design, Windows Media Audio, Twin-VQ, ATRAC-3, Dolby Digital AC-3, ePAC, RealAudio, FM, AM, PCM.
Noise addition	Adding white noise with constant level of 40dB lower than total averaged music power (SNR: 40dB).
Time scale modification	Pitch invariant time scaling of +/- 4%.
Wow and flutter	0.5% rms, from DC to 250Hz.
Echo addition	Delay up to 100 milliseconds, feedback coefficient up to 0.5.
Down mixing and surround sound processing	Stereo to mono, 6 channel to stereo, SRS, spatializer, Dolby surround, Dolby headphone.
Sample rate conversion	44.1 kHz to 16 kHz, 48 kHz to 44.1 kHz, 96 kHz to 48/44.1 kHz.
Dynamic range reduction	Threshold of 50dB, 16dB maximum compression. Rate: 10-millisecond attack, 3-second recovery.
Amplitude compression	16 bits to 8 bits.

try to extract a different mark *W'* while using the same key *K*. The *false positive rate* (FPR) is then defined as the number of successful test runs divided by the total number of test runs. A successful test run is said to occur whenever a false positive is detected.

However, a big problem arises when one takes into account the required false positive rate for some schemes. For example, a popular application such as DVD watermarking requires a false positive rate of 1 in 10^{12} (Cox et al., 2002). In order to verify that this rate is accomplished one would need to run the described experiment during several years. Other applications such as proof of ownership in court are rare, and thus require a lower false positive rate. Nonetheless, a false rate probability of 10^{-6}, required for the mentioned application, can be difficult to test.

MEASURING PERCEPTIBILITY

Digital content consumers are aware of many aspects of emerging watermarking technologies. However, only one prevails over all of them: users are concerned with the appearance of perceptible (audible) artifacts due to the use of a watermarking scheme. Watermarks are supposed to be imperceptible (Cox et al., 2002). Given this fact, one must carefully measure the amount of distortion that the listener will perceive on a watermarked audio file, as compared to its unmarked counterpart. Formal listening tests have been considered the only relevant method for judging audio quality, as traditional objective measures such as the signal-to-noise ratio (SNR) or total-harmonic-distortion[16] (THD) have never been shown to reliably relate to the perceived audio quality, as they can not be used to distinguish inaudible artifacts from audible noise (ITU, 2001; Kutter & Hartung, 2000; Thiede & Kabot, 1996). There is a need to adopt an objective measurement test for perceptibility of audio watermarking schemes.

Furthermore, one must be careful, as perceptibility must not be viewed as a binary condition (Arnold & Schilz, 2002; Cox et al., 2002). Different levels of perceptibility can be achieved by a watermarking scheme; that is, listeners will perceive the presence of the watermark in different ways. Auditory sensitivities vary significantly from individual to individual. As a consequence, any measure of perceptibility that is not binary should accurately reflect the probability of the watermark being detected by a listener.

In this section a practical and automated evaluation of watermark perceptibility is proposed. In order to do so, the human auditory system (HAS) is first described. Then a formal listening test is presented, and finally a psychoacoustical model for automation of such a procedure is outlined.

Human Auditory System (HAS)

Figure 4, taken from Robinson (2002), presents the physiology of the human auditory system. Each one of its components is now described.

The *pinna* directionally filters incoming sounds, producing a spectral coloration known as *head related transfer function* (or HRTF). This function enables human listeners to localize the sound source in three dimensions.

The *ear canal* filters the sound, attenuating both low and high frequencies. As a result, a resonance arises around 5 kHz. After this, small bones known as the *timpanic membrane* (or ear drum), *malleus* and *incus* transmit the sound pressure wave through the middle ear. The outer and middle ear perform a band pass filter operation on the input signal.

The sound wave arrives at the fluid-filled *cochlea,* a coil within the ear that is partially protected by a bone. Inside the cochlea resides the *basilar membrane* (BM), which semi-divides it. The basilar membrane acts as a spectrum analyzer, as it divides the signal into frequency components. Each point on the membrane resonates at a different frequency, and the spacing of these resonant frequencies along the BM is almost logarithmic. The effective frequency selectivity is related to the width of the filter characteristic at each point.

The *outer hair cells,* distributed along the length of the BM, react to feedback from the brainstem. They alter their length to change the resonant properties of the BM. As a consequence, the frequency response of the membrane becomes amplitude dependent.

Figure 4. Overview of the human auditory system (HAS)

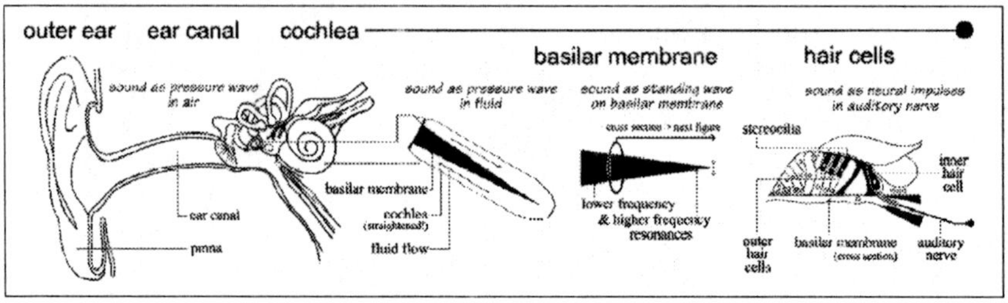

Finally, the inner hair cells of the basilar membrane fire when the BM moves upward. In doing so, they transduce the sound wave at each point into a signal on the auditory nerve. In this way the signal is half wave rectified. Each cell needs a certain time to recover between successive firings, so the average response during a steady tone is lower than at its onset. This means that the inner hair cells act as an automatic gain control.

The net result of the process described above is that an audio signal, which has a relatively wide-bandwidth, and large dynamic range, is encoded for transmission along the nerves. Each one of these nerves offers a much narrower bandwidth, and limited dynamic range. In addition, a critical process has happened during these steps. Any information that is lost due to the transduction process within the cochlea is not available to the brain. In other words, the cochlea acts as a lossy coder. The vast majority of what we cannot hear is attributable to this transduction process (Robinson & Hawksford, 1999).

Detailed modeling of the components and processes just described will be necessary when creating an auditory model for the evaluation of watermarked audio. In fact, by representing the audio signal at the basilar membrane, one can effectively model what is effectively perceived by a human listener.

Perceptual Phenomena

As was just stated, one can model the processes that take place inside the HAS in order to represent how a listener responds to auditory stimuli. Given its characteristics, the HAS responds differently depending on the frequency and loudness of the input. This means that all components of a watermark may not be equally perceptible. Moreover, it also denotes the need of using a perceptual model to effectively measure the amount of distortion that is imposed on an audio signal when a mark is embedded. Given this fact, in this section the main processes that need to be included on a perceptual model are presented.

Sensitivity refers to the ear's response to direct stimuli. In experiments designed to measure sensitivity, listeners are presented with isolated stimuli and their perception of these stimuli is tested. For example, a common test consists of measuring the minimum sound intensity required to hear a particular frequency

(Cox et al., 2002). The main characteristics measured for sensitivity are *frequency* and *loudness.*

The responses of the HAS are frequency dependent; variations in frequency are perceived as different tones. Tests show that the ear is most sensitive to frequencies around 3kHz and that sensitivity declines at very low (20 Hz) and very high (20 kHz) frequencies.

Regarding loudness, different tests have been performed to measure sensitivity. As a general result, one can state that the HAS is able to discern smaller changes when the average intensity is louder. In other words, the human ear is more sensitive to changes in louder signals than in quieter ones.

The second phenomenon that needs to be taken into account is *masking.* A signal that is clearly audible if presented alone can be completely inaudible in the presence of another signal, the masker. This effect is known as masking, and the masked signal is called the *maskee.* For example, a tone might become inaudible in the presence of a second tone at a nearby frequency that is louder. In other words, masking is a measure of a listener's response to one stimulus in the presence of another.

Two different kinds of masking can occur: simultaneous masking and temporal masking (Swanson et al., 1998). In simultaneous masking, both the masker and the maskee are presented at the same time and are quasi-stationary (ITU, 2001). If the masker has a discrete bandwidth, the threshold of hearing is raised even for frequencies below or above the masker. In the situation where a noise-like signal is masking a tonal signal, the amount of masking is almost frequency independent; if the sound pressure of the maskee is about 5 dB below that of the masker, then it becomes inaudible. For other cases, the amount of masking depends on the frequency of the masker.

In temporal masking, the masker and the maskee are presented at different times. Shortly after the decay of a masker, the masked threshold is closer to simultaneous masking of this masker than to the absolute threshold (ITU, 2001). Depending on the duration of the masker, the decay time of the threshold can vary between five ms and 150 ms. Furthermore, weak signals just before loud signals are masked. The duration of this backward masking effect is about five ms.

The third effect that has to be considered is *pooling.* When multiple frequencies are changed rather than just one, it is necessary to know how to combine the sensitivity and masking information for each frequency. Combining the perceptibilities of separate distortions gives a single estimate for the overall change in the work. This is known as pooling. In order to calculate this phenomenon, it is common to apply the formula:

$$D(A,A') = \left(\sum_i |d[i]|^p \right)^{\frac{1}{p}}$$

where $d[i]$ is an estimate of the likelihood that an individual will notice the difference between A and A' in a temporal sample (Cox et al., 2002). In the case of audio, a value of $p=1$ is sometimes appropriate, which turns the equation into a linear summation.

ABX Listening Test

Audio quality is usually evaluated by performing a listening test. In particular, the ABX listening test is commonly used when evaluating the quality of watermarked signals. Other tests for audio watermark quality evaluation, such as the one described in Arnold and Schilz (2002), follow a similar methodology as well. Given this, it becomes desirable to create an automatic model that predicts the response observed from a human listener in such a procedure.

In an ABX test the listener is presented with three different audio clips: selection A (in this case the non-watermarked audio), selection B (the watermarked audio) and X (either the watermarked or non-watermarked audio), drawn at random. The listener is then asked to decide if selection X is equal to A or B. The number of correct answers is the basis to decide if the watermarked audio is perceptually different than the original audio and one will, therefore, declare the watermarking algorithm as "perceptible". In the other case, if the watermarked audio is perceptually equal to the original audio, the watermarking algorithm will be declared as *transparent,* or imperceptible. In the particular case of Arnold and Schilz (2002), the level of transparency is assumed to be determined by the noise-to-mask ratio (NMR).

The ABX test is fully described in ITU Recommendation ITU-R BS.1116, and has been successfully used for subjective measurement of impaired audio signals. Normally only one attribute is used for quality evaluation. It is also defined that this attribute represents any and all detected differences between the original signal and the signal under test. It is known as *basic audio quality* (BAQ), and is calculated as the difference between the grade given to the impaired signal and the grade given to the original signal. Each one of these grades uses the five-level impairment scale that was presented previously. Given this fact, values for the BAQ range between 0 and -4, where 0 corresponds to an imperceptible impairment and -4 to one judged as very annoying.

Although its results are highly reliable, there are many problems related to performing an ABX test for watermark quality evaluation. One of them is the subjective nature of the test, as the perception conditions of the listener may vary with time. Another problem arises from the high costs associated with the test. These costs include the setup of audio equipment[17], construction of a noise-free listening room, and the costs of employing individuals with extraordinarily acute hearing. Finally, the time required to perform extensive testing also poses a problem to this alternative.

Given these facts it becomes desirable to automate the ABX listening test, and incorporate it into a perceptual model of the HAS. If this is implemented, then the task measuring perceptibility can be fully automated and thus watermarking schemes can be effectively and thoroughly evaluated. Fortunately, several perceptual models for audio processing have been proposed. Specifically, in the field of audio coding, psychoacoustic models have been successfully implemented to evaluate the perceptual quality of coded audio. These models can be used as a baseline performance tool for measuring the perceptibility of audio watermarking schemes; thus they are now presented.

A Perceptual Model

A perceptual model used for evaluation of watermarked content must compare the quality of two different audio signals in a way that is similar to the ABX listening test. These two signals correspond to the original audio cover A and the watermarked audio file A'. An ideal system will receive both signals as an input, process them through an auditory model, and compare the representations given by this model (Thiede et al., 1998). Finally it will return a score for the watermarked file A' in the five-level impairment scale. More importantly, the results of such an objective test must be highly correlated with those achieved under a subjective listening test (ITU, 2001). The general architecture of such a perceptual measurement system is depicted in Figure 5.

The auditory model used to process the input signals will have a similar structure to that of the HAS. In general terms, the response of each one of the components of the HAS is modeled by a series of filters. In particular, a synopsis of the models proposed in Robinson and Hawksford (1999), Thiede and Kabot (1996), Thiede et al. (1998), and ITU (2001) is now presented.

The filtering performed by the pinna and ear canal is simulated by an FIR filter, which has been derived from experiments with a dummy head. More realistic approaches can use measurements from human subjects.

Figure 5. Architecture of a perceptual measurement system

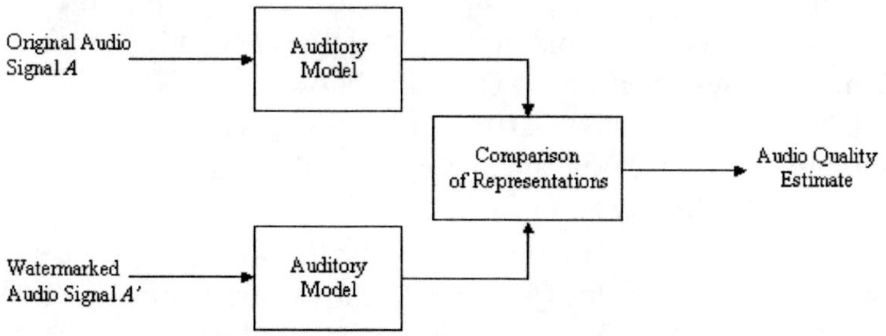

After this prefiltering, the audio signal has to be converted to a basilar membrane representation. That is, the amplitude dependent response of the basilar membrane needs to be simulated. In order to do this, the first step consists of processing the input signal through a bank of amplitude dependant filters, each one adapted to the frequency response of a point on the basilar membrane. The center frequency of each filter should be linearly spaced on the Bark scale, a commonly used frequency scale[18]. The actual number of filters to be used depends on the particular implementation. Other approaches might use a fast Fourier transform to decompose the signal, but this creates a trade-off between temporal and spectral resolution (Thiede & Kabot, 1996).

At each point in the basilar membrane, its movement is transduced into an electrical signal by the hair cells. The firing of individual cells is pseudorandom, but when the individual signals are combined, the proper motion of the BM is derived. Simulating the individual response of each hair cell and combining these responses is a difficult task, so other practical solutions have to be applied. In particular, Robinson and Hawksford (1999) implement a solution based on calculating the half wave response of the cells, and then using a series of feedback loops to simulate the increased sensitivity of the inner hair cells to the onset of sounds. Other schemes might just convolve the signal with a spreading function, to simulate the dispersion of energy along the basilar membrane, and then convert the signal back to decibels (ITU, 2001). Independently of the method used, the basilar membrane representation is obtained at this point.

After a basilar membrane representation has been obtained for both the original audio signal *A,* and the watermarked audio signal *A',* the perceived difference between the two has to be calculated. The difference between the signals at each frequency band has to be calculated, and then it must be determined at what level these differences will become audible for a human listener (Robinson & Hawksford, 1999). In the case of the ITU Recommendation ITU-R BS.1387, this task is done by calculating a series of model variables, such as excitation, modulation and loudness patterns, and using them as an input to an artificial neural network with one hidden layer (ITU, 2001). In the model proposed in Robinson and Hawksford (1999), this is done as a summation over time (over an interval of 20 ms) along with weighting of the signal and peak suppression.

The result of this process is an objective difference between the two signals. In the case of the ITU model, the result is given in a negative five-level impairment scale, just like the BAQ, and is known as the *objective difference grade* (ODG). For other models, the difference is given in implementation-dependant units. In both cases, a mapping or scaling function, from the model units to the ITU-R. 500 scale, must be used.

For the ITU model, this mapping could be trivial, as all that is needed is to add a value of five to the value of the ODG. However, a more precise mapping function could be developed. The ODG has a resolution of one decimal, and the model was not specifically designed for the evaluation watermarking schemes. Given this, a nonlinear mapping (for example using a logarithmic function) could be more appropriate.

For other systems, determining such a function will depend on the particular implementation of the auditory model; nonetheless such a function should exist, as a correlation between objective and subjective measures was stated as an initial requirement. For example, in the case of Thiede and Kabot (1996), a sigmoidal mapping function is used. Furthermore, the parameters for the mapping function can be calculated using a control group consisting of widely available listening test data.

The resulting grade, in the five-level scale, is defined as the perceptibility of the audio watermark. This means that in order to estimate the perceptibility of the watermarking scheme, several test runs must be performed. Again, these test runs should embed a random mark on a cover signal, and a large and representative set of audio cover signals must be used. The perceptibility test score is finally calculated by averaging the different results obtained for each one of the individual tests.

FINAL BENCHMARK SCORE

In the previous sections, three different testing procedures have been proposed, in order to measure the fidelity, robustness and perceptibility of a watermarking scheme. Each one of these tests has resulted in several scores, some of which may be more useful than others. In this section, these scores are combined in order to obtain a final benchmarking score. As a result, fair comparison amongst competing technologies is possible, as the final watermarking scheme evaluation score is obtained.

In addition, another issue is addressed at this point: defining the specific parameters to be used for each attack while performing the robustness test. While the different attacks were explained in the sixth section, the strength at which they should be applied was not specified. As a general rule of thumb, it was just stated that these operations should be tested up to the point where noticeable distortion is introduced on the audio cover file.

As it has been previously discussed, addressing these two topics can prove to be a difficult task. Moreover, a single answer might not be appropriate for every possible watermarking application. Given this fact, one should develop and use a set of application-specific evaluation templates to overcome this restriction. In order to do so, an *evaluation template* is defined as a set of guidelines that specifies the specific parameters to be used for the different tests performed, and also denotes the relative importance of each one of the tests performed on the watermarking scheme. Two fundamental concepts have been incorporated into that of evaluation templates: evaluation profiles and application specific benchmarking.

Evaluation profiles have been proposed in Petitcolas (2000) as a method for testing different levels of robustness. Their sole purpose is to establish the set of tests and media to be used when evaluating a marking algorithm. For example, Table 4, which summarizes the robustness requirements imposed by various organizations, constitutes a general-purpose evaluation profile. More specific profiles have to be developed when evaluating more specific watermarking systems. For example, one should test a marking scheme intended for advertisement broadcast monitoring with a set of recordings similar to those that will be used in a real world situation. There is no point in testing such an algorithm with a set of high-fidelity musical recordings. Evaluation profiles are thus a part of the proposed evaluation templates.

Application specific benchmarking, in turn, is proposed in Pereira et al. (2001) and Voloshynovskiy, Pereira, Iquise and Pun (2001) and consists of averaging the results of the different tests performed to a marking scheme, using a set of weights that is specific to the intended application of the watermarking algorithm. In other words, attacks are weighted as a function of applications (Pereira et al., 2001). In the specific case of the evaluation templates proposed in this document, two different sets of weights should be specified: those used when measuring one of the three fundamental characteristics of the algorithm (i.e., fidelity, robustness and perceptibility); and those used when combining these measures into a single benchmarking score.

After the different weights have been established, the *overall watermarking scheme score* is calculated as a simple weighted average, with the formula:

$$Score = w_f * s_f + w_r * s_r + w_p * s_p$$

where w represents the assigned weight for a test, s to the score received on a test, and the subscripts f, r, p denote the fidelity, robustness and perceptibility tests respectively. In turn, the values of s_f, s_r, and s_p are also determined using a weighted average for the different measures obtained on the specific subtests.

The use of an evaluation template is a simple, yet powerful idea. It allows for a fair comparison of watermarking schemes, and for ease of automated testing. After these templates have been defined, one needs only to select the intended application of the watermarking scheme that is to be evaluated, and the rest of the operations can be performed automatically. Nonetheless, time has to be devoted to the task of carefully defining the set of evaluation templates for the different applications sought to be tested. A very simple, general-purpose evaluation template is shown next, as an example.

Application: General Purpose Audio Watermarking		
Final Score Weights: Fidelity = 1/3, Robustness = 1/3, Perceptibility = 1/3		
	FIDELITY TEST	
Measure	**Parameters**	**Weight**
Quality	N/A	0.75
Data Payload	Watermark length = 100 bits, score calculated as BER.	0.125
Speed	Watermark length = 50 bits, score calculated as 1 if embedding time is less than 2 minutes, 0 otherwise.	0.125
	ROBUSTNESS TEST	
Measure	**Parameters**	**Weight**
D/A Conversion	D/A ↔ A/D twice.	1/14
Equalization	10 band graphic equalizer with the following characteristics: Freq. (Hz) 31 62 125 250 500 1k 2k 4k 8k 16k Gain (db) -6 +6 -6 +3 -6 +6 -6 +6 -6 +6	1/14
Band-pass filtering	100 Hz – 6 kHz, 12dB/oct.	1/14
Time stretch and pitch change	+/- 10% compression and decompression	1/14
Codecs	AAC, MPEG-4 AAC with perceptual noise substitution, MPEG-1 Audio Layer 3, Windows Media Audio, and Twin-VQ at 128 kbps.	1/14
Noise addition	Adding white noise with constant level of 40dB lower than total averaged music power (SNR: 40dB)	1/14
Time scale modification	Pitch invariant time scaling of +/- 4%	1/14
Wow and flutter	0.5% rms, from DC to 250Hz	1/14
Echo addition	Delay = 100 milliseconds, feedback coefficient = 0.5	1/14
Down mixing	Stereo to mono, and Dolby surround	1/14
Sample rate conversion	44.1 kHz to 16 kHz	1/14
Dynamic range reduction	Threshold of 50dB, 16dB maximum compression Rate: 10 millisecond attack, 3 second recovery	1/14
Amplitude compression	16 bits to 8 bits	1/14
	PERCEPTIBILITY TEST	
Measure	**Parameters**	**Weight**
Watermark perceptibility	N/A	1

Presenting the Results

The main result of the benchmark presented here is the overall watermarking scheme score that has just been explained. It corresponds to a single, numerical result. As a consequence, comparison between similar schemes is both quick and easy. Having such a comprehensive quality measure is sufficient in most cases.

Under some circumstances the intermediate scores might also be important, as one might want to know more about the particular characteristics of a

Table 5. Useful graphs when evaluating a specific watermarking scheme

Graph Type	Perceptual Quality	Robustness Measure	Strength of a Specific Attack	Data Payload
Robustness to an attack	*fixed*	*variable*	*variable*	*fixed*
Perceptual Quality vs. Payload	*variable*	*fixed*	*Fixed*	*variable*
Attack strength vs. Perceptual Quality	*variable*	*fixed*	*variable*	*fixed*
ROC	*fixed*	*fixed*	*fixed/variable*	*fixed*

For example, one might just be interested in the perceptibility score of the echo watermarking algorithm, or in the robustness against uniform noise for two different schemes. For these cases, the use of graphs, as proposed in Kutter and Hartung (2000) and Kutter and Petitcolas (1999, 2000) is recommended.

The graphs should plot the variance in two different parameters, with the remaining parameters fixed. That is, the test setup conditions should remain constant along different test runs. Finally, several test runs should be performed, and the results averaged. As a consequence, a set of variable and fixed parameters for performing the comparisons are possible, and thus several graphs can be plotted. Some of the most useful graphs, based on the discussion presented in Kutter and Petitcolas (1999), along with their corresponding variables and constants, are summarized in Table 5.

Of special interest to some watermark developers is the use of receiver operating characteristic (ROC) graphs, as they show the relation between false positives and false negatives for a given watermarking system. "They are useful for assessing the overall behavior and reliability of the watermarking scheme being tested" (Petitcolas & Anderson, 1999).

In order to understand ROC graphs, one should remember that a watermark decoder can be viewed as a system that performs two different steps: first it decides if a watermark is present on the audio signal *A'*, and then it tries to recover the embedded watermark *W*. The first step can be viewed as a form of hypothesis testing (Kutter & Hartung, 2000), where the decoder decides between the alternative hypothesis (a watermark is present), and the null hypothesis (the watermark is not present). Given these two options, two different errors can occur, as was stated in the third section: a false positive, and a false negative.

ROC graphs plot the true positive fraction (TPF) on the Y-axis, and the false positive fraction (FPF) on the X-axis. The TPF is defined by the formula:

$$TPF = \frac{TP}{TP + FN}$$

where TP is the number of true positive test results, and FN is the number of false negative tests. Conversely, the FPF is defined by:

$$FPF = \frac{FP}{TN + FP}$$

where TN is the number of false-positive results, and FP the number of true negative results. An optimal detector will have a curve that goes from the bottom left corner to the top left, and then to the top right corner (Kutter & Petitcolas, 2000). Finally, it must be stated that the same number of watermarked and unwatermarked audio samples should be used for the test, although false-positive testing can be time-consuming, as was previously discussed in this document.

Automated Evaluation

The watermarking benchmark proposed here can be implemented for the automated evaluation of different watermarking schemes. In fact, this idea has been included in test design, and has motivated some key decisions, such as the use of a computational model of the ear instead of a formal listening test. Moreover, the establishment of an automated test for watermarking systems is an industry need. This assertion is derived from the following fact: to evaluate the quality of a watermarking scheme one can do one of the following three options (Petitcolas, 2000):

- Trust the watermark developer and his or her claims about watermark performance.
- Thoroughly test the scheme oneself.
- Have the watermarking scheme evaluated by a trusted third party.

Only the third option provides an objective solution to this problem, as long as the evaluation methodology and results are transparent to the public (Petitcolas et al., 2001). This means that anybody should be able to reproduce the results easily. As a conclusion, the industry needs to establish a trusted evaluation authority in order to objectively evaluate its watermarking products. The establishment of watermark certification programs has been proposed, and projects such as the Certimark and StirMark benchmarks are under development (Certimark, 2001; Kutter & Petitcolas, 2000; Pereira et al., 2001; Petitcolas et al., 2001). However, these programs seem to be aimed mainly at testing of image watermarking systems (Meerwald & Pereira, 2002). A similar initiative for audio watermark testing has yet to be proposed.

Nonetheless, one problem remains unsolved: watermarking scheme developers may not be willing to give the source code for their embedding and recovery systems to a testing authority. If this is the situation, then both watermark embedding and recovery processes must be performed at the developer's side, while the rest of the operations can be performed by the watermark tester. The problem with this scheme is that the watermark developer could cheat and always report the watermark as being recovered by the detector. Even if a basic zero knowledge protocol is used in the testing procedure, the developer can cheat, as he or she will have access to both the original audio file A and the modified, watermarked file $\tilde{A}$ that has been previously processed by the tester. The cheat is possible because the developer can estimate the value of the watermarked file A', even if it has always been kept secured by the tester (Petitcolas, 2000), and then try to extract the mark from this estimated signal. Given this fact, one partial solution consists of giving the watermark decoder to the evaluator, while the developer maintains control over the watermark embedder, or vice versa[19].

Hopefully, as the need for thorough testing of watermarking systems increases, watermark developers will be more willing to give out access to their systems for thorough evaluation. Furthermore, if a common testing interface is agreed upon by watermark developers, then they will not need to release the source code for their products; a compiled library will be enough for practical testing of the implemented scheme if it follows a previously defined set of design guidelines. Nonetheless, it is uncertain if both the watermarking industry and community will undergo such an effort.

CONCLUSIONS

Digital watermarking schemes can prove to be a valuable technique for copyright control of digital material. Different applications and properties of digital watermarks have been reviewed in this chapter, specifically as they apply to digital audio. However, a problem arises as different claims are made about the quality of the watermarking schemes being developed; every developer measures the quality of their respective schemes using a different set of procedures and metrics, making it impossible to perform objective comparisons among their products.

As the problem just described can affect the credibility of watermarking system developers, as well as the acceptance of this emerging technology by content owners, this document has presented a practical test for measuring the quality of digital audio watermarking techniques. The implementation and further development of such a test can prove to be beneficial not only to the industry, but also to the growing field of researchers currently working on the subject.

Nonetheless, several problems arise while implementing a widely accepted benchmark for watermarking schemes. Most of these problems have been presented in this document, but others have not been thoroughly discussed. One of these problems consists of including the growing number of attacks against marking systems that are proposed every year. These attacks get more complex and thus their implementation becomes more difficult (Meerwald & Pereira, 2002; Voloshynovskiy, Pereira, Pun et al., 2001); nonetheless, they need to be implemented and included if real world testing is sought.

Another problem arises when other aspects of the systems are to be evaluated. For example, user interfaces can be very important in determining whether a watermarking product will be widely accepted (Craver et al., 2000). Its evaluation is not directly related to the architecture and performance of a marking system, but it certainly will have an impact on its acceptance.

Legal constraints can also affect watermark testing, as patents might protect some of the techniques used for watermark evaluation. In other situations, the use of certain watermarking schemes in court as acceptable proofs of ownership cannot be guaranteed, and a case-by-case study must be performed (Craver, Yeo et al., 1998; Lai & Buonaiuti, 2000). Such legal attacks depend on many factors, such as the economic power of the disputing parties.

While these difficulties are important, they should not be considered severe and must not undermine the importance of implementing a widely accepted benchmarking for audio watermarking systems. Instead, they show the need for further development of the current testing techniques. The industry has seen that ambiguous requirements and unmethodical testing can prove to be a disaster, as they can lead to the development of unreliable systems (Craver et al., 2001).

Finally, the importance of a specific benchmark for audio watermarking must be stated. Most of the available literature on watermarking relates to the specific field of image watermarking. In a similar way, the development of testing techniques for watermarking has focused on the marking of digital images. Benchmarks currently being developed, such as Stirmark and Certimark, will be extended in the future to manage digital audio content (Certimark, 2001; Kutter & Petitcolas, 2000); however, this might not be an easy task, as the metrics used in these benchmarks have been optimized for the evaluation of image watermarking techniques. It is in this aspect that the test proposed in this document proves to be valuable, as it proposes the use of a psychoacoustical model in order to measure the perceptual quality of audio watermarking schemes. Other aspects, such as the use of a communications model as the base for the test design, are novel as well, and hopefully will be incorporated into the watermark benchmarking initiatives currently under development.

REFERENCES

Acken, J.M. (1998, July). How watermarking adds value to digital content. *Communications of the ACM, 41,* 75-77.

Arnold, M. (2000). Audio watermarking: Features, applications and algorithms. Paper presented at the *IEEE International Conference on Multimedia and Expo 2000.*

Arnold, M., & Schilz, K. (2002, January). Quality evaluation of watermarked audio tracks. Paper presented at the *Proceedings of the SPIE, Security and Watermarking of Multimedia Contents IV*, San Jose, CA.

Bassia, P., & Pitas, I. (1998, August). Robust audio watermarking in the time domain. Paper presented at the *9th European Signal Processing Conference (EUSIPCO'98)*, Island of Rhodes, Greece.

Bender, W., Gruhl, D., Morimoto, N., & Lu, A. (1996). Techniques for data hiding. *IBM Systems Journal, 35*(5).

Boney, L., Tewfik, A.H., & Hamdy, K.N. (1996, June). Digital watermarks for audio signals. Paper presented at the *IEEE International Conference on Multimedia Computing and Systems*, Hiroshima, Japan.

Certimark. (2001). *Certimark benchmark, metrics & parameters* (D22). Geneva, Switzerland.

Chen, B. (2000). *Design and analysis of digital watermarking, information embedding, and data hiding systems.* MIT, Boston.

Chen, B., & Wornell, G.W. (1999, January). Dither modulation: A new approach to digital watermarking and information embedding. Paper presented at the *SPIE: Security and Watermarking of Multimedia Contents*, San Jose, CA.

Chen, B., & Wornell, G.W. (2000, June). Quantization index modulation: A class of provably good methods for digital watermarking and information embedding. Paper presented at the *International Symposium on Information Theory ISIT-2000*, Sorrento, Italy.

Cox, I.J., Miller, M.L., & Bloom, J.A. (2000, March). Watermarking applications and their properties. Paper presented at the *International Conference on Information Technology: Coding and Computing, ITCC 2000*, Las Vegas, NV.

Cox, I.J., Miller, M.L., & Bloom, J.A. (2002). *Digital watermarking* (1st ed.). San Francisco: Morgan Kaufmann.

Cox, I.J., Miller, M.L., Linnartz, J.-P.M.G., & Kalker, T. (1999). A review of watermarking principles and practices. In K.K. Parhi & T. Nishitani (Eds.), *Digital signal processing in multimedia systems* (pp. 461-485). Marcell Dekker.

Craver, S., Memon, N., Yeo, B.-L., & Yeung, M.M. (1998). Resolving rightful ownerships with invisible watermarking techniques: Limitations, attacks and implications. *IEEE Journal on Selected Areas in Communications, 16*(4), 573-586.

Craver, S., Memon, N., & Yeung, M.M. (1996). *Can invisible watermarks resolve rightful ownerships?* (RC 20509). IBM Research.

Craver, S., Perrig, A., & Petitcolas, F.A.P. (2000). Robustness of copyright marking systems. In F.A.P. Petitcolas & S. Katzenbeisser (Eds.), *Information hiding: Techniques for steganography and digital watermarking* (1st ed., pp. 149-174). Boston, MA: Artech House.

Craver, S., Wu, M., Liu, B., Stubblefield, A., Swartzlander, B., Wallach, D.S., Dean, D., & Felten, E.W. (2001, August). Reading between the lines: Lessons from the SDMI challenge. Paper presented at the *USENIX Security Symposium*, Washington, DC.

Craver, S., Yeo, B.-L., & Yeung, M.M. (1998, July). Technical trials and legal tribulations. *Communications of the ACM, 41,* 45-54.

Czerwinski, S., Fromm, R., & Hodes, T. (1999). *Digital music distribution and audio watermarking* (IS 219). University of California - Berkeley.

Dannenberg, R., & Mazzoni, D. (2002). *Audacity* (Version 0.98). Pittsburgh, PA.

Dugelay, J.-L., & Roche, S. (2000). A survey of current watermarking techniques. In F. A.P. Petitcolas & S. Katzenbeisser (Eds.), *Information hiding: Techniques for steganography and digital watermarking* (1st ed., pp. 121-148). Boston, MA: Artech House.

Gordy, J.D., & Burton, L.T. (2000, August). Performance evaluation of digital audio watermarking algorithms. Paper presented at the *43rd Midwest Symposium on Circuits and Systems*, Lansing, MI.

Initiative, S.D.M. (2000). *Call for proposals for Phase II screening technology, Version 1.0: Secure Digital Music Initiative.*

ITU. (2001). *Method for objective measurements of perceived audio quality* (ITU-R BS.1387). Geneva: International Telecommunication Union.

JASRAC. (2001). *Announcement of evaluation test results for "STEP 2001", International evaluation project for digital watermark technology for music.* Tokyo: Japan Society for the Rights of Authors, Composers and Publishers.

Johnson, N.F., Duric, Z., & Jajodia, S. (2001). *Information hiding: Steganography and watermarking - Attacks and countermeasures* (1st ed.). Boston: Kluwer Academic Publishers.

Johnson, N.F., & Katzenbeisser, S.C. (2000). A survey of steganographic techniques. In F.A.P. Petitcolas & S. Katzenbeisser (Eds.), *Information hiding: Techniques for steganography and digital watermarking* (1st ed., pp. 43-78). Boston, MA: Artech House.

Katzenbeisser, S., & Veith, H. (2002, January). Securing symmetric watermarking schemes against protocol attacks. Paper presented at the *Proceedings of the SPIE, Security and Watermarking of Multimedia Contents IV*, San Jose, CA.

Katzenbeisser, S.C. (2000). Principles of steganography. In F.A.P. Petitcolas & S. Katzenbeisser (Eds.), *Information hiding: Techniques for steganography and digital watermarking* (1st ed., pp. 17-41). Boston, MA: Artech House.

Kirovski, D., & Malvar, H. (2001, April). Robust cover communication over a public audio channel using spread spectrum. Paper presented at the *Information Hiding Workshop*, Pittsburgh, PA.

Kuczynski, A. (2000, January 6). Radio squeezes empty air space for profit. *The New York Times.*

Kutter, M., & Hartung, F. (2000). Introduction to watermarking techniques. In F.A.P. Petitcolas & S. Katzenbeisser (Eds.), *Information hiding: Techniques for steganography and digital watermarking* (1st ed., pp. 97-120). Boston, MA: Artech House.

Kutter, M., & Petitcolas, F.A.P. (1999, January). A fair benchmark for image watermarking systems. Paper presented at the *Electronic Imaging '99. Security and Watermarking of Multimedia Contents*, San Jose, CA.

Kutter, M., & Petitcolas, F.A.P. (2000). Fair evaluation methods for image watermarking systems. *Journal of Electronic Imaging, 9*(4), 445-455.

Lai, S., & Buonaiuti, F.M. (2000). Copyright on the Internet and watermarking. In F.A. P. Petitcolas & S. Katzenbeisser (Eds.), *Information hiding: Techniques for steganography and digital watermarking* (1st ed., pp. 191-213). Boston, MA: Artech House.

Meerwald, P., & Pereira, S. (2002, January). Attacks, applications, and evaluation of known watermarking algorithms with Checkmark. Paper presented at the *Proceedings of the SPIE, Security and Watermarking of Multimedia Contents IV*, San Jose, CA.

Memon, N., & Wong, P.W. (1998, July). Protecting digital media content. *Communications of the ACM, 41,* 35-43.

Mintzer, F., Braudaway, G.W., & Bell, A.E. (1998, July). Opportunities for watermarking standards. *Communications of the ACM, 41,* 57-64.

Mintzer, F., Magerlein, K.A., & Braudaway, G.W. (1996). *Color correct digital watermarking of images.*

Pereira, S., Voloshynovskiy, S., Madueño, M., Marchand-Maillet, S., & Pun, T. (2001, April). Second generation benchmarking and application oriented evaluation. Paper presented at the *Information Hiding Workshop*, Pittsburgh, PA.

Petitcolas, F.A.P. (2000). Watermarking schemes evaluation. *IEEE Signal Processing, 17*(5), 58-64.

Petitcolas, F.A.P., & Anderson, R.J. (1998, September). Weaknesses of copyright marking systems. Paper presented at the *Multimedia and*

Security Workshop at the 6th ACM International Multimedia Conference, Bristol UK.

Petitcolas, F.A.P., & Anderson, R.J. (1999, June). Evaluation of copyright marking systems. Paper presented at the *IEEE Multimedia Systems*, Florence, Italy.

Petitcolas, F.A.P., Anderson, R.J., & G., K.M. (1998, April). Attacks on copyright marking systems. Paper presented at the *Second Workshop on Information Hiding*, Portland, OR.

Petitcolas, F.A.P., Anderson, R.J., & G., K. M. (1999, July). Information hiding – A survey. Paper presented at the *IEEE.*

Petitcolas, F.A.P., Steinebach, M., Raynal, F., Dittmann, J., Fontaine, C., & Fatès, N. (2001, January 22-26). A public automated Web-based evaluation service for watermarking schemes: StirMark Benchmark. Paper presented at the *Electronic Imaging 2001, Security and Watermarking of Multimedia Contents*, San Jose, CA.

Piron, L., Arnold, M., Kutter, M., Funk, W., Boucqueau, J.M., & Craven, F. (1999, January). OCTALIS benchmarking: Comparison of four watermarking techniques. Paper presented at the *Proceedings of SPIE: Security and Watermarking of Multimedia Contents*, San Jose, CA.

RLE. (1999). *Leaving a mark without a trace* [RLE Currents 11(2)]. Available online: http://rleweb.mit.edu/Publications/currents/cur11-1/11-1watermark.htm.

Robinson, D.J.M. (2002). *Perceptual model for assessment of coded audio.* University of Essex, Essex.

Robinson, D.J.M., & Hawksford, M.J. (1999, September). Time-domain auditory model for the assessment of high-quality coded audio. Paper presented at the *107th Conference of the Audio Engineering Society*, New York.

Secure Digital Music Initiative. (2000). *Call for proposal for Phase II screening technology* (FRWG 000224-01).

Swanson, M.D., Zhu, B., Tewfik, A.H., & Boney, L. (1998). Robust audio watermarking using perceptual masking. *Signal Processing, 66*(3), 337-355.

Thiede, T., & Kabot, E. (1996). A new perceptual quality measure for bit rate reduced audio. Paper presented at the *100th AES Convention*, Copenhagen, Denmark.

Thiede, T., Treurniet, W.C., Bitto, R., Sporer, T., Brandenburg, K., Schmidmer, C., Keyhl, K., G., B. J., Colomes, C., Stoll, G., & Feiten, B. (1998). PEAQ - der künftige ITU-Standard zur objektiven messung der wahrgenommenen audioqualität. Paper presented at the *Tonmeistertagung Karlsruhe*, Munich, Germany.

Voloshynovskiy, S., Pereira, S., Iquise, V., & Pun, T. (2001, June). Attack modelling: Towards a second generation benchmark. Paper presented at the *Signal Processing*.

Voloshynovskiy, S., Pereira, S., Pun, T., Eggers, J.J., & Su, J.K. (2001, August). Attacks on digital watermarks: Classification, estimation-based attacks and benchmarks. *IEEE Communications Magazine, 39,* 118-127.

Yeung, M.M. (1998, July). Digital watermarking. *Communications of the ACM, 41,* 31-33.

Zhao, J., Koch, E., & Luo, C. (1998, July). In business today and tomorrow. *Communications of the ACM, 41,* 67-72.

ENDNOTES

1 It must be stated that when information is digital there is no difference between an original and a bit by bit copy. This constitutes the core of the threat to art works, such as music recordings, as any copy has the same quality as the original. This problem did not exist with technologies such as cassette recorders, since the fidelity of a second-generation copy was not high enough to consider the technology a threat.

2 A test subject is defined as a specific implementation of a watermarking algorithm, based on one of the general techniques presented in this document.

3 It is implied that the transmission of a watermark is considered a communication process, where the content creator embeds a watermark into a work, which acts as a channel. The watermark is meant to be recovered later by a receiver, but there is no guarantee that the recovery will be successful, as the channel is prone to some tampering. This assumption will be further explained later in the document.

4 Or a copy of such, given the digital nature of the medium.

5 A cover is the same thing as a work. C, the set of all possible covers (or all possible works), is known as content.

6 This pattern is also known as a pseudo-noise (PN) sequence. Even though the watermark message and the PN-sequence are different, it is the latter one we refer to as the watermark W.

7 The fingerprinting mechanism implemented by the DiVX, where each player had an embedder rather than a decoder, constitutes an interesting and uncommon case.

8 This in accordance to Kerckhoff's principle.

9 In the case of an audio recording, the symbol □ along with the owner name must be printed on the surface of the physical media.

10 The registration fee at the Office of Copyrights and Patents can be found online at: http://www.loc.gov/copyright.

11 In fact, the call for proposal for Phase II of SDMI requires this functionality (Initiative, 2000).

12 This is very similar to the use of serial numbers in software packages.

13 Some of the literature refers to this distortion as beating.

14 This is known as an oracle attack.

15 $$C(x)=E\left((x-\bar{x})(x-\bar{x})^{*}\right)$$

16 THD is the amount of undesirable harmonics present in an output audio signal, expressed as a percentage. The lower the percentage the better.

17 A description of the equipment used on a formal listening test can be found in Arnold and Schilz (2002).

18 1 Bark corresponds to 100 Hz, and 24 Bark correspond to 15000 Hz.

19 This decision will be motivated by the economics of the system; that is, by what part of the systems is considered more valuable by the developer.

Chapter IV

Digital Audio Watermarking

Changsheng Xu, Institute for Infocomm Research, Singapore

Qi Tian, Institute for Infocomm Research, Singapore

ABSTRACT

This chapter provides a comprehensive survey and summary of the technical achievements in the research area of digital audio watermarking. In order to give a big picture of the current status of this area, this chapter covers the research aspects of performance evaluation for audio watermarking, human auditory system, digital watermarking for PCM audio, digital watermarking for wav-table synthesis audio, and digital watermarking for compressed audio. Based on the current technology used in digital audio watermarking and the demand from real-world applications, future promising directions are identified.

INTRODUCTION

The recent growth of networked multimedia systems has increased the need for the protection of digital media. This is particularly important for the protection and enhancement of intellectual property rights. Digital media includes text, digital audio, video and images. The ubiquity of digital media in Internet and digital library applications has called for new methods in digital copyright protection and new measures in data security. Digital watermarking techniques have been developed to meet the needs for these growing concerns and have become an active research area.

Digital watermark is an invisible structure to be embedded into the host media. To be effective, a watermark must be imperceptible within its host, discrete to prevent unauthorized removal, easily extracted by the owner, and robust to incidental and intentional distortions. Many watermarking techniques in images and video are proposed, mainly focusing on the invisibility of the watermark and its robustness against various signal manipulations and hostile attacks. Most of recent work can be grouped into two categories: spatial domain methods (Pitas, 1996; Wolfgang & Delp, 1996) and frequency domain methods (Cox et al., 1995; Delaigle et al., 1996; Swanson et al., 1996). There is a current trend towards approaches that make use of information about the human visual system (HVS) to produce a more robust watermark. Such techniques use explicit information about the HVS to exploit the limited dynamic range of the human eye.

Compared with digital video and image watermarking, digital audio watermarking provides a special challenge because the human auditory system (HAS) is extremely more sensitive than the HVS. The HAS is sensitive to a dynamic range of amplitude of one billion to one and of frequency of one thousand to one. Sensitivity to additive random noise is also acute. The perturbations in a sound file can be detected as low as one part in ten million (80dB below ambient level). Although the limit of perceptible noise increases as the noise contents of the host audio signal increases, the typical allowable noise level is very low. While the HAS has a large dynamic range, it often has a fairly small differential range. As a result, loud sounds tend to mask out quiet sounds. Additionally, while the HAS has very low sensitivity to the amplitude and relative phase of the sound, it is unable to perceive absolute phase. Finally, there are some environmental distortions so common as to be ignored by the listener in most cases. There is always a conflict between inaudibility and robustness in digital audio watermarking. How to achieve an optimal balance between inaudibility and robustness of watermarked audio is a big challenge.

The aim of this chapter is to provide a comprehensive survey and summary of the technical achievements in the research area of digital audio watermarking. In order to give a big picture of the current status of this area, this chapter covers the research aspects of performance evaluation for audio watermarking, human auditory system, digital watermarking for PCM audio, digital watermarking for wav-table synthesis audio, and digital watermarking for compressed audio. Based on the current technology used in digital audio watermarking and the demand from real-world applications, future promising directions are identified.

PERFORMANCE EVALUATION FOR AUDIO WATERMARKING

Digital audio watermarking can be applied into many applications, including copyright protection, authentication, trace of illegal distribution, captioning and digital right management (DRM). Since different applications have different requirements, the criteria used to evaluate the performance of digital audio watermarking techniques may be more important in some applications than in others. Most of the requirements are conflicting and there is no unique set of requirements that all digital audio watermarking techniques must satisfy. Some important performance evaluation criteria are described in following subsections. These criteria also can be used in image and video watermarking.

Perceptual Quality

One of the basic requirements of digital audio watermarking is that the embedded watermark cannot affect the perceptual quality of the host audio signal; that is, the embedded watermark should not be detectable by a listener. This is important in some applications, such as copyright protection and usage tracking. In addition, digital watermarking should not produce artefacts that are perceptually dissimilar from those that may be detected in an original host signal.

Usually, signal-to-noise ratio (SNR) of the original host signal vs. the embedded watermark can be used as a quantitative quality measure (Gordy & Bruton, 2000).

$$SNR = 10\log_{10}\left\{\frac{\sum_{n=0}^{N-1} x^2(n)}{\sum_{n=0}^{N-1}[\tilde{x}(n) - x(n)]^2}\right\} \quad (1)$$

where $x(n)$ is the host signal of length N samples and $\tilde{x}(n)$ is the watermarked signal.

Another subjective quality measure is listening test. In listening test, subjects (called golden ears) are selected to listen to the test sample pairs with and without watermarks and give the grades corresponding to different impairment scales. There are a number of listening test methods, such as "Perceptual Audio Quality Measure (PAQM)" (Beerends & Stemerdink, 1992).

Bit Rate

Bit rate is a measure to reflect the amount of watermark data that may be reliably embedded within a host signal per unit of time, such as bits per second. Some watermarking applications, such as insertion of a serial number or author identification, require relevant small amounts of data embedded repeatedly in the host signal. However, high bit rate is desirable in some envisioned applications such as covert communication in order to embed a significant fraction of the amount of data in the host signal.

Usually, the reliability is measured as the bit error rate (BER) of extracted watermark data (Gordy & Bruton, 2000). For embedded and extracted watermark sequences of length B bits, the BER (in percent) is given by the expression:

$$BER = \frac{100}{B}\sum_{n=0}^{B-1}\begin{cases}1, \tilde{w}(n) \neq w(n)\\0, \tilde{w}(n) = w(n)\end{cases} \quad \textbf{(2)}$$

where $w(n) \in \{-1,1\}$ is a bipolar binary sequence of bits to be embedded within the host signal, for $0 \leq m \leq B\text{-}1$, and $\tilde{w}(n)$ denotes the set of watermark bits extracted from the watermarked signal.

Robustness

Robustness is another important requirement for digital audio watermarking. Watermarked audio signals may frequently suffer common signal processing operations and malicious attacks. Although these operations and attacks may not affect the perceived quality of the host signal, they may corrupt the embedded data within the host signal. A good and reliable audio watermarking algorithm should survive the following manipulations (MUSE Project, 1998):

- additive and multiplicative noise;
- linear and nonlinear filtering, for example, lowpass filtering;
- data compression, for example, MPEG audio layer 3, Dobly AC-3;
- local exchange of samples, for example, permutations;
- quantization of sample values;
- temporal scaling, for example, stretch by 10%;
- equalization, for example, +6 dB at 1 kHz and -6 dB at 4 kHz;
- removal of insertion of samples;
- averaging multiple watermarked copies of a signal;
- D/A and A/D conversions;
- frequency response distortion;
- group-delay distortions;

- downmixing, for example, stereo to mono;
- overdubbing, for example, placing another track into the audio.

Robustness can be measured by the bit error rate (BER) of the extracted watermark data as a function of the amount of distortion introduced by a given manipulation.

Security

In order to prevent an unauthorized user from detecting the presence of embedded data and remove the embedded data, the watermark embedding procedure must be secure in many applications. Different applications have different security requirements. The most stringent requirements arise in covert communication scenarios. Security of data embedding procedures is interpreted in the same way as security of encryption techniques. A secure data embedding procedure cannot be broken unless the authorized user has access to a secret key that controls the insertion of the data in the host signal. Hence, a data embedding scheme is truly secure if knowing the exact algorithm for embedding the data does not help an unauthorized party detect the presence of embedded data. An unauthorized user should not be able to extract the data in a reasonable amount of time even if he or she knows that the host signal contains data and is familiar with the exact algorithm for embedding the data. Usually, the watermark embedding method should open to the public, but the secret key is not released. In some applications, for example, covert communications, the data may also be encrypted prior to insertion in a host signal.

Computational Complexity

Computational complexity refers to the processing required to embed watermark data into a host signal, and/or to extract the data from the signal. It is essential and critical for the applications that require online watermark embedding and extraction. Algorithm complexity is also important to influence the choice of implementation structure or DSP architecture. Although there are many ways to measure complexity, such as complexity analysis (or "Big-O" analysis) and actual CPU timings (in seconds), for practical applications more quantitative values are required (Cox et al., 1997).

HUMAN AUDITORY SYSTEM

The human auditory system (HAS) model has been successfully applied in perceptual audio coding such as MPEG Audio Codec (Brandenburg & Stoll, 1992). Similarly, HAS model can also be used in digital watermarking to embed the data into the host audio signal more transparently and robustly.

Audio masking is a phenomenon where a weaker but audible signal (the maskee) can be made inaudible (masked) by a simultaneously occurring stronger signal (the masker) (Noll, 1993). The masking effect depends on the frequency and temporal characteristics of both the maskee and the masker.

Frequency masking refers to masking between frequency components in the audio signal. If masker and maskee are close enough to each other in frequency, the masker may make the maskee inaudible. A masking threshold can be measured below which any signal will not be audible. The masking threshold depends on the sound pressure level (SPL) and the frequency of the masker, and on the characteristics of masker and maskee. For example, with the masking threshold for the SPL=60 dB masker at around 1 kHz, the SPL of the maskee can be surprisingly high — it will be masked as long as its SPL is below the masking threshold. The slope of the masking threshold is steeper towards lower frequencies; that is, higher frequencies are more easily masked. It should be noted that it is easier for a broadband noise to mask a tonal than for a tonal signal to mask out a broadband noise. Noise and low-level signal contributions are masked inside and outside the particular critical band if their SPL is below the masking threshold. If the source signal consists of many simultaneous maskers, a global masking threshold can be computed that describes the threshold of just noticeable distortions as a function of frequency. The calculation of the global masking threshold is based on the high-resolution short-term amplitude spectrum of the audio signal and sufficient for critical-band-based analyses. In a first step all individual masking thresholds are determined, depending on signal level, type of masker (noise or tone), and frequency range. Next, the global masking threshold is determined by adding all individual masking thresholds and threshold in quiet. Adding threshold in quiet ensures that computed global masking threshold is not below the threshold in quiet. The effects of masking reaching over critical band bounds must be included in the calculation. Finally, the global signal-to-mask ratio (SMR) is determined as the ratio of the maximum of the signal power and the global masking threshold. Frequency masking models can be readily obtained from the current generation of high quality audio codes, for example, the masking model defined in ISO-MPEG Audio Psychoacoustic Model 1, for Layer 1 (ISO/IEC IS 11172, 1993).

In addition to frequency masking, two time domain phenomena also play an important role in human auditory perception, pre-masking and post-masking. The temporal masking effects occur before and after a masking signal has been switched on and off respectively. Pre-masking effects make weaker signals inaudible before the stronger masker is switched on, and post-masking effects make weaker signals inaudible after the stronger masker is switched off. Pre-masking occurs from five to 20 ms before the masker is switched on, while post-masking occurs from 50 to 200 ms after the masker is turned off.

DIGITAL WATERMARKING FOR PCM AUDIO

Digital audio can be classified into three categories: PCM audio, WAV-table synthesis audio and compressed audio. Most current audio watermarking techniques mainly focus on PCM audio. The popular methods include low-bit coding, phase coding, spread spectrum coding, echo hiding, perceptual masking and content-adaptive watermarking.

Low Bit Coding

The basic idea in low bit coding technique is to embed the watermark in an audio signal by replacing the least significant bit of each sampling point by a coded binary string corresponding to the watermark. For example, in a 16-bits per sample representation, the least four bits can be used for hiding. The retrieval of the hidden data in low-bit coding is done by reading out the value from the low bits. The stego key is the position of altered bits. Low-bit coding is the simplest way to embed data into digital audio and can be applied in all ranges of transmission rates with digital communication modes. Ideally, the channel capacity will be 8kbps in an 8kHz sampled sequence and 44kbps in a 44kHz sampled sequence for a noiseless channel application. In return for this large channel capacity, audio noise is introduced. The impact of this noise is a direct function of the content of the original signal; for example, a live sports event contains crowd noise that makes the noise resultant from low-bit encoding.

The major disadvantage of the low bit coding method is its poor immunity to manipulations. Encoded information can be destroyed by channel noise, re-sampling, and so forth, unless it is coded using redundancy techniques, which reduces the data rate one to two orders of magnitude. In practice, it is useful only in closed, digital-to-digital environments.

Turner (1989) proposed a method for inserting an identification string into a digital audio signal by substituting the "insignificant" bits of randomly selected audio samples with the bits of an identification code. Bits are deemed "insignificant" if their alteration is inaudible. Unfortunately, Turner's method may easily be circumvented. For example, if it is known that the algorithm only affects the least significant two bits of a word, then it is possible to randomly flip all such bits, thereby destroying any existing identification code. Bassia and Pitas (1998) proposed a watermarking scheme to embed a watermark in the time domain of a digital audio signal by slightly modifying the amplitude of each audio sample. The characteristics of this modification are determined both by the original signal and the copyright owner. The detection procedure does not use the original audio signal. But this method can only detect whether an audio signal contains a watermark or not. It cannot indicate the watermark information embedded in the audio signal. Aris Technologies, Inc. (Wolosewicz & Jemeli, 1998) proposed a technique to embed data by modifying signal peaks with their MusiCode product. Temporal peaks within a segment of host audio signal are modified to fall within quantized amplitude levels. The quantization pattern of the peaks is used to distinguish the embedded data. In Cooperman and Moskowitz (1997), Fourier transform coefficients are computed on non-overlapping audio blocks. The least significant bits of the transform coefficients are replaced by the embedded data. The DICE company offers a product based on this algorithm.

Phase Coding

Phase coding is one of the most effective coding schemes in term of the signal-to-noise ratio because experiments indicate that listeners might not hear any difference caused by a smooth phase shift, even though the signal pattern may change dramatically. When the phase relation between each frequency components is dramatically changed, phase dispersion and "rain barrel" distortions occur. However, as long as the modification of the phase is within certain limits an inaudible coding can be achieved.

In phase coding, a hidden datum is represented by a particular phase or phase change in the phase spectral. If the audio signal is divided into segments, data are usually hidden only in the first segment under two conditions. First, the phase difference between each segment needs to be preserved. The second condition states that the final phase spectral with embedded data needs to be smoothed; otherwise, an abrupt phase change causes hearing awareness. Once the embedding procedure is finished, the last step is to update the phase spectral of each of the remaining segments by adding back the relative phase. Consequently, the embedded signal can be constructed from this set of new phase spectral. For the extraction process, the hidden data can be obtained by detecting the phase values from the phase spectral of the first segment. The stego key in this implementation includes the phase shift and the size of one segment. Phase coding can be used in both analog and digital modes but it is sensitive to most audio compressing algorithms.

The procedure for phase coding (Bender et al., 1996) is as follows:

1. Break the sound sequence s[i], ($0 \le i \le I$-1) into a series of N short segments, $s_n[i]$ where ($0 \le n \le N$-1).
2. Apply a K-points discrete Fourier transform (DFT) to n-th segment, $s_n[i]$, where ($K = I/N$), and create a matrix of the phase, $\phi_n(\omega_k)$, and magnitude, $A_n(\omega_k)$ for ($0 \le k \le K$-1).
3. Store the phase difference between each adjacent segment for ($0 \le n \le N$-1):

$$\Delta\phi_{n+1}(\omega_k) = \phi_{n+1}(\omega_k) - \phi_n(\omega_k) \qquad \textbf{(3)}$$

4. A binary set of data is represented as a $\phi_{data} = \pi/2$ or $-\pi/2$ representing 0 or 1:

$$\phi_0' = \phi_{data}' \tag{4}$$

5. Re-create phase matrices for n>0 by using the phase difference:

$$\begin{bmatrix} (\phi_1'(\omega_k) = \phi_0'(\omega_k) + \Delta\phi_1(\omega_k)) \\ \cdots \\ (\phi_n'(\omega_k) = \phi_{n-1}'(\omega_k) + \Delta\phi_n(\omega_k)) \\ \cdots \\ (\phi_N'(\omega_k) = \phi_{N-1}'(\omega_k) + \Delta\phi_N(\omega_k)) \end{bmatrix} \tag{5}$$

6. Use the modified phase matrix $\phi_n'(\omega_k)$ and the original magnitude matrix $A_n(\omega_k)$ to reconstruct the sound signal by applying the inverse DFT.

For the decoding process, the synchronization of the sequence is done before the decoding. The length of the segment, the DFT points, and the data interval must be known at the receiver. The value of the underlying phase of the first segment is detected as a 0 or 1, which represents the coded binary string. Since $\phi_0'(\omega_k)$ is modified, the absolute phases of the following segments are modified respectively. However, the relative phase difference of each adjacent frame is preserved. It is this relative difference in phase that the ear is most sensitive to.

Phase coding is also applied to data hiding in speech signals (Yardimci et al., 1997).

Spread Spectrum Coding

The basic spread spectrum technique is designed to encrypt a stream of information by spreading the encrypted data across as much of the frequency spectrum as possible. It turns out that many spread spectrum techniques adapt well to data hiding in audio signals. Because the hidden data are usually not expected to be destroyed by operations such as compressing and cropping, broadband spread spectrum-based techniques, which make small modifications to a large number of bits for each hidden datum, are expected to be robust against the operations. In a normal communication channel, it is often desirable to concentrate the information in as narrow a region of the frequency spectrum as possible. Among many different variations on the idea of spread spectrum communication, Direct Sequence (DS) is currently considered. In general, spreading is accomplished by modulating the original signal with a sequence of random binary pulses (referred to as chip) with values 1 and -1. The chip rate is an integer multiple of the data rate. The bandwidth expansion is typically of the order of 100 and higher.

For the embedding process, the data to be embedded are coded as a binary string using error-correction coding so that errors caused by channel noise and original signal modification can be suppressed. Then, the code is multiplied by the carrier wave and the pseudo-random noise sequence, which has a wide frequency spectrum. As a consequence, the frequency spectrum of the data is spread over the available frequency band. The spread data sequence is then attenuated and added to the original signal as additive random noise. For extraction, the same binary pseudo-random noise sequence applied for the embedding will be synchronously (in phase) multiplied with the embedded signal.

Unlike phase coding, DS introduces additive random noise to the audio signal. To keep the noise level low and inaudible, the spread code is attenuated (without adaptation) to roughly 0.5% of the dynamic range of the original audio signal. The combination of simple repetition technique and error correction coding ensure the integrity of the code. A short segment of the binary code string is concatenated and added to the original signal so that transient noise can be reduced by averaging over the segment in the extraction process.

Most audio watermarking techniques are based on the spread spectrum scheme and are inherently projection techniques on a given key-defined direction. In Tilki and Beex (1996), Fourier transform coefficients over the middle frequency bands are replaced with spectral components from a signature sequence. The middle frequency band is selected so that the data remain outside of the more sensitive low frequency range. The signature is of short time duration and has a low amplitude relative to the local audio signal. The technique is described as robust to noise and the wow and flutter of analogue tapes. In Wolosewicz (1998), the high frequency portion of an audio segment is replaced with embedded data. Ideally, the algorithm looks for segments in the audio with high energy. The significant low frequency energy helps to perceptually hide the embedded high frequency data. In addition, the segment should have low energy to ensure that significant components in the audio are not replaced with the embedded data. In a typical implementation, a block of approximately 675 bits of data is encoded using a spread spectrum algorithm with a 10kHz carrier waveform. The duration of the resulting data block is 0.0675 seconds. The data block is repeated in several locations according to the constraints imposed on the audio spectrum. In another spread spectrum implementation, Pruess et al. (1994) proposed to embed data into the host audio signal as coloured noise. The data are coloured by shaping a pseudo-noise sequence according to the shape of the original signal. The data are embedded within a preselected band of the audio spectrum after proportionally shaping them by the corresponding audio signal frequency components. Since the shaping helps to perceptually hide the embedded data, the inventors claim the composite audio signal is not readily distinguishable from the original audio signal. The data may be recovered by essentially reversing the embedding operation using a whitening filter. Solana Technology

Development Corp. (Lee et al., 1998) later introduced a similar approach with their Electronic DNA product. Time domain modelling, for example, linear predictive coding, or fast Fourier transform is used to determine the spectral shape. Moses (1995) proposed a technique to embed data by encoding them as one or more whitened direct sequence spread spectrum signals and/or a narrowband FSK data signal and transmitted at the time, frequency and level determined by a neural network such that the signal is masked by the audio signal. The neural network monitors the audio channel to determine opportunities to insert the data such that the inserted data are masked.

Echo Hiding

Echo hiding (Gruhl et al., 1996) is a method for embedding information into an audio signal. It seeks to do so in a robust fashion, while not perceivably degrading the original signal. Echo hiding has applications in providing proof of the ownership, annotation, and assurance of content integrity. Therefore, the embedded data should not be sensitive to removal by common transform to the embedded audio, such as filtering, re-sampling, block editing, or lossy data compression.

Echo hiding embeds data into a host audio signal by introducing an echo. The data are hidden by varying three parameters of the echo: initial amplitude, decay rate, and delay. As the delay between the original and the echo decreases, the two signals blend. At a certain point, the human ear cannot distinguish between the two signals. The echo is perceived as added resonance. The coder uses two delay times, one to represent a binary one and another to represent binary zero. Both delay times are below the threshold at which the human ear can resolve the echo. In addition to decreasing the delay time, the echo can also be ensured unperceivable by setting the initial amplitude and the delay rate below the audible threshold of the human ear.

For the embedding process, the original audio signal ($v(t)$) is divided into segments and one echo is embedded in each segment. In a simple case, the embedded signal ($c(t)$) can, for example, be expressed as follows:

$$c(t)=v(t)+av(t-d) \tag{6}$$

where a is an amplitude factor. The stego key is the two echo delay times, of d and d'.

The extraction is based on the autocorrelation of the cepstrum (i.e., $\log F(c(t))$) of the embedded signal. The result in the time domain is $F^{-1}(\log(F(c(t))^2)$. The decision of a d or a d' delay can be made by examining the position of a spike that appears in the autocorrelation diagram. Echo hiding can effectively place unperceivable information into an audio stream. It is robust to noise and does not require a high data transmission channel. The drawback of echo hiding is its unsafe stego key, so it is easy to be detected by attackers.

Perceptual Masking

Swanson et al. (1998) proposed a robust audio watermarking approach using perceptual masking. The major contributions of this method include:

- *A perception-based watermarking procedure.* The embedded watermark adapts to each individual host signal. In particular, the temporal and frequency distribution of the watermark are dictated by the temporal and frequency masking characteristics of the host audio signal. As a result, the amplitude (strength) of the watermark increases and decreases with the host signal, for example, lower amplitude in "quiet" regions of the audio. This guarantees that the embedded watermark is inaudible while having the maximum possible energy. Maximizing the energy of the watermark adds robustness to attacks.
- *An author representation that solves the deadlock problem.* An author is represented with a pseudo-random sequence created by a pseudo-random generator and two keys. One key is author-dependent, while the second key is signal-dependent. The representation is able to resolve rightful ownership in the face of multiple ownership claims.
- *A dual watermark.* The watermarking scheme uses the original audio signal to detect the presence of a watermark. The procedure can handle virtually all types of distortions, including cropping, temporal rescaling, and so forth using a generalized likelihood ratio test. As a result, the watermarking procedure is a powerful digital copyright protection tool. This procedure is integrated with a second watermark, which does not require the original signal. The dual watermarks also address the deadlock problem.

Each audio signal is watermarked with a unique noise-like sequence shaped by the masking phenomena. The watermark consists of (1) an author representation, and (2) spectral and temporal shaping using the masking effects of the human auditory system. The watermarking scheme is based on a repeated application of a basic watermarking operation on smaller segments of the audio signal. The length N audio signal is first segmented into blocks $s_i(k)$ of length 512 samples, $i = 0, 1, ..., \lfloor N/512 \rfloor -1$, and $k = 0, 1, ..., 511$. The block size of 512 samples is dictated by the frequency masking model. For each audio segment $s_i(k)$, the algorithm works as follows.

1. compute the power spectrum $S_i(k)$ of the audio segment $s_i(k)$;
2. compute the frequency mask $M_i(k)$ of the power spectrum $S_i(k)$;
3. use the mask $M_i(k)$ to weight the noise-like author representation for that audio block, creating the shaped author signature $P_i(k) = Y_i(k)M_i(k)$;

4. compute the inverse FFT of the shaped noise $p_i(k) = IFFT(P_i(k))$;
5. compute the temporal mask $t_i(k)$ of $s_i(k)$;
6. use the temporal mask $t_i(k)$ to further shape the frequency shaped noise, creating the watermark $w_i(k) = t_i(k)p_i(k)$ of that audio segment;
7. create the watermarked block $s_i'(k) = s_i(k) + w_i(k)$.

The overall watermark for a signal is simply the concatenation of the watermark segments w_i for all of the length 512 audio blocks. The author signature y_i for block i is computed in terms of the personal author key x_1 and signal-dependent key x_2 computed from block s_i.

The dual localization effects of the frequency and temporal masking control the watermark in both domains. Frequency-domain shaping alone is not enough to guarantee that the watermark will be inaudible. Frequency-domain masking computations are based on a Fourier transform analysis. A fixed length Fourier transform does not provide good time localization for some applications. In particular, a watermark computed using frequency-domain masking will spread in time over the entire analysis block. If the signal energy is concentrated in a time interval that is shorter than the analysis block length, the watermark is not masked outside of that subinterval. This leads to audible distortion, for example, pre-echoes. The temporal mask guarantees that the "quiet" regions are not disturbed by the watermark.

Content-Adaptive Watermarking

A novel content-adaptive watermarking scheme is described in Xu and Feng (2002). The embedding design is based on audio content and the human auditory system. With the content-adaptive embedding scheme, the embedding parameter for setting up the embedding process will vary with the content of the audio signal. For example, because the content of a frame of digital violin music is very different from that of a recording of a large symphony orchestra in terms of spectral details, these two respective music frames are treated differently. By doing so, the embedded watermark signal will better match the host audio signal so that the embedded signal is perceptually negligible. The content-adaptive method couples audio content with the embedded watermark signal. Consequently, it is difficult to remove the embedded signal without destroying the host audio signal. Since the embedding parameters depend on the host audio signal, the tamper-resistance of this watermark embedding technique is also increased.

In broad terms, this technique involves segmenting an audio signal into frames in time domain, classifying the frames as belonging to one of several known classes, and then encoding each frame with an appropriate embedding scheme. The particular scheme chosen is tailored to the relevant class of audio signal according to its properties in frequency domain. To implement the content-adaptive embedding, two techniques are disclosed. They are audio frame classification and embedding scheme design.

Figure 1 illustrates the watermark embedding scheme. The input original signal is divided into frames by audio segmentation. Feature measures are extracted from each frame to represent the characteristics of the audio signal of that frame. Based on the feature measures, the audio frame is classified into one of the pre-defined classes and an embedding scheme is selected accordingly, which is tailored to the class. Using the selected embedding scheme, a watermark is embedded into the audio frame using multiple-bit hopping and hiding method. In this scheme, the feature extraction method is exactly the same as the one used in the training processing. The parameters of the classifier and the embedding schemes are generated in the training process.

Figure 2 depicts the training process for an adaptive embedding model. Adaptive embedding, or content-sensitive embedding, embeds watermark differently for different types of audio signals. In order to do so, a training process is run for each category of audio signal to define embedding schemes that are well suited to the particular category of audio signal. The training process analyses an audio signal to find an optimal way to classify audio frames into classes and then design embedding schemes for each of those classes. To achieve this objective, the training data should be sufficient to be statistically significant. Audio signal frames are clustered into data clusters and each of them forms a partition in the feature vector space and has a centroid as its representation. Since the audio frames in a cluster are similar, embedding schemes can be designed according to the centroid of the cluster and the human audio system model. The design of embedding schemes may need a lot of testing to ensure the inaudibility and robustness. Consequently, an embedding scheme is designed for each class/cluster of signal that is best suited to the host signal. In the process,

Figure 1. Watermark embedding scheme for PCM audio

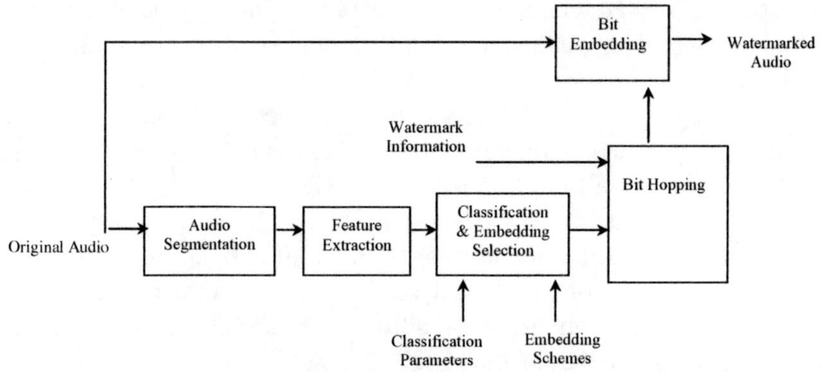

Figure 2. Training and embedding scheme design

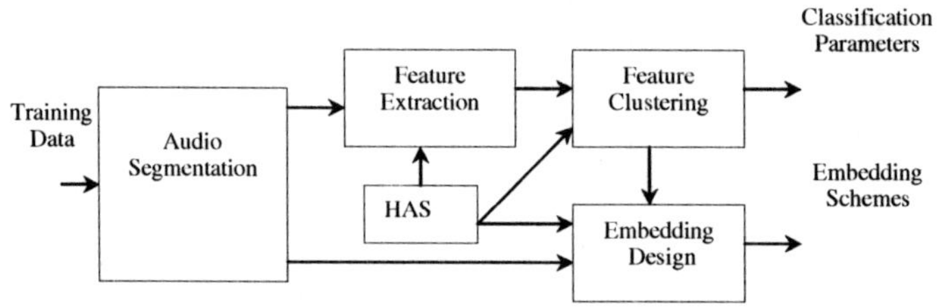

inaudibility or the sensitivity of the human auditory system and resistance to attackers must be taken into considerations.

The training process needs to be performed only once for a category of audio signals. The derived classification parameters and the embedding schemes are used to embed watermarks in all audio signals in that category.

As shown in Figure 1 in the audio classification and embedding scheme selection, similar pre-processing will be conducted to convert the incoming audio signal into feature frame sequences. Each frame is classified into one of the predefined classes. An embedding scheme for a frame is chosen, which is referred to as *content-adaptive embedding scheme.* In this way, the watermark code is embedded frame by frame into the host audio signal.

Figure 3 illustrates the scheme of watermark extraction. The input signal is converted into a sequence of frames by feature extraction. For the watermarked audio signal, it will be segmented into frames using the same segmentation method as in embedding process. Then the bit detection is conducted to extract bit delays on a frame-by-frame basis. Because a single bit of the watermark is hopped into multiple bits through bit hopping in the embedding process, multiple delays are detected in each frame. This method is more robust against attackers compared with the single bit hiding technique. Firstly, one frame is encoded with multiple bits, and any attackers do not know the coding parameters. Secondly, the embedded signal is weaker and well hidden as a consequence of using multiple bits.

The key step of the bit detection involves the detection of the spacing between the bits. To do this, the magnitude (at relevant locations in each audio frame) of an autocorrelation of an embedded signal's cepstrum (Gruhl et al., 1996) is examined. Cepstral analysis utilises a form of a homomorphic system that coverts the convolution operation into an addition operation. It is useful in detecting the existence of embedded bits. From the autocorrelation of the cepstrum, the embedded bits in each audio frame can be found according to a "power spike" at each delay of the bits.

Figure 3. Watermark extracting scheme for PCM audio

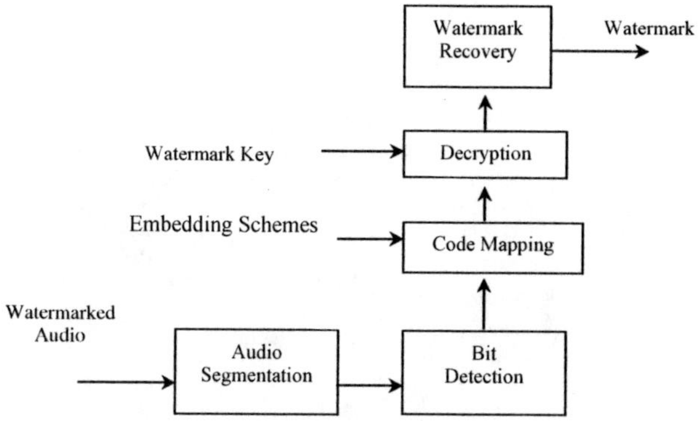

DIGITAL WATERMARKING FOR WAV-TABLE SYNTHESIS AUDIO

Architectures of WAV-Table Audio

Typically, watermarking is applied directly to data samples themselves, whether this is still image data, video frames or audio segments. However, such systems fail to address the issue of audio coding systems, where digital audio data are not available, but a form of representing the audio data for later reproduction according to a protocol is. It is well known that tracks of digital audio data can require large amounts of storage and high data transfer rates, whereas synthesis architecture coding protocols such as the Musical Instrument Digital Interface (MIDI) have corresponding requirements that are several orders of magnitude lower for the same audio data. MIDI audio files are not files made entirely of sampled audio data (i.e., actual audio sounds), but instead contain synthesizer instructions, or MIDI message, to reproduce the audio data. The synthesizer instructions contain much smaller amounts of sampled audio data. That is, a synthesizer generates actual sounds from the instructions in a MIDI audio file. Expanding upon MIDI, Downloadable Sounds (DLS) is a synthesizer architecture specification that requires a hardware or software synthesizer to support all of its components (Downloadable Sounds Level 1, 1997). DLS is a typical WAV-table synthesis audio and permits additional instruments to be defined and downloaded to a synthesizer besides the standard 128 instruments provided by the MIDI system. The DLS file format stores both samples of digital sound data and articulation parameters to create at least one sound instrument. An instrument contains "regions" that point to WAVE "files" also embedded in the DLS file. Each region specifies an MIDI note and velocity range that will trigger the corresponding sound and also contains articulation information such as enve-

Figure 4. DLS file structure

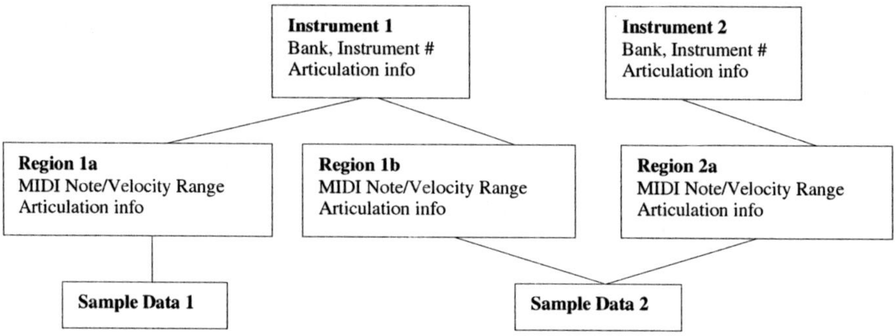

lopes and loop points. Articulation information can be specified for each individual region or for the entire instrument. Figure 4 illustrates the DLS file structure.

DLS is expected to become a new standard in musical industry, because of its specific advantages. On the one hand, when compared with MIDI, DLS provides a common playback experience and an unlimited sound palette for both instruments and sound effects. On the other hand, when compared with PCM audio, it has true audio interactivity and, as noted hereinbefore, smaller storage requirement. One of the objectives of DLS design is that the specification must be open and non-proprietary. Therefore, how to effectively protect its copyright is important. A novel digital watermarking method for WT synthesis audio, including DLS, is proposed in Xu et al. (2001). Watermark embedding and extraction schemes for WT audio are described in the following subsections.

Watermark Embedding Scheme

Figure 5 illustrates the watermark embedding scheme for WT audio. Generally, a WT audio file contains two parts: articulation parameters and sample data such as DLS, or only contains articulation parameters such as MIDI. Unlike traditional PCM audio, the sample data in WT audio are not the prevalent components. On the contrary, it is the articulation parameters in WT audio that control how to play the sounds. Therefore, in the embedding scheme watermarks are embedded into both sample data (if they are included in the WT audio) and articulation parameters. Firstly, original WT audio is divided into sample data and articulation parameters. Then, two different embedding schemes are used to process them respectively and form the relevant watermarked outputs. Finally, the watermarked WT audio is generated by integrating the watermarked sample data and articulation parameters.

Figure 5. Watermark embedding scheme for WAV-table synthesis audio

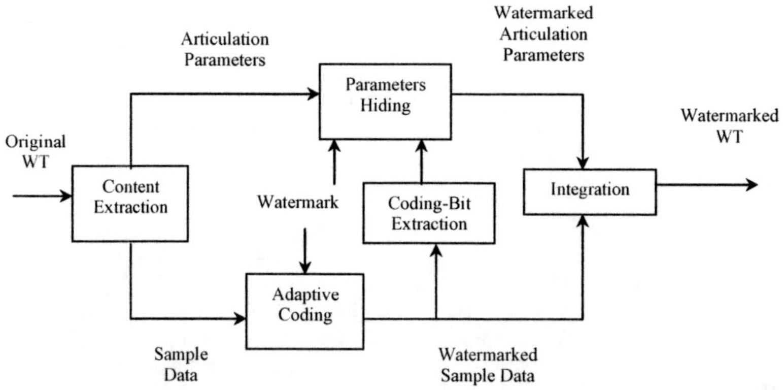

Adaptive Coding Based on Finite Automaton

Figure 6 shows the scheme of adaptive coding. In this scheme, techniques (finite automaton and redundancy) are proposed to improve the robustness. In addition, the bits of sample data are adaptively coded according to HAS so as to guarantee the minimum distortion of original sample data. The watermark message is firstly converted into a string of binary sequence. Each bit of the sequence will replace a corresponding bit of the sample points. The particular location in sample points is determined by finite automaton and HAS. The number of sample points is calculated according to the redundancy technique.

Adaptive bit coding has, however, low immunity to manipulations. Embedded information can be destroyed by channel noise, re-sampling, and other operations. Adaptive bit coding technique is used based on several considerations. Firstly, unlike sampled digital audio, WT audio is a parameterised digital audio, so it is difficult to attack it using the typical signal processing techniques such as adding noise and re-sampling. Secondly, the size of wave sample in WT audio is very small, and therefore it is unsuitable to embed a watermark into the samples in the frequency domain. Finally, in order to ensure robustness, the watermarked bit sequence of sample data is embedded into the articulation parameters of WT audio. If the sample data are distorted, the embedded information can be used to restore the watermarked bit of the sample data.

The functionality of a finite automaton *M* can be described as a quintuple:

$$M = < X, Y, S, \delta, \lambda > \qquad \textbf{(7)}$$

where *X* is a non-empty finite set (the input alphabet of *M*), *Y* is a non-empty finite set (the output alphabet of *M*), *S* is a non-empty finite set (the state alphabet of *M*), $\delta : S \times X \rightarrow S$ is a single-valued mapping (the next state function of *M*) and $\lambda : S \times X \rightarrow Y$ is a single-valued mapping (the output function of *M*).

Figure 6. Adaptive-bit coding scheme

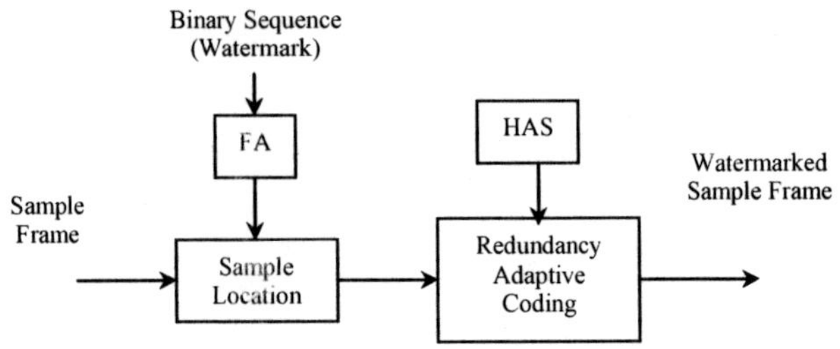

The elements X, Y, S, δ, λ are expressed as follows:

$$X = \{0,1\} \quad \textbf{(8)}$$

$$Y = \{y_1, y_2, y_3, y_4\} \quad \textbf{(9)}$$

$$S = \{S_0, S_1, S_2, S_3, S_4\} \quad \textbf{(10)}$$

$$S_{i+1} = \delta(S_i, x) \quad \textbf{(11)}$$

$$y_i = \lambda(S_i, x) \quad \textbf{(12)}$$

where y_i (i=1,2,3,4) is the number of sample points that are jumped off when embedding bit corresponding to relevant states, and S_i $(i = 0 - 4)$ is five kinds of states corresponding to 0, 00, 01, 10 and 11 respectively, and S_0 is to be supposed the initial state. The state transfer diagram of finite automaton is shown in Figure 7. An example procedure of redundancy low-bit coding method based on FA and HAS is described as follows:

1. Convert the watermark message into binary sequence;
2. Determine the values of the elements in FA; that is, the number of sample points that will be jumped off corresponding relevant states:
   y_1: state 00
   y_2: state 01
   y_3: state 10
   y_4: state 11
3. Determine the redundant number for 0 and 1 bit to be embedded:
   r_0: the embedded number for 0 bit;
   r_1: the embedded number for 1 bit;

Figure 7. Finite automaton

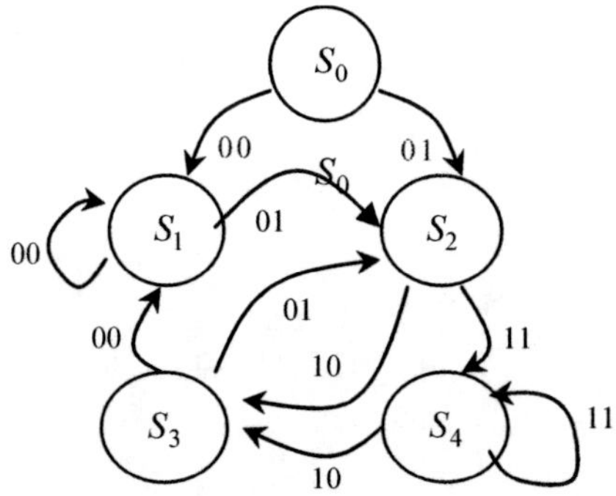

4. Determine the HAS threshold T;
5. For each bit of the binary sequence corresponding to watermark message and the sample point in the WT sample data,
   (a) Compare the amplitude value A of sample point with HAS threshold T; if $A<T$ then go to next point, else
   (b) Step over $y_i (i = 1,2,3,4)$ number of points and replace the lowest bit of $r_j (j = 0,1)$ number of points by the bit of the binary sequence;
   (c) Repeat until all bits in binary sequence are processed.

Parameters Hiding

In order to improve the robustness of watermarked WT audio, the watermark (and watermarked bit sequence if necessary) is also embedded into articulation parameters. This process is shown in Figure 8. Watermark and watermarked bit sequence are encrypted and form a data stream. In the meantime, some virtual parameters are generated to be used to embed the watermark data stream into the WT articulation parameters. Because the location of the parameters is not known to attackers, the embedded data are difficult to be detected and removed in the presence of attacks. On the other hand, it can ensure the correction of detection if the watermarks in WT sample data are distorted when both watermark and watermarked bit sequence are embedded into the articulation parameters.

The basic idea of the parameters hiding scheme is to embed the watermark information into the articulation parameters of WT audio by generating some virtual parameters. The Downloadable Sounds (DLS) Level 1 is used as an example to illustrate how to hide watermark information in articulation parameters.

1. Encrypt the watermark binary sequence and watermarked low-bits sequence;

Figure 8. Parameters hiding scheme

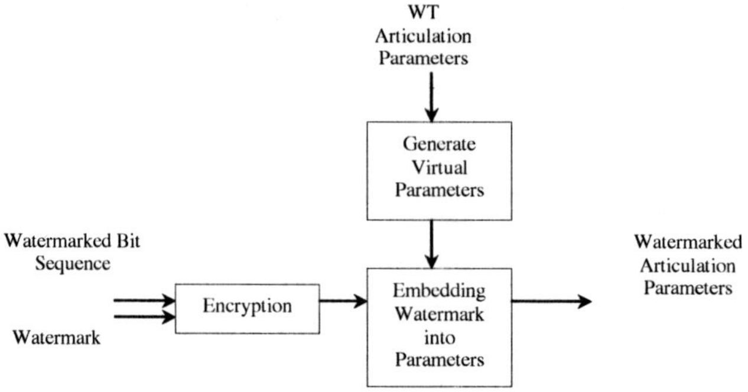

2. Segment the encrypted data stream into *n* parts;
3. Create a virtual instrument in DLS file, and use its parameters to hide the watermark information.

The virtual instrument collection to hide watermark information can be described as follows:

```
LIST 'ins'
        LIST 'INFO'
                 Inam "Instrument name"
        <dlid> (watermark Info part 1)
        <insh> (watermark Info part 2)
        LIST 'lrgn'
                 LIST 'rgn'
                         <rgnh> (watermark Info part 3)
                         <wsmp> (watermark Info part 4)
                         <wlnk> (watermark Info part 5)
                 LIST 'rgn'
                            .
                            .
                            .
                 ...
                 LIST 'lart'
                          <art1> (watermark Info part n)
```

Watermark Extraction Scheme

Figure 9 shows the scheme of watermark extraction. In the extraction process, the original WT audio is not needed. For a watermarked WT audio, it is also divided into sample data and articulation parameters at first. Then the

Figure 9. Watermark extraction scheme for WAV-table synthesis audio

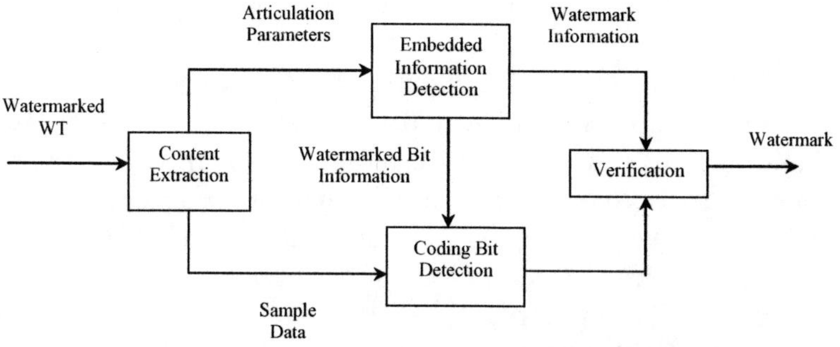

watermark sequence in the coding bits of the sample data and the encrypted watermark information in the articulation parameters are detected. If the watermark sequence in sample data is obtained, it will be compared with the watermark in articulation parameters to make the verification. If the sample data suffered from distortions and the watermark sequence cannot be detected, the watermarked bit sequence in the articulation parameters will be used to restore the watermarked bit information in the sample data and make the detection in the restored data. Similarly, the detected watermark will be verified by comparing with that embedded in articulation parameters.

DIGITAL WATERMARKING FOR COMPRESSED AUDIO

Compression algorithms for digital audio can preserve audio quality as well as reduce bit rate dramatically, increase network bandwidth, and save density storage of audio content. Among various kinds of compressed digital audio currently used, MP3 is the most popular one and gets more and more welcomed by music users. MP3 audio compression is based on psycho-acoustic models of the human auditory system. It is an ideal format for distributing high-quality sound files online because it can offer near-CD quality at the compression ratio of 11 to one (128kb/s).

Compressed Domain Watermarking

One possible method to protect compressed audio is to decompress it first, then embed a watermark into decompressed audio, and finally recompress the watermarked decompressed audio. This can probably ensure the robustness of the watermark, but it is too time consuming because the compression process will take a long time. For example, it will take more than 30 minutes to compress a five- to six-minute audio of WAV format to MP3 format with the bit rate of 128k/sec. So it is not suitable for online transaction and distribution. In order to improve the embedding speed, several embedding schemes in compressed domain have been proposed.

In Sandford et al. (1997), the auxiliary information is embedded as a watermark into the host signal created by a lossy compression technique. Obviously, this method has low robustness since the watermark can be removed easily without affecting the quality of the host audio signal by decompressing the compressed audio. In Petitcolas (1999), a watermarking method (MP3Stego) for MP3 files is proposed. MP3Stego hides information in MP3 files during the compression process. The watermark data are first compressed, encrypted and then hidden in the MP3 bit stream. The hiding process takes place at the heart of the Layer III encoding process, namely in the inner_loop. The inner loop quantizes the input data and increases the quantizer step size until the quantized data can be coded with the available number of bits. Another loop checks that the distortions introduced by the quantization do not exceed the threshold defined by the psychoacoustic model. The part2_3_length variable contains the number of main_data bits used for scalefactors and Huffman code data in the MP3 bit stream. The bits were encoded by changing the end loop condition of the inner loop. Only randomly chosen part2_3_length values were modified and the selection was done by using a pseudo-random bit generator based on SHA-1. This scheme is very weak in robustness. The author acknowledged that any attacker could remove the hidden watermark information by uncompressing the bit stream and recompressing it. On the other hand, MP3Stego does not directly embed a watermark in compressed domain. The processed object is PCM audio and the watermark is embedded during the compress process, so it is time consuming. Qiao and Klara (1999) propose a non-invertible watermarking scheme to embed a watermark in the compressed domain. The watermark is constructed by a random sequence created by applying an encryption algorithm (DES) to compressed audio frames. Then, the watermark is embedded in scale factors and encoded samples of the compressed audio. The watermarking scheme can avoid expensive decoding/re-encoding, but the original audio stream must be presented in the verification process.

Horvatic et al. (2000) propose a content-based scheme for compressed domain audio stream. Block diagram of watermark embedding for MPEG-1 audio stream is outlined as Figure 10. Compressed audio stream is partially interpreted. Quantized audio samples obtained from interpreted audio stream are modified by adding ECC (error correction code) encoded watermark. If modified quantized samples introduce audible distortion or the corresponding bit-rate is changed, watermark robustness is decreased and the step is repeated. Otherwise, modified quantized samples are packed into a watermarked bitstream.

The most significant feature of compressed-domain watermarking is that watermark can be detected extremely fast and using minimal computing

Figure10. Compressed-domain watermarking

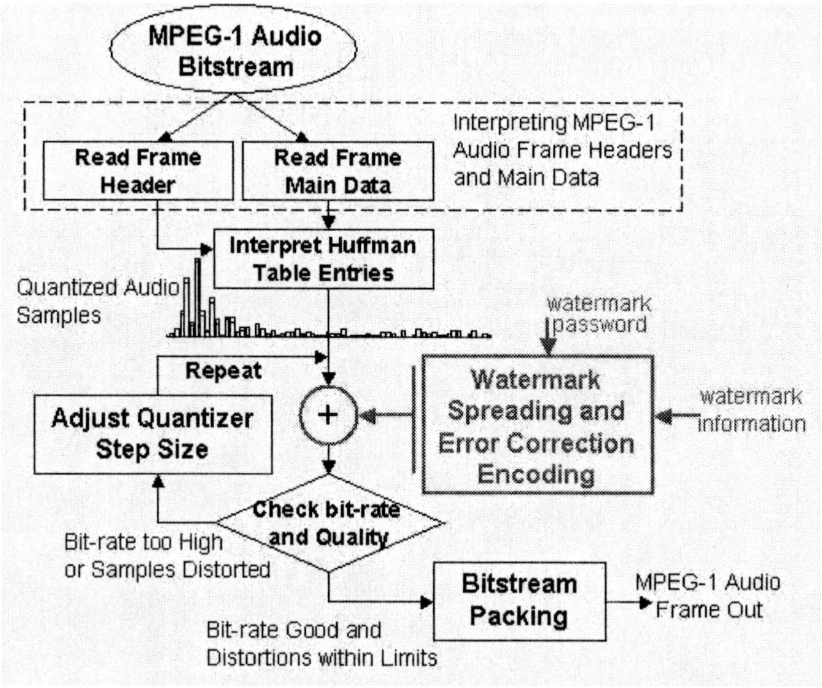

resources. Watermark detection becomes part of the MPEG-1 decoding process and does not interfere with audio playback while adding little additional processing. Block diagram of watermark detection for MPEG-1 audio stream integrated within the ISO MPEG-1 Audio Decoder is outlined as Figure 11.

This compressed domain watermarking method has minimal resource consumption and ability to integrate a watermarking module directly into real-time IP streaming applications including live broadcasting, video/audio on demand, secure IP telephony, high quality video conferencing, and others. Based on desired bitrate and perceptual quality, watermark robustness is adaptive and watermark energy automatically adapts to the bitrate and audio distortion limits. It is able to sustain significant packet loss. Successive watermarks are interlaced with marks used for watermark synchronisation when audio stream is exposed to packet loss or bit-rate conversion. This method also uses key-based random sequences to modulate watermark information prior to embedding to enable existence of multiple watermarks simultaneously.

Figure 11. Compressed-domain watermark detection

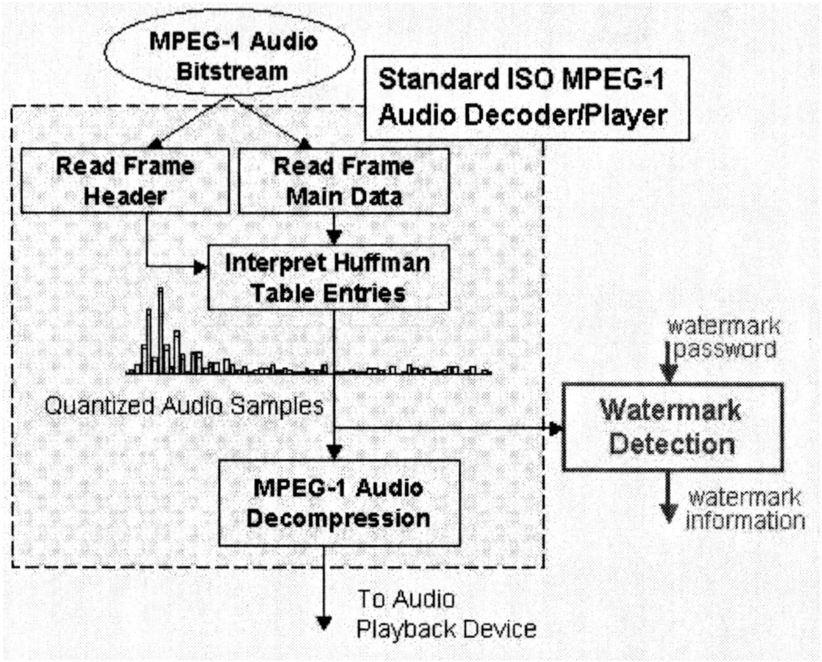

Partially Uncompressed Domain Watermarking

In order to improve the robustness of the watermark embedded into the compressed audio as well as ensure the embedding speed, a content-based watermark embedding scheme is proposed in Xu et al. (2001). According to this scheme the watermark will be embedded in partially uncompressed domain and the embedding scheme is highly related to audio content. Figure 12 illustrates the block diagram of the content-based watermark embedding scheme in partially uncompressed domain.

How to select the suitable frames to embed watermark from compressed audio is important. The incoming compressed audio is first segmented into frames according to the coding algorithm. All the frames are decoded from compressed domain to uncompressed domain. Then the feature extraction model (Xu & Feng, 2002) and the psychoacoustic model (Moore, 1997) are applied to each decoded frame to calculate the features of the audio content and masking threshold in each frame. According to the features and masking threshold, a pre-designed filter bank (Kahrs & Branderburg, 1998) is used to select the candidate frames suitable for embedding watermark. The watermark will be embedded into these selected frames using an adaptive multiple bit hopping and hiding scheme (Xu et al., 2001) depicted in Figure 13. The embedded frames will be re-encoded to generate the coded frames using the coding algorithm. Finally, the re-

Figure 12. Content-based watermark embedding scheme for compressed audio

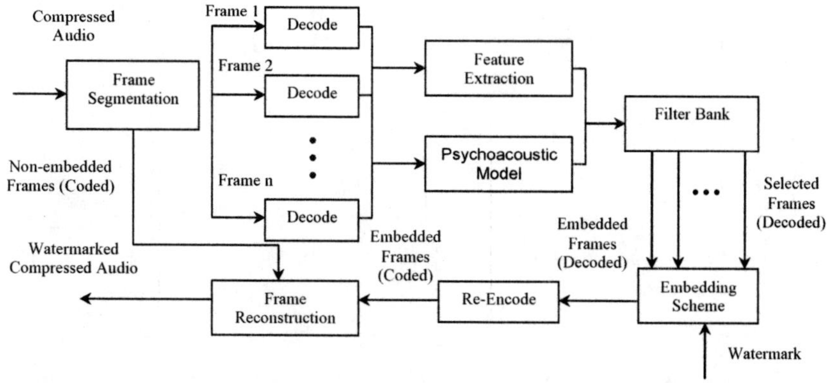

encoded frames and the non-embedded frames will be reconstructed to generate the watermarked compressed audio. Compared with embedding schemes in wholly uncompressed domain, this scheme can not only get the same performance in audibility and robustness but also embed the watermark much faster. It is suitable for online embedding and distribution. Compared with the embedding schemes in compressed domain, this scheme has high robustness for embedded watermark.

Figure 13 illustrates the block diagram of detailed watermark embedding scheme for decoded frames from the compressed audio. Since audio coding is a lossy processing, the embedded watermark must exist after audio compression. Furthermore, the embedded watermark must not affect the audio quality perceptually. In order to satisfy these requirements, the embedding scheme fully considers the human auditory system and the features of audio content. For the decoded frames from the original compressed audio that will be selected to embed watermark, feature parameters (Xu & Feng, 2002) are extracted from each selected frame to represent the characteristics of the audio content in that frame. In the meantime, each selected frame will pass through a psycho-acoustic model (Moore, 1997) to determine the ratio of the signal energy to the masking threshold. Based on the feature parameters and masking threshold, the embedding scheme for each selected frame is designed. The watermark is embedded into these frames using a multiple-bit hopping and hiding method (Xu et al., 2001). The watermarked audio frame will be compressed to generate the compressed audio frame.

In order to correctly detect the watermark from a compressed audio, the frames embedded watermark must be extracted at first. Figure 14 illustrates how to extract the frames including watermark from a compressed audio. This

Figure 13. Watermark embedding scheme for single frame

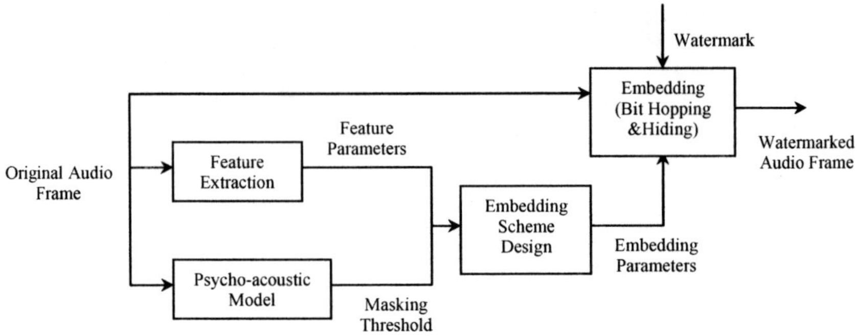

Figure 14. Frames and watermark extraction scheme for compressed audio

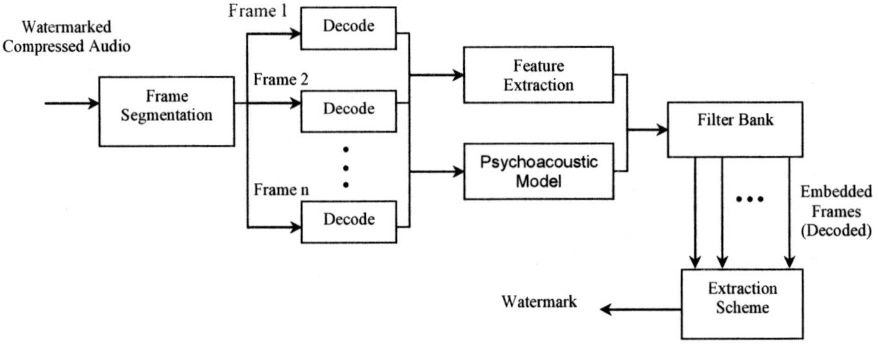

process is similar to the watermark embedding scheme to select candidate frames to embed watermark. The watermarked compressed audio is first segmented into frames according to the coding algorithm. These frames are decoded and each decoded frame is analyzed by the feature extraction model (Xu & Feng, 2002) and the psychoacoustic model (Moore, 1997). According to the calculated feature parameters and masking threshold, a filter bank (Kahrs & Branderburg, 1998) is applied to select the frames including watermark information. The watermark will be detected from these frames using the extraction scheme depicted as Figure 15.

Figure 15 illustrates the block diagram of watermark extraction from the selected frames. For each incoming frame, the magnitude (at relevant locations in each audio frame) of the autocorrelation of the embedded signal's cepstrum is examined. From the diagram of autocorrelation of the cepstrum, the bits of a watermark in each frame can be found according to a "power spike" at each delay of the embedded bits. Since the multiple-bit hopping method is used to embed the bits into the frames, for detected bits in each frame, they will pass

Figure 15. Watermark extraction in uncompressed domain

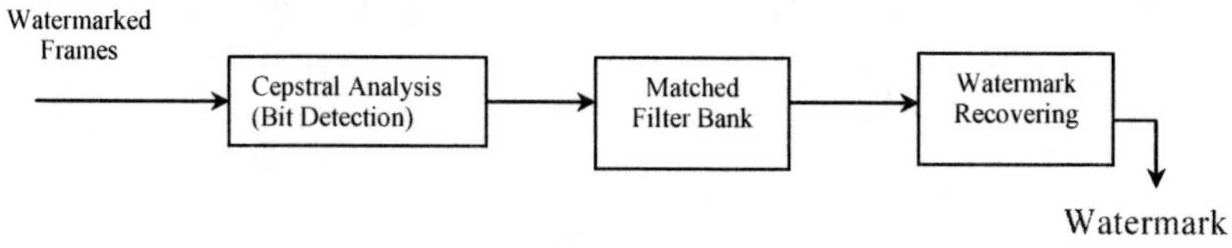

through a matched filter bank that can map the bits into the actual code (1 or 0). Finally, the watermark is recovered by correlating the detected codes with the original watermark.

CONCLUSIONS AND FUTURE RESEARCH DIRECTIONS

This chapter reviews past and current technical achievements in digital audio watermarking. Performance evaluation of audio watermarking and the human auditory system model, which are important to design a watermarking scheme, are introduced. Digital audio can be classified into three categories: PCM audio, WAV-table synthesis audio and compressed audio. Digital watermarking for PCM audio, usually based on time domain and frequency domain embedding and extraction schemes, has received significant achievement and is the most mature audio watermarking approach to date. Digital watermarking for compressed audio, especially embedding watermark directly in compressed domain, still has a lot of work to do to improve the robustness to decompressing and re-compressing attack. Digital watermarking for WAV-table synthesis audio is a new research direction in audio watermarking. WAV-table synthesis audio is expected to become a new standard in musical industry because of its specific advantages. One of the objectives of WAV-table synthesis audio design is that the specification must be open and non-proprietary. Therefore, how to effectively protect its copyright is important. A novel digital watermarking method for WAV-table synthesis audio is introduced in this chapter.

Since several requirements for audio watermarking are conflicting and the human auditory system is very sensitive, how to obtain an optimal balance among these requirements is a big challenge for audio watermarking. An overview of the requirements and challenges for audio watermarking indicates that, while some general rules apply, they are often application-dependent. Content-adaptive watermark embedding is another direction in digital audio watermarking. By content-adaptive, the embedding parameter for setting up the embedding process will vary with the content of the audio signal. By doing so, the embedded watermark signal will better match the host audio signal so that the embedded signal is perceptually negligible. The content-adaptive method couples audio content with embedded watermark signal. Consequently, it is difficult to remove the embedded signal without destroying the host audio signal.

REFERENCES

Bassia, P., & Pitas, I. (1998). Robust audio watermarking in the time domain. *IX European Signal Processing Conference* (EUSIPCO'98), September 8-11, *1,* 13-16, Rhodes, Greece.

Beerends, J., & Stemerdink, J. (1992). A perceptual audio quality measurement based on a psychoacoustic sound representation. *Journal of AES, 40*(12), 963-972.

Bender, W., Gruhl, D., Morimoto, N., & Lu, A. (1996). Techniques for data hiding. *IBM Systems Journal, 35*(3/4), 313-336.

Brandenburg, K., & Stoll, G. 1992). *The ISO/MPEG-Audio Codec: A generic standard for coding of high quality digital audio.* The 92nd AES Convention, Wien, Marz.

Cooperman, M., & Moskowitz, M. (1997). Steganographic method and device, US Patent 5,613,004.

Cox, I.J., Kilian, J., Leighton, T., & Shamoon, T. (1995). *Secure spread spectrum watermarking for multimedia.* Technical Report 95-10, NEC Research Institute.

Cox, I.J., Kilian, J., Leighton, T., & Shamoon, T. (1997). Secure spread spectrum watermarking for multimedia. *IEEE Transactions on Image Processing, 6*(12), 1673-1687.

Delaigle, J.F., Vleeschouver, C., & Macq, B. (1996). Digital watermarking. *Proceedings of SPIE, Optical Security and Counterfeit Deterrence Techniques, 2659,* (pp. 99-110).

Downloadable Sounds Level 1, Version 1.0. (1997). The MIDI Manufacturers Association, CA, USA.

Gordy, J.D., & Bruton, L.T. (2000). Performance evaluation of digital audio watermarking algorithms. *Proceedings of IEEE MWSCAS 2000.*

Gruhl, D., Lu, A., & Bender, W. (1996). Echo hiding. *Proceedings of Information Hiding Workshop*, (pp. 295-315). University of Cambridge.

Horvatic, P., Zhao, J., & Thorwirth, N.J. (2000). Robust audio watermarking based on secure spread spectrum and auditory perception model. In S. Qing (Ed.), *International Federation for Information Processing (IFIP): Information security for global information infrastructures* (pp. 181-190). Boston, MA: Kluwer Academic Publishers.

ISO/IEC IS 11172. (1993). *Information technology – Coding of moving pictures and associated audio for digital storage up to about 1.5 Mbits/s.*

Kahrs, M., & Branderburg, K. (1998). *Applications of digital signal processing to audio and acoustics.* Kluwer Academic Publishers.

Lee, C., Moallemi, K., & Warren, R. (1998). Method and apparatus for transporting auxiliary data in audio signals, US Patent 5,822,360.

Moore, B.J.C. (1997). *An introduction to the psychology of hearing* (4th ed.). Academic Press.

Moses, D. (1995). *Simultaneous transmission data and audio signals by means of perceptual coding,* US Patent 5,473,631.

MUSE Project: Embedded signalling. Available online: www.ifpi.org/technology/muse_embed.html.

Noll, P. (1993). Wideband speech and audio coding. *IEEE Communications Magazine, 31*(11), 34-44.

Petitcolas, F. Available online: http://www.cl.cam.ac.uk/~fapp2/steganography/mp3stego/ Cambridge University, UK.

Pitas, I. (1996). A method for signature casting on digital images. *Proceedings of IEEE International Conference on Image Processing,* (vol. 3, pp. 215-218).

Preuss, R., Roukos, S., Huggins, A., Gish, H., Bergamo, M., & Peterson, P. (1994). *Embedded signalling,* US patent 5,319,735.

Qiao, L., & Klara, N. (1999, January). Non-invertible watermarking scheme for MPEG audio, *Proceedings of SPIE Multimedia Security Conference,* San Jose, CA.

Sandford, S. (1997). *Compression embedding,* US Patent 5,778,102.

Swanson, M.D., Zhu, B., & Tewfik, A.H. (1996). Transparent robust image watermarking. *Proc. IEEE Int. Conf. on Image Processing, 3,* 211-214.

Swanson, M.D., Zhu, B., Tewfik, A.H., & Boney, L. (1998). Robust audio watermarking using perceptual masking. *Signal Processing, 66,* 337-355.

Tilki, J.F., & Beex, A.A. (1996). Encoding a hidden digital signature onto an audio signal using psychoacoustic masking. *Proc. of 7th Int. Conf. on Sig. Proc. Apps. and Tech.,* (pp. 476-480).

Turner, L.F. (1989). *Digital data security system,* Patent IPN WO 89/08915.

Wolfgang, R.B., & Delp, E.J. (1996). A watermark for digital images. *Proc. IEEE Int. Conf. On Image Processing,* (vol. 3, pp. 219-222).

Wolosewicz, J. (1998). *Apparatus and method for encoding and decoding information in audio signals,* US Patent 5,774,452.

Wolosewicz, J., & Jemeli, K. (1998). *Apparatus and method for encoding and decoding information in analog signals,* US Patent 5,828,325.

Xu, C., & Feng, D. (2002). Robust and efficient content-based digital audio watermarking. *ACM Journal of Multimedia Systems, 8*(5), 353-368.

Xu, C., Feng, D., & Zhu, Y. (2001). Copyright protection for WAV-table synthesis audio using digital watermarking. Lecture Note in Computer Science 2195. In H.-Y. Shum, M. Liao & S.-F. Chang (Eds.), *Advances in multimedia information processing* (pp. 772-779). *The Second IEEE Pacific-Rim Conference on Multimedia, PCM 2001*, Beijing, P.R. China

Xu, C., Zhu, Y., & Feng, D. (2001a). Digital audio watermarking based-on multiple-bit hopping and human auditory system. *ACM International Conference on Multimedia,* pp. 568-571, Ottawa, Canada.

Xu, C., Zhu, Y., & Feng, D. (2001b). A robust and fast watermarking scheme for compressed audio. *IEEE International Conference on Multimedia and Expo,* pp. 253-256, Tokyo, Japan.

Yardimci, Y., Cetin, A.E., & Ansari, R. (1997). Data hiding in speech using phase coding. *ESCA, Eurospeech97*, Greece, pp. 1679-1682.

Chapter V

Design Principles for Active Audio and Video Fingerprinting

Martin Steinebach, Fraunhofer IPSI, Germany

Jana Dittmann, Otto-von-Guericke-University Magdeburg, Germany

ABSTRACT

Active fingerprinting combines digital media watermarking and codes for collusion-secure customer identification. This requires specialized strategies for watermark embedding to lessen the thread of attacks like marked media comparison or mixing. We introduce basic technologies for fingerprinting and digital watermarking and possible attacks against active fingerprinting. Based on this, we provide test results, discuss the consequences and suggest an optimized embedding method for audio fingerprinting.

INTRODUCTION

Robust digital watermarking is the enabling technology for a number of approaches related to copyright protection mechanisms: Proof of ownership on copyrighted material, detection of the originator of illegally made copies and monitoring the usage of the copyrighted multimedia data are typical examples where watermarking is applied. A general overview about digital watermarking can be found in a variety of existing publications, for example in Cox, Miller and Bloom (2002) or Dittmann, Wohlmacher and Nahrstedt (2001).

While stopping the reproduction of illegal copies may be the first goal for copyright holders, discouraging pirates from distributing copies is the more realistic goal today. It can be observed that current copy protection or digital rights management systems tend to fail in stopping pirates (Pfitzmann, Federrath, & Kuhn, 2002). One important reason for this is the fact that media data usually leave a controlled digital environment when they are consumed, enabling analogue copies of high quality of material protect with digital mechanisms. Under these circumstances, the challenge is to find the most discouraging method making it especially dangerous for pirates to distribute copies. Identification of a copyrighted work by embedding a watermark or retrieving a passive fingerprint (Allamanche, Herre, Helmuth, Fröba, Kasten, & Cremer, 2001) is necessary for preventing large-scale production of illegal CD or DVD copies, but does not stop people from distributing single copies or uploading them to file-sharing networks. Here a method that enables the copyright holder to trace an illegal copy to its source would be much more effective, as pirates would loose their anonymity and therefore have to fear detection and punishment.

Embedding unique customer identification as a watermark into data to identify illegal copies of documents is called fingerprinting. Basically, watermarks, labels or codes embedded into multimedia data to enforce copyright must uniquely identify the data as property of the copyright holder. They also must be difficult to be removed, even after various media transformation processes. Thus the goal of a label is to always remain present in the data. Digital fingerprinting, which embeds customer information into the data to enable detection of license infringement, raises the additional problem that we produce different copies for each customer. Attackers can compare several fingerprinted copies to find and destroy the embedded identification string by altering the data in those places where a difference was detected.

In this chapter, we introduce a method for embedding customer identification into multimedia data: Active digital fingerprinting is a combination of robust digital watermarking and the creation of a collision-secure customer vector. In literature we also find the term *collusion secure fingerprinting* or *coalition attack secure fingerprinting.* There is also another mechanism often called fingerprinting in multimedia security, the identification of content with robust hash algorithms; see for example in Haitsma, Kalker and Oostveen (2001). To be able to distinguish both methods, robust hashes are called *passive fingerprinting* and collision-free customer identification watermarks are called *active fingerprinting.* Whenever we write fingerprinting in this chapter, we mean active fingerprinting.

MOTIVATION

To achieve customer identification directly connected to the copy of the media to be protected, embedding a robust watermark with a customer identification number — called ID from hereon — is a first solution. This prevents the removal of the ID in most cases, as watermarking algorithms become robust to most media processing, like lossy compression or DA/AD conversion.

A simple example:

The content provider wants to sell four copies of an audio file to his customers. To be able to trace the source of an illegal distribution of the file, he embeds a different bit sequence in each copy. For customer A, he embeds "00," for B "01," for C "10" and for D "11".

If he finds a copy of the audio file only sold to those four customers, he could try to retrieve the watermark from the copy. As he uses a robust watermarking algorithm, he is able to find the watermark and to identify the source. For example, he detects the watermark "01" and concludes the source is B. In the case of very strong attacks — which would reduce the quality and make the copies less attractive — he may not be able to detect the watermark, but when the copy is of little value, he does not worry about this.

But due to watermarking characteristics, a much more dangerous situation can occur: Imagine A and D know each other and want to distribute illegal copies of the audio file. They know the file is watermarked and have a certain level of understanding regarding this technology. Therefore they compare both copies to each other, showing differences at certain positions. Knowing most watermarking algorithms can be confused in this way, they now mix both copies, creating a copy consisting of both customers' copies.

This could render the watermarking algorithm unable to detect the watermarking information embedded. The illegal copy would be of good quality but still not traceable. Even worse, this could lead to pointing at a third customer who is innocent: If A's "00" and D's "11" are mixed, depending on the attacking algorithm and the watermarking method, it can happen that "01" or "10" is detected and B or C are accused.

A possible solution to this problem is to embed checksums together with the customer ID, significantly reducing the probability of false accusations, as the randomly generated new watermark will not fit to the checksum and the

Figure 1. Coalition attack scheme

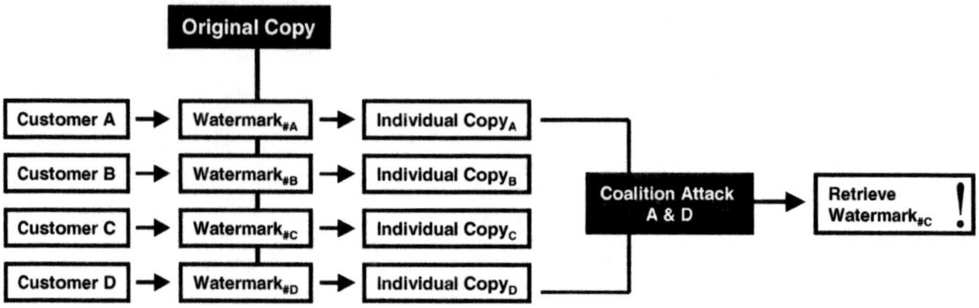

watermark becomes useless. Still, no customer identification takes place and the attack is successful. Therefore, a collusion-robust method for customer identification is required.

BASIC TECHNOLOGIES

Before we discuss optimisation methods for active digital fingerprinting, we need to provide an overview to customer identification codes and to identify requirements regarding digital watermarking in this scenario.

From Dittmann, Behr, Stabenau, Schmitt, Schwenk and Ueberberg (1999), a digital fingerprinting scheme consists of:

- a number of marking positions in the document
- a watermarking embedder to embed letters from a certain alphabet — most often bits — at these marking positions
- a fingerprint generator, which selects the letters to be embedded for each marking position depending on the customer
- a watermarking detector to retrieve a watermark from a marked copy
- a fingerprint interpreter, which outputs at least one customer from the retrieved watermarking information

Different copies of a document containing digital fingerprints differ at most at the marking positions. An attack — as already described — to remove a fingerprint therefore consists of comparing two or more fingerprinted documents and altering these documents randomly in those places where a difference was detected. If three or more documents are compared, a majority decision can be applied to improve this kind of attack: For the area where the documents differ, one will choose the value that is present in most of the documents. The only marking positions the pirates cannot detect are those positions that contain the same letter in all the compared documents. We call the set of these marking positions the intersection of the different fingerprints.

The major challenge of active digital fingerprinting is to create a sequence of bits (or letters) that is robust against these comparisons. Even if the attackers can identify differences between their copies, mixing the copies must not lead to a copy in which none of the attackers can be identified.

Active Fingerprinting

To solve the problem of the coalition attack, we use the Boneh-Shaw fingerprint and the Schwenk-Ueberberg fingerprint algorithm (Boneh & Shaw, 1995; Dittmann et al., 1999). Both algorithms offer the possibility to find the customers who have committed the coalition attack. As an application example, we have applied both schemes in a video fingerprinting solution with coalition resistance in Dittmann, Hauer, Vielhauer, Schwenk and Saar (2001) and an analysis of the resistants of audio watermarking in Steinebach, Dittmann and Saar (2002). In the following two subchapters we summarize the two fingerprinting schemes.

Schwenk Fingerprint Scheme

The Schwenk et al. approach (Dittmann et al., 1999) puts the information to trace the pirates into the intersection of up to *d* fingerprints. This allows us in the best case (e.g., automated attacks like computing the average of fingerprinted images) to detect all pirates. In the worst case (removal of individually selected marks), we can detect the pirates with a negligibly small one-sided error probability; that is, we will never accuse innocent customers.

The fingerprint vector is spread over the marking positions. The marking positions for each customer are the same in every customer copy and the intersection of different fingerprints can therefore not be detected. With the remaining marked points, the intersection of all used copies, it is possible to follow up on all customers who have worked together. Another important parameter is the number *n* of copies that can be generated with such a scheme. The scheme uses techniques from finite projective geometry (Beutelspacher & Rosenbaum, 1998; Hirschfeld, 1998) to construct d-detecting fingerprinting schemes with q+1 possible copies. This scheme needs $n=q^d+q^{d-1}+...+q+1$ marking positions in the document. As we see, this can be a huge length and can cause problems with the capacity of the watermarking scheme. The idea to build the customer vector is based on finite geometries and the detailed mathematical background will be provided in the final section.

Boneh-Shaw Fingerprint Scheme

The scheme of Boneh and Shaw (1995) is also used to recognize the coalition attack, but it is another scheme. Here it is noticeable that we do not necessarily find all pirates, with a (any arbitrary small) probability *e* that we get the wrong customer, and each fingerprint has a different number of zeros.

The number of customers is q and with q and e you can get the repeats d. The fingerprint vector consists of $(q-1)$ blocks of the length d ("d-blocks"), and the total length of the embedded fingerprint computes as $d*(q-1)$. Depending on the repeats the customer vector can be very long and cause problems with the capacity of the watermarking algorithm. The idea to build the fingerprinting vector for each customer is simple: The first customer has the value one in all marked points; for the second customer all marked points without the fist "d-block" are ones; in the third all marked points without the first two "d-blocks" are ones, and so forth. The last customer has the value 0 in all marked points.

With a permutation of the fingerprint vector we get a higher security, because the pirates can find differences between the copies, but they cannot assign it to a special d-block. In the final version we provide the detailed mathematical background.

Digital Watermarking

Digital watermarking is in general a method of embedding information into a cover file. In our case, the cover consists of audio or video files. Depending on the application scenario, the information embedded will differ. Even the basic concept of the watermarking algorithms may change, as there are robust, fragile and invertible watermarking schemes (Cox et al., 2001; Dittmann, 2000; Dittmann et al., 2001; Petticolas & Katzenbeisser, 2000). For copyright protection, usually robust watermarking is applied. Still, numerous requirements need to be identified to adjust a watermarking algorithm to a specific scenario. In this section, we discuss the watermarking requirements with respect to the active fingerprinting application.

Fingerprinting can only take place if the customer is known. This is the case in, for example, Web shop environments, more generally speaking in on-demand-scenarios that require customer authentication. Copies of songs ripped from CDs bought anonymously in stores cannot be marked this way. Embedding a fingerprint in an on-demand situation induces a number of requirements to the watermarking algorithms:

- *Transparency* is a common requirement for marking digital media in e-commerce environments, as the quality of the content acting as a cover for the watermark must not be reduced.
- *Robustness* is necessary against common media operations like lossy compression and format changes.
- *Payload* must be high enough to include the fingerprint, which usually consists of a long bit vector. This can become a critical requirement.

- *Security* is of special importance in this case, as the existence of several copies of the same cover with different embedded fingerprints enables a number of specialized attacks commonly called *coalition attacks.*
- *Complexity* has to be low enough to enable online and real-time marking. A customer who wants to download a song is not willing to stay online for a long time until his or her personalized copy is available. As there will be multiple customers at the same time and media data may have a playing time of an hour or more, either streaming concepts or multiple real-time embedding speed will be necessary. Furthermore, in most cases non-blind methods are suitable where the original is needed during retrieval or detection.
- *Verification* should be performed in a secret environment. The content provider uses a secret watermarking key to embed and retrieve the watermarks. Customers do not know this key as attackers could easily verify their success with it.

This scenario-specific list of parameters shows the difference to common copyright protection environments: While robustness and transparency are of similar interest, in our scenario payload, security and complexity become more important. As active fingerprinting will only be applied if the content provider has to be prepared for attacks against more simple customer identification schemes, security is of special interest. One can assume that specialized attacks against the watermarks will take place. Complexity needs to be low in comparison to embedding a copyright notice, as in active fingerprinting each copy sold needs to be watermarked. This easily can become a bottleneck if the algorithms are not designed accordingly. In general, active fingerprints are much longer than copyright notes, inducing higher payload requirements in our scenario.

To summarize these observations, it becomes clear that not all watermarking algorithms suitable for robust copyright watermarking will be equally suited for active fingerprinting. Only those algorithms that provide high security, high payload and a low complexity in addition to a high transparency and good robustness may be chosen as a watermarking method.

ADJUSTING WATERMARKING ALGORITHMS TO ACTIVE FINGERPRINTING

To apply active fingerprinting in tracing illegal copies we need a digital watermarking algorithm. Current digital watermarking techniques may embed the generated fingerprinting information redundantly and randomly over the media file. With a random distribution, the intersection of the proposed fingerprints may be destroyed by coalition attacks. Therefore it is important to ensure that one bit with a certain position in the fingerprint vector is always embedded at the same place in the media file for every copy. Only then an intersection is undetectable for an attacker.

Audio Watermarking

To use the properties of the fingerprinting mechanisms to identify the customers who attacked the watermark we build a watermarking scheme with a fixed number of marking positions in each copy of the audio file (Steinebach et al., 2002). These marking positions can be selected based on a secret key and a psycho-acoustic model to find secure and transparent positions. The fingerprinting algorithm generates the fingerprint vector over the binary alphabet {0,1}. The watermarking algorithm embeds this binary vector at the chosen marking positions.

Watermarking algorithms use different methods to embed a message into a cover. The way the message is embedded is relevant for the security of the watermarking and fingerprinting combination: A PCM audio stream consists of a sequence of audio samples over time. Our algorithm uses a group of successive samples, for example, 2048, to embed a single bit of the complete message. Figure 2 illustrates this: The bit sequence 01011 is embedded in a 1-second audio segment by separating the audio into groups of samples and embedding one bit in each of the segments.

This leads to the following situation: If two different bit vectors are embedded in two copies of the same cover with the same key, the two copies differ exactly in those segments where different bits have been embedded as information. Figure 3 shows two embedded bit vectors "01011" and "00001". Both have been embedded in the same cover audio file. If A and B compare their copies, they find equal segments at positions 1, 3 and 5 and different segments at positions 2 and 4.

Figure 2. Audio watermarking over time

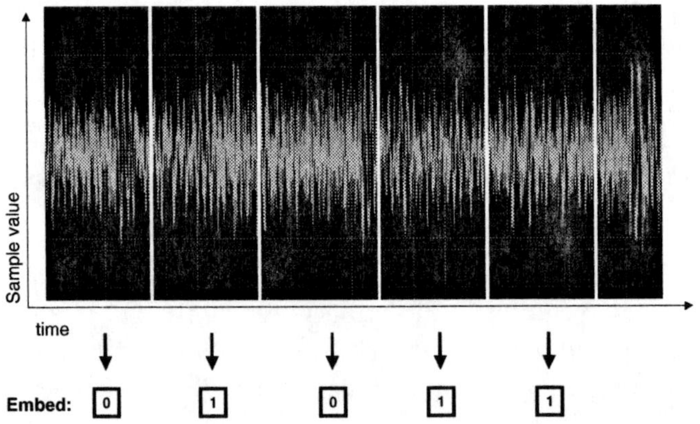

Figure 3. Different embedded bit vectors lead to different segments in the copies

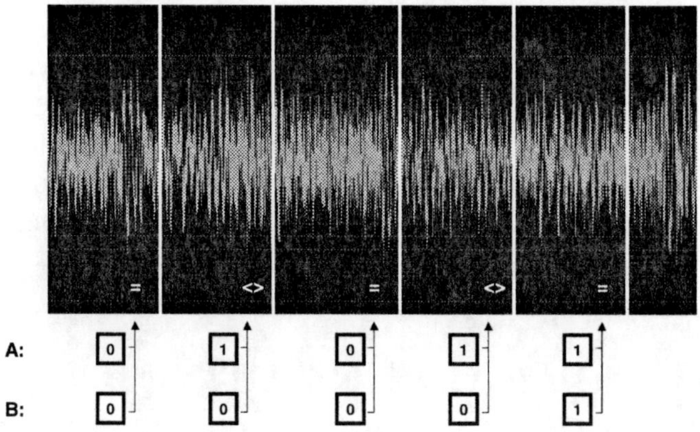

Video Watermarking

In Dittmann et al. (2001) we have introduced for Schwenk Fingerprint Scheme and the Boneh-Shaw Fingerprint Scheme, a video fingerprinting solution and the coalition resistance. To mark the video, we generate positions within the frame to embed the watermark information (in the video the positions stand for scenes). Each customer has his or her own fingerprint, which contains a number of "1" and "0". Each fingerprint vector is assigned to marking positions in the document to prevent the coalition attack. The only marking positions the pirates cannot detect are those positions that contain the same letter in all the compared documents. We call the set of these marking positions the intersection of the different fingerprints.

Three general problems emerge during the development of the watermark (Dittmann et al., 2001):

- *Robustness.* To improve the robustness against the coalition attack, we embed one fingerprint vector bit in a whole scene. So we reach a resistance against statistical attacks, like average calculation of look alike frames. With this method we can make the frame cutting and frame changing ineffective. We have not contemplated the cutting of a whole scene yet. In the current prototype we mark a group of pictures GOP for one fingerprint bit. We add a pseudo-random sequence to the first AC values of the luminance DCT blocks of an intracoded macroblock in all I-Frames of the video.
- *Capacity.* The basis of the video watermark is an algorithm, which was developed for still images (Dittmann et al., 1999). In still images the whole fingerprint is embedded into the image and the capacity is restricted. With the I-Frame in a video, the capacity is much better. To achieve high

robustness, we embed one watermark information bit into a scene. Thus the video must have a minimal length. Additional to the embedding of the watermark, the data rate can increase. The problem of synchronization between the audio and video stream can arise or data rate is raised. Basically, with the embedding of the watermark we must synchronize the audio and video stream.

- *Transparence.* To improve the transparency we use a visual model. With the visual model the watermark strength is calculated for every marking position individually. Additionally, we use the same marking position for each frame.

DESIGNING ACTIVE FINGERPRINTING ALGORITHMS

Combining customer fingerprints and existing robust watermarking algorithms to provide active fingerprinting is only a first approach to solve the challenge of customer tracking. While existing algorithms may offer parameters to optimise them for this application, new algorithms especially designed for this purpose may lead to superior performance in this domain. In this section, we discuss approaches on digital watermarking algorithm design for active fingerprinting.

Fingerprinting-Optimised Audio Watermarking

For identifying users that took part in a coalition attack, it could be helpful to change the embedding algorithm so that a rule could be set for mixing two fingerprints. If every time an embedded "0" and "1" are mixed, one specific bit occurs, we would receive a bit vector much more easy to interpret. In the case of the Schwenk algorithm, mixing a "0" and a "1" should always result in a "0" as the "1"s are used to identify the group of attackers.

An example:

Fingerprint A =	0010101
Fingerprint B =	0110001
Possible results of A&B coalition attack = #1	0110101
#2	0010101
#3	0110001
#4	0010001

The fingerprints A and B differ at position 2 and 5. This leads to 2^2 possible results of a fingerprint attack. Figure 4 shows the reason for this behaviour: Both

Figure 4. Even-strength watermarking leads to undeterminable results after coalition attacks

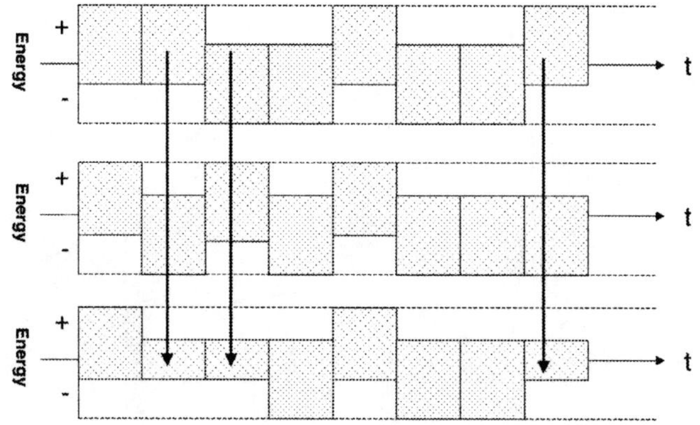

0 and 1 are embedded at equal strength. A coalition attack results in traces of both bits at similar strengths at the same position. The watermark detector will therefore have a comparatively random bit at these positions.

After an optimisation for the Schwenk fingerprint the only possible result of a coalition attack with the fingerprints A and B from the example above should be "0010001" identifying both attackers by the shared "1"s at position 3 and 6. At the positions 2 and 5 where the bit values of both fingerprints differ, both times the "0" was dominant in the attack.

This characteristic can be achieved by using different embedding strengths for both bits. In the case of middle or mix attacks this would result in the bit embedded with more strength surviving the coalition attacks. Figure 5 illustrates this concept. Bit values are embedded as a positive or negative energy. Now if we embed a bit, we use more energy for one bit type then the other. When the two energy levels are later mixed by a coalition attack, the energy type embedded with more strength is dominant. For the Schwenk algorithm, the bit 0 would be embedded with more energy then bit 1.

In Figure 5, the positive embedding energy is stronger then the negative one. In the last row the result of a coalition attack is shown: Whenever a positive and a negative energy position is mixed, the result is positive and the retrieved watermarking bit can be predetermined.

Figure 5. Different watermarking strengths for 0 and 1 lead to predetermined results after coalition attacks

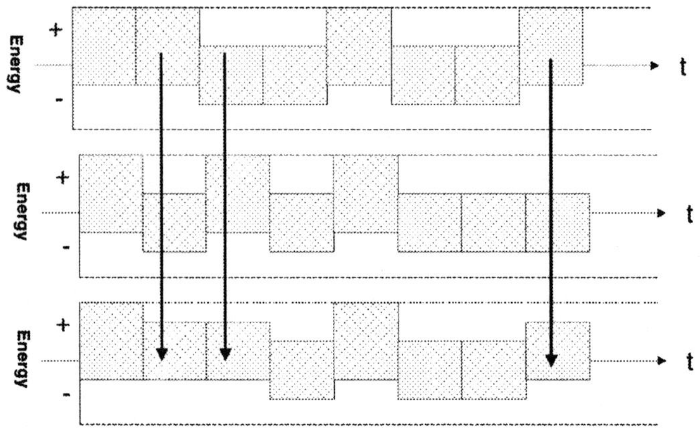

EXAMPLE SCENARIO: CINEMA APPLICATION

Fingerprinting media files today is seen as a promising way of discouraging illegal transfers of copyrighted material. Therefore example scenarios for this technology come from media distribution, especially where a small number of copies exist but leaking of these copies to the public results in major damage.

One appropriate example is the distribution of movies: In recent times copies of movies often happen to be available via Internet as illegal copies before or at the same day they are shown in cinemas. This leads to two possible leaks in distribution:

1. If the movie is available before it is shown in the cinema, some promotional copy of the movie may have been used as a master.
2. If the movie is available right when shown in the cinema, someone may have recorded it with a small video camera.

Tracing illegal copies is more difficult in (2) then in (1). The two leaks strongly differ with regards to the watermarking parameters:

- Robustness in (1) is only necessary against digital video format change if the promotion copy is on DVD, or against high-quality digitisation if the copy is on videotape. Leak (2) requires robustness against a low quality analogue to digital conversion, as the movie is recorded by a small digital camera in a noisy surrounding.

- Transparency, on the other hand, needs to be higher or at least more reliable in (2) than in (1), as a low audio or video quality caused by embedding the watermark will not be accepted by movie theatres and customers.
- The required payload of the watermark may also be higher in (2) than in (1), as one can assume there will be fewer promotional copies than actual movie copies for the cinemas. This leads to more individual customers to be identified by the fingerprints, making them significantly longer.

While, therefore leak (2) may be more challenging then (1), both can be addressed with the same strategy:

- Create a movie master
- Create the required amount of fingerprinted copies from this master
- Distribute the fingerprinted copies
- Search for occurring illegal copies
- Retrieve the fingerprint from the copy
- Identify the leak with the help of the fingerprint

Attacks against Fingerprinted Copies

As a movie consists of video as well as audio information, watermarking algorithms for both media types can be used for fingerprint embedding. While the watermarking algorithms may be able to satisfy all the scenario-dependent requirements stated above, the fingerprint may also be subject to specialized attacks as soon as it becomes known to the public that fingerprinting is used for tracing copies. This is unavoidable if discouragement is desired.

Let us assume we fingerprint promotional DVDs for tracing leaks (1) using an MPEG video watermark. Two recipients of the promotional copies wanting to distribute illegal copies and willing to work together now can start coalition attacks to remove or corrupt the fingerprints.

The coalition security implies, for example, the following attacks:

(a) Attacks to separate frame areas
(b) Attacks to whole frame
(c) Attacks to whole scenes

The time and practical effort grows from (a) to (c). The video must be split in the important areas. Additionally there must be knowledge about the MPEG video format. The attack over whole frames, like the exchange of frames, is only possible with visually similar frames, because with different frames the semantics of the frames can be destroyed. Only for attacks over whole scenes the watermark has no robustness, because one bit of the fingerprint vector will be cut out. But with the cut off of whole scenes the semantics of the video will be decreased.

Optimisation Potential

To be less vulnerable against coalition attacks, we introduced a strategy for fingerprinting-optimised audio watermarking in this chapter. This strategy can be applied in the cinema-application if a certain loss of audio quality is acceptable, which may be the case in promotional copy distribution.

First test results with embedding the bits 0 and 1 of the audio watermark with different energy are promising. Depending on the energy difference, error rates after coalition attacks are reduced by up to 50%. Error rates have been calculated by counting the number of times bit 1 has been replaced by bit 0 after a coalition attack.

Figure 6 shows that the reduction of error rates is related to the increase of energy difference between bit 0 and bit 1. If both are embedded at equal strength (0 dB difference), the error rate is above 50%. On the other hand, at a difference of 12 dB, almost no errors occurred.

If the quality loss caused by the strong watermark for bit 1 can be accepted, embedding watermark bits with differing energy seems to be an improvement regarding robustness against coalition attacks. In our example, to reduce the error rate below 10%, we would need an embedding difference of 6 dB, which produces a quality loss similar to mp3 encoding at 192 kbps. This should be acceptable for a huge number of applications.

Figure 6. Error rates of fingerprints

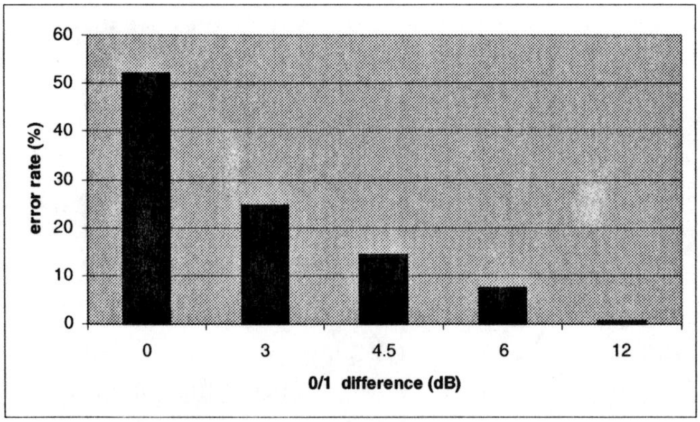

SUMMARY AND CONCLUSIONS

Altogether, digital watermarking to embed fingerprinting information is a pragmatic approach to discourage the illegal use of the copied data. The wide variety of existing watermarking algorithms reflects the business relevance. Beside the robustness to common media transformations, coalition attacks raise importance and become a critical factor for example in the design of cinema applications. As, for example, a special session "Cinema application" at SPIE 2003 shows, the combination of secure fingerprint schemes and the watermarking algorithms itself seems to be still an open problem. Reasons are in most cases the limited capacity for embedding the collusion secure fingerprint as well as synchronisation problems.

Besides the development of watermarking algorithms and collusion secure fingerprint vector design our future goal is to design interactive tools that strengthen the producers' acceptance to use digital watermarking techniques to offer their data in a more secure way in the digital marketplace.

REFERENCES

Allamanche, E., Herre, J., Helmuth, O., Fröba, B., Kasten, T., & Cremer, M. (2001). Content-based identification of audio material using MPEG-7 low level description. *Proceedings of the International Symposium of Music Information Retrieval.*

Beutelspacher, A., & Rosenbaum, U. (1998). *Projective geometry.* Cambridge University Press.

Boneh, D., & Shaw, J. (1995). Collusion-secure fingerprinting for digital data. *Proceedings of CRYPTO'95,* LNCS 963, (pp. 452-465). Springer.

Cox, I., Miller, M., & Bloom, J. (2002). *Digital watermarking,* ISBN 1-55860-714-5. San Diego, CA: Academic Press.

Dittmann, J. (2000). *Digitale wasserzeichen,* ISBN 3-540- 66661-3. Springer Verlag.

Dittmann, J., Behr, A., Stabenau, M., Schmitt, P., Schwenk, J., & Ueberberg, J. (1999). Combining digital watermarks and collusion secure fingerprints for digital images. *Proceedings of SPIE, 3657,* (pp. 3657-51). San Jose, CA: Electronic Imaging.

Dittmann, J., Hauer, E., Vielhauer, C., Schwenk, J., & Saar, E. (2001). Customer identification for MPEG video based on digital fingerprints. *Proceedings of Advances in Multimedia Information Processing - PCM 2001, The Second IEEE Pacific Rim Conference on Multimedia,* Beijing, China, ISBN 3-540-42680-9, (pp. 383-390). Berlin: Springer Verlag.

Dittmann, J., Wohlmacher, P., & Nahrstedt, K. (2001, October-December). Multimedia and security – Using cryptographic and watermarking algorithms. ISSN 1070-986X *IEEE MultiMedia, 8*(4), 54-65.

Haitsma, J., Kalker, T., & Oostveen, J. (2001). Robust audio hashing for content identification. *Proceedings of the Content-Based Multimedia Indexing.*

Hirschfeld, J.W.P. (1998). *Projective geometries over finite fields* (2nd ed.). Oxford University Press.

Petticolas, F., & Katzenbeisser, S. (2000). *Information hiding techniques for steganography and digital watermarking.* Artech House Computer Security Series, ISBN: 1580530354.

Pfitzmann, A., Federrath, J., & Kuhn, M. (2002). *DRM-studie dmmv-technischer teil.*

Steinebach, M., Dittmann, J., & Saar, E. (2002, September 26 - 27). Combined fingerprinting attacks against digital audio watermarking: Methods, results and solutions. In B. Jerman-Blazic & T. Klobucar (Eds.), *Proceedings of Advanced Communications and Multimedia Security, IFIP TC6 / TC11 6th Joint Working Conference on Communications and Multimedia Security*, Portoroz, Slovenia (pp. 197 - 212, ISBN 1-4020-7206-6). Kluwer Academic Publishers.

Chapter VI

Issues on Image Authentication

Ching-Yung Lin, IBM T.J. Watson Research Center, USA

ABSTRACT

Multimedia authentication distinguishes itself from other data integrity security issues because of its unique property of content integrity in several different levels — from signal syntax levels to semantic levels. In this section, we describe several image authentication issues, including the mathematical forms of optimal multimedia authentication systems, a description of robust digital signature, the theoretical bound of information hiding capacity of images, an introduction of the self-authentication-and-recovery image (SARI) system, and a novel technique for image/video authentication in the semantic level. This chapter provides an overview of these image authentication issues.

INTRODUCTION

The well-known adage that "seeing is believing" is no longer true due to the pervasive and powerful multimedia manipulation tools. Such development has decreased the credibility that multimedia data such as photos, video or audio clips, printed documents, and so forth used to command. To ensure trustworthiness, multimedia authentication techniques are being developed to protect multimedia data by verifying the information integrity, the alleged source of data, and the reality of data. This distinguishes from other generic message authentication in its unique requirements of *integrity*. Message authentication techniques usually cannot allow any single bit of data change. However, multimedia data are generally compressed and quality enhanced. Thus, accepting lossy compressed multimedia and some content-preserving filtering is an essential requirement in many applications.

Multimedia authentication distinguishes itself from other data integrity security issues because of its unique property of content integrity in several different levels - from signal syntax levels to semantic levels. In contrast to the data integrity issues that do not allow any changes on the data, multimedia can be considered as authentic if it is manipulated in a sense that its "content" is preserved. Content, which is an ambiguous concept, can indicate several different meanings of multimedia data. Figure 1 shows several layers of content description (Jaimes & Chang, 2000). Among them, the first three layers in the syntax level may be explicitly described by machines. For instance, compression, filtering, or some other signal level manipulations can be explicitly modeled. Thus, it is possible to clearly distinguish them from malicious manipulations, such as crop-and-replacement, without any false alarm and with a negligible miss rate (Lin & Chang, 2001). However, an authentication system based on syntax-level modeling may meet its limits if the overall manipulation is a combination of various types of acceptable changes and the final manipulated multimedia data are still similar to the original in the semantic sense. For instance, a picture of President Clinton and the First Lady walking on the lawn may be semantically authentic even if the color of lawn changes or some background trees are removed, as long as the head of the First Lady is not changed. Therefore, we consider a semantic authentication system that checks the semantic content is required and is closer to the way human beings conduct authentication.

Several syntax level authentication methods have been discussed. Schneider and Chang first proposed the concept of salient feature extraction and similarity measure for image content authentication (Schneider & Chang, 1996). They also discussed issues of embedding such signatures into the image. However, their work lacked a comprehensive analysis of adequate features and embedding schemes. Bhattacha and Kutter proposed a method that extracts "salient" image feature points by using a scale interaction model and Mexican-hat wavelets (1998). Queluz proposed techniques to generate digital signature based on moments and edges of an image (Queluz, 1999). Fridrich divided images into 64x64 pixel blocks. For each block, quasi-VQ codes were embedded using the spread spectrum method (Fridirch, 1998). Lu and Liao proposed several schemes for structured digital signatures for authentication. Lin and Chang proposed a unique *self-authentication-and-recovery image* (SARI) system (2001). SARI utilizes a semi-fragile watermarking technique that distinguishes acceptable JPEG lossy compression, brightness and contrast changes from malicious attacks. The authenticator can identify the positions of corrupted blocks, and recover them with approximations of the original ones. SARI is based on the invariant feature codes and the zero-error information hiding capacity of images.

Figure 1. Conceptual framework for visual information (Jaimes & Chang, 2000)

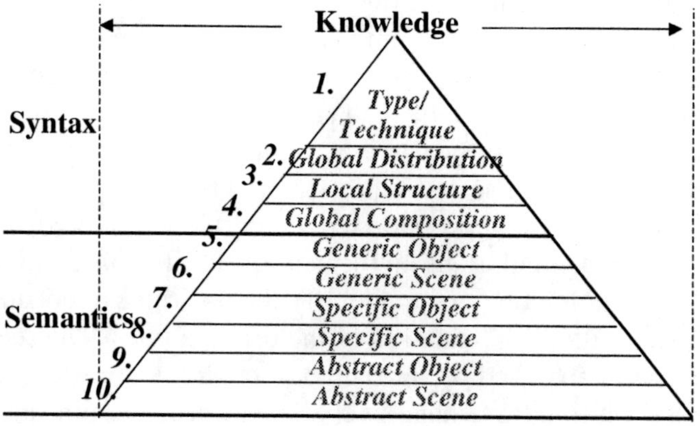

Experiments have demonstrated the effectiveness of the syntax level authentication system.

An authentication system could be evaluated based on the following requirements:

- *Sensitivity.* The authenticator is sensitive to malicious manipulations such as crop-and-replacement.
- *Robustness.* The authenticator is robust to acceptable manipulations such as lossy compression, or other content-preserving manipulations.
- *Security.* The embedded information bits cannot be forged or manipulated. For instance, if the embedded watermarks are independent of the content, then an attacker can copy watermarks from one multimedia data to another.
- *Portability.* It is desired to conduct authentication from the received content without needing separate data. Watermarks have better portability than digital signatures.
- *Location of manipulated area.* The authenticator should be able to detect location of altered areas, and verify other areas as authentic.
- *Recovery capability.* The authenticator may need the ability to recover the lost content in the manipulated areas (at least approximately).

These are the essential requirements of an "ideal" authenticator.

In this chapter, we first show how to formulate these requirements into rigorous quantative measures in a theoretical framework. Then, we show a robust digital signature method that is secure based on public key infrastructure, robust to several acceptable manipulations, sensitive to malicious changes and able to detect the manipulated area. Next, we will have a brief introduction of watermarking and then show the solution of an important issue in watermarking — what is the upper bound of embedding watermark codes in an image such that the watermark information is guaranteed to be reconstructible in amplitude-bounded noisy environments.

Using the techniques for embedded error-free watermark codes in images, we show a self-authentication-and-recovery image (SARI) watermarking system. SARI utilizes a novel semi-fragile watermarking technique that accepts quantization-based lossy compression to a quantifiable quality level and some content-preserving manipulations on the watermarked image, and rejects malicious attacks. The authenticator can identify the positions of corrupted blocks, and recover them with approximation of the original ones. The security of the proposed method is achieved by utilizing the public key infrastructure. SARI system provides solutions to two major challenges in developing authentication watermarks: how to extract short, robust and invariant information to substitute fragile image-based hash functions, and how to embed information that is guaranteed to survive quantization-based lossy compression. Also, recovery bits are generated and embedded for recovering approximate pixel values in corrupted areas.

In the last part of this chapter, we describe a novel technique for image/video authentication in the semantic level. This method uses statistical learning, visual object segmentation and classification schemes for semantic understanding of visual content. Then, we further embed either the classification output or the user annotated model labels into multimedia data as watermarks. A robust rotation, scaling, and translation public watermarking method is used for embedding information (Lin, Wu, Bloom, Miller, Cox, & Lui, 2001). The authentication process is executed by comparing the classification result with the information carried by the watermark. This method leads the authentication system to learn the semantic content of multimedia data and perform authentication tasks in a model-based semantic level.

CHARACTERISTICS OF MULTIMEDIA AUTHENTICATION SYSTEM

Multimedia authentication is centered on an extended detection issue, but involves more parties and more measures than traditional detection problems. A generic detection system, such as a radar system that detects missile attack, or a pattern recognition system that detects specific fish, considers the system performance from the detector's point of view. These detectors make decisions based on the features of collected data. They cannot interfere in the features, for example, time of the appearance of missiles or the size, shape and weight of fish.

In general, classic detection theorems consider only two measures, the probabilities of miss and false alarm, and the Neyman-Pearson criteria, usually applied to determine the operating points on the receiver operating characteristic (ROC) plot.

On the other hand, an authentication system involves three active parties: the *watermark embedder,* the *authenticator,* and the *attacker.* In an authentication system, the embedders interfere in the features of the collected data. This makes a multimedia authentication system involve the characteristics of communication, signal detection and security. The authenticator plays a traditional role of detector, which can be evaluated by the probabilities of miss and false alarm. For the embedder, the evaluation metric is mainly related to the visual quality of the watermark-embedded images. When we consider the attacker's role in evaluating the overall multimedia authentication system, we are mainly concerned with the probability of successful attack, based on the parameters chosen by the watermark embedder, authenticator, and the level of attacker's knowledge about the secret information in the system. In summary, we need four measures: the *visual quality* of watermarked image at embedder, Q_I, the *probability of false alarm* (in mistaking acceptable manipulations at authenticator), P_{FA}, the *probability of miss* (in detecting malicious manipulations at authenticator), P_M, and the *probability of successful attack* by attacker, P_S, for a multimedia authentication watermarking system. In addition, how easily an attacker acquires knowledge can be interpreted related to the security level of the system. This may be measured by the computation required to break cryptographic keys and the possible breaking points of system protocol (Schneier, 1996). To our knowledge, how to measure security level quantatively in a multimedia authentication system is still an open issue.

We can measure Q_I by peak signal-noise ratio (PSNR) or just-noticeable distortion (JND). PSNR is well known for its advantage of computational efficiency and the disadvantage of not being able to reflect subjective image quality properly. JND is a measure that indicates the visibility of the changes to a pixel, an area, or the whole frames between two images in comparison (Lu & Liao, 2003; Watson, 1993). The fact that some coefficient changes are not noticeable is due to the human vision masking effect. The maximum unnoticeable changes (or equivalently, the minimal noticeable changes) are called masks, which represent 1 JND. A more detailed discussion of JNDs can be found in Lin (2000).

From the authenticator's point of view, authentication is a hypothesis test based on the observed data, **Z**, which is obtained after manipulations of an image, $\boldsymbol{I}$:

Hypothesis 1 (H_1): $\boldsymbol{Z} = \boldsymbol{M}_A(\boldsymbol{I})$
Hypothesis 2 (H_2): $\boldsymbol{Z} = \boldsymbol{M}_N(\boldsymbol{I})$

and a specific classifier, $g(\,)$, is used to decide which hypothesis is true. $\boldsymbol{M}_A(\,)$ and $\boldsymbol{M}_N(\,)$ represent acceptable and unacceptable manipulations, respectively. Then, the probability of false alarm, P_{FA} and P_M can be expressed as:

$$P_{FA} = \mathrm{E}[\ P(\ g(\mathbf{Z}) = 2 \mid H_1)\ ] = \mathrm{E}[\ P(g(\mathbf{Z}) = 2 \mid \boldsymbol{M}_A(\,\boldsymbol{I}\,)\,)\ ], \qquad \mathbf{(1)}$$

and

$$P_M = \mathrm{E}[\ P(\ g(\mathbf{Z}) = 1 \mid H_2)\ ] = \mathrm{E}[\ P(\ g(\mathbf{Z}) = 1 \mid \boldsymbol{M}_N(\,\boldsymbol{I}\,)\,)\ ]. \qquad \mathbf{(2)}$$

The expectation value is measured over the probability distributions of H_1 or H_2. These probabilities are measures of each fixed classifier, because the authenticator chooses a specific classifier to optimize performance. Equations (1) and (2) are modeled from the classic statistical point of view. From the Bayesian theories' viewpoints, the instances of the given item and the classifier items are reversed and the classifiers are random 0. Bayesian theories consider two priors, $P(H_1 = true) = p_1$, and $P(H_2 = true) = 1 - p_1 = p_2$, are available, while classic statistical theories did not acknowledge the existence of these two probabilities.

For the authenticator, the discrimination classifier, *g*, is fixed and optimized based on the parameters sent by the embedder. On the other hand, we assume the attacker may assume a specific classifier based on the best knowledge or assume random classifiers in the case of lacking embedder knowledge. Without knowledge about the attacker's approaches, we may assume the attacker's method comes from a random pool, *G*. The probability of the attacker's success can be represented as:

$$P_S = \mathrm{E}[\ \mathrm{P}(\ \mathrm{G}_{\boldsymbol{\Theta}}(\mathbf{Z}) = 1 \mid \boldsymbol{M}_{N0}(\,\boldsymbol{I}\,))\ ], \qquad \mathbf{(3)}$$

that is, the probability of the attacker's success is an expectation value. In Equation (3), $\boldsymbol{\Theta}$ is treated as a random variable and its probability distribution function (pdf) is a subjective prior measure about how much knowledge the attacker has about the security of the system. A subjective pdf clearly point out that P_S is the *degree of belief* of the attacker but not the *physical property* of an event 0. Different levels of security knowledge can be indicated by different probability distribution functions of $\boldsymbol{\Theta}$, that is, $f(\boldsymbol{\Theta})$ can be modeled as a delta function, which is one at the true value of $\boldsymbol{\Theta}$ and zero elsewhere, if the attacker knows exactly how the authenticator authenticates the image. We should note that P_S is a measure of a known fixed manipulation to the attacker.

An authentication system wishes to minimize the probabilities of false alarm, miss, and attack success subject to constraints on the visual quality of embedded image. If there are penalties (costs) of each probability, then the total cost of the system can be represented by:

$$C_Q = c_1 \mathrm{E}[P_{FA}] + c_2 \mathrm{E}[P_M] + c_3 \mathrm{E}[P_S]. \tag{4}$$

where we take the expectation of P_{FA}, P_M and P_S based on prior probabilities of various manipulation and attack types, and c_1, c_2 and c_3 are costs of the three kinds of errors. There are no universal models for these prior probabilities. Some examples and analyses of them can be seen in Lin and Chang (2001).

Theoretically, we can extend Neyman-Pearson criteria to get an operating point (of these three probabilities) for the authentication system, based on the maximally tolerable quality degradation:

$$q_i = arg_{QI} \; min \; C_Q \tag{5}$$

In general, as the embedded code length increases, the three probabilities, P_{FA}, P_M and P_S decrease while the image quality is fixed. The information hiding capacity of an image is the critical operational point of the system. There are no general-form solutions to Equations (4) and (5). But, given the information hiding capacity, if we model manipulations and attacks using Gaussian distributions and model quality loss using PSNR, we then can obtain closed form answers of them, although we may have over-simplified the calculations via assuming a lot of prior probabilities.

ROBUST DIGITAL SIGNATURE

The digital signature method introduced by Diffie and Hellman in 1976 provides a technique to verify the integrity and the alleged source of data simultaneously. If machines play the role of signer, as the trustworthy camera technique proposed by Friedman in 1993, digital signatures may provide a sense of reality. We should note that the trustworthiness of the signers is always a concern. Because multimedia data are usually distributed, transcoded, and reinterpreted by many interim entities (e.g., editors, agents), it becomes important to guarantee end-to-end trustworthiness between the origin source and the final recipient. Figure 2 shows a comparison of systems using traditional digital signatures (TDS) and robust digital signatures (RDS). RDS-based system reduces both the required number of trusted intermediate parties and the risk of forgery. It also verifies authenticity directly from the original machine signer, which could, in a sense, provide a proof of reality.

A simple structure of RDS algorithm is shown in Figure 3. An RDS is an encrypted form of the feature codes of the multimedia data. When a user needs to authenticate the received data, he should decrypt this signature and compare

Figure 2. Multimedia authentication: (a) Using traditional digital signatures (TDS) – Trust all parties and verify multiple digital signatures; (b) Using robust digital signature (RDS) – Trust only the original signer and verify single signature

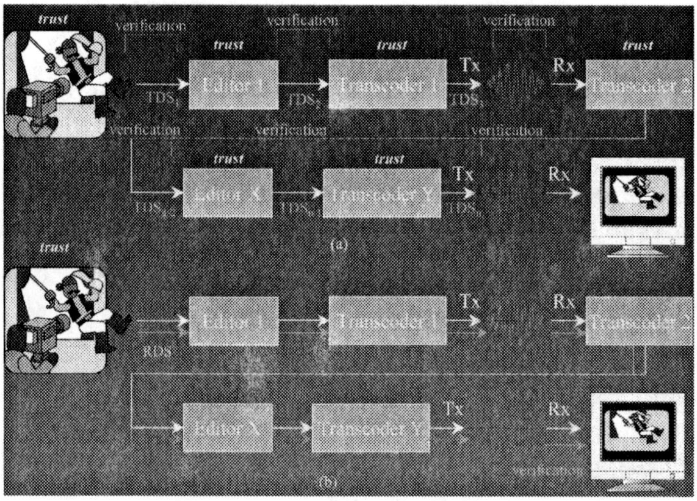

the feature codes to their corresponding values in the signature. If the derived feature codes match the range space of the original feature codes after acceptable manipulations, this multimedia data is said to be "authentic". How to extract (short) feature codes that are invariant to acceptable manipulations but sensitive to malicious changes is the main challenge of RDS.

We found that some strictly quantitative invariants and predictable properties can be extracted when multimedia data was transcoded by quantization-based compressions. For instance, because all DCT coefficient matrices of images are divided by the same quantization table in the JPEG compression process, the relationship between two DCT coefficients of the same coordinate

Figure 3. Generation and authentication of robust digital signatures

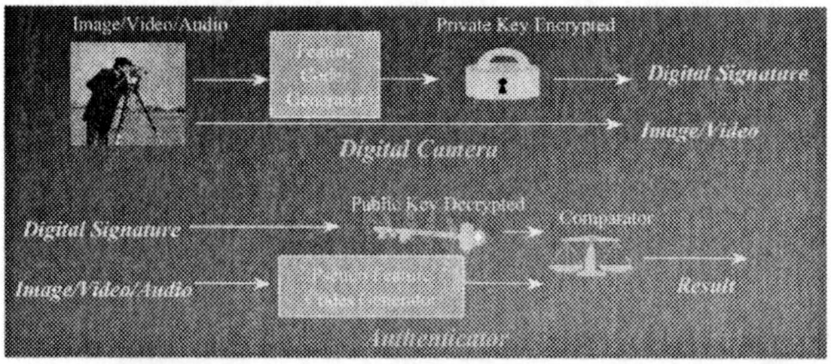

position should remain the same after the quantization process. Furthermore, due to the rounding effect after quantization, the relationship of the two may be the same or become equal. In other words, if one coefficient Fp(n) in the position n of block p is larger than the other coefficient Fq(n) in the position n of block q, then after compression, their relationship, Fp'(n)≥Fq'(n), where Fp'(n) = Integer Round (Fp(n)/Q)×Q and Fq'(n) = Integer Round (Fq(n)/Q)×Q, is guaranteed. It can be summarized as Theorem 1:

Theorem 1:

- if $Fp(n) > Fq(n)$ then $Fp'(n) \geq Fq'(n)$,
- if $Fp(n) < Fq(n)$ then $Fp'(n) \leq Fq'(n)$,
- if $Fp(n) = Fq(n)$ then $Fp'(n) = Fq'(n)$.

This property holds for any number of decoding, re-encoding processes, as well as intensity and contrast changes.

The signature generation process is as follows: each 8×8 block of an image captured is transformed to the DCT coefficients, and sent to the image analyzer. The feature codes are generated according to two crypto key-dependent controllable parameters: mapping function, W, and selected positions, b. Given a block p in an image, the mapping function is used for selecting the other block to form a block pair, that is, q = W(p). A coefficient position set, b, is used to indicate which positions in an 8×8 block are selected. The feature codes of the image records the relationship of the difference value, Fp(n)-Fq(n) at the b selected positions. This process is applied to all blocks to ensure the whole image is protected. In the last step, the feature codes are encrypted with a private key by using the public key encryption method.

Given a signature derived from the original image and a JPEG compressed image bitstream, for authentication, at the first step, we have to decrypt the signature and reconstruct DCT coefficients. Because the feature codes decrypted from the signature record the relationship of the difference values and zero, they indicate the sign of the difference of DCT coefficients, despite the changes of the coefficients incurred by lossy JPEG compression. If these constraints are not satisfied, we can claim that this image has been manipulated by another method.

Some parameters can be used to allow this system to be applied in various situations. For instance, we can set tolerance bounds on the authenticator to allow systems to accept some other minor manipulations, such as low-pass filtering, median filtering, and so forth. Or, multilayer feature codes can be used to increase the security and sensitivity of the system.

Similar to the image authentication system, video authentication signatures that are robust to the transcoding processes can be generated. Systems can generate RDS based on different transcoding application scenario: for example, dynamic rate shaping, rate control with/without drift error correction, consistent/inconsistent frame types transcoding, and so forth.

WATERMARKING CAPACITY FOR DIGITAL IMAGES

In watermarking schemes, multimedia data are considered as a communication channel to transmit messages. An important theoretical issue of watermarking is: how much information can be reliably transmitted as watermarks without causing noticeable quality losses?

Theoretical capacity issues of digital watermarking have not been fully understood. Most of the previous works on watermarking capacity (e.g., Barn, Bartolini, De Rosa, & Piva, 1999; Queluz, 1999; Servetto, Podilchuk, & Ramchandran, 1998) directly apply Shannon's well-known channel capacity bound:

$$C = \frac{1}{2}\log_2(1 + \frac{P}{N}) \quad \textbf{(6)}$$

which provides a theoretic capacity bound of an analog-value time-discrete communication channel in a static transmission environment, that is, where the (codeword) signal power constraint, *P,* and the noise power constraint, *N,* are constants (Shannon, 1948). Transmitting message rate at this bound, the probability of decoding error can approach zero if the length of codeword approaches infinite, which implies that infinite transmission samples are expected.

Considering multimedia data, we found there are difficulties if we directly apply Equation (6). The first is the number of channels. If the whole image is a channel, then this is not a static transmission environment because the signal power constraints are not uniform throughout the pixels, based on the human vision properties. If the image is a composition of parallel channels, then this capacity is meaningless because there is only one or few sample(s) in each channel. The second difficulty is the issue of digitized values in the multimedia data. Contrary to floating point values, which have infinite states, integer value has only finite states. This makes a difference in both the applicable embedding watermark values and the effect of noises. The third obstacle is that we will not know how large the watermark signals can be without an extensive study of human vision system models, which is usually ignored in most previous watermarking research, perhaps because of its difficulties and complexity. The fourth hurdle is related to noise modeling.

Figure 4. Watermarking: Multimedia data as a communication channel

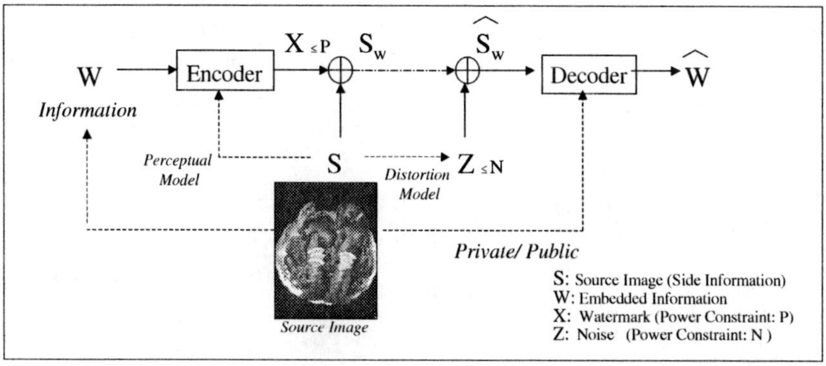

Despite the existence of various distortion/attacks, additive noises might be the easiest case. Other distortions may be modeled as additive noises if the distorted image can be synchronized/registered. There are other issues such as private or public watermarking and questions as to whether noise magnitudes are bounded. For instance, Equation (6) is a capacity bound derived for Gaussian noises and is an upper bound for all kinds of additive noises. However, in an environment with finite states and bounded noises, transmission error can actually be zero, instead of approaching zero as in Equation (6). This motivated a research of zero-error capacity initialed by Shannon (1956). Quantization, if an upper bound on the quantization step exists, is an example of such a noise. We can find the zero-error capacity of a digital image if quantization is the only source of distortion, such as in JPEG.

A broad study of theoretical watermarking capacity based on the above four obstacles can be found in Lin (2000). In Lin and Chang (2001), we showed the watermarking capacity based on multivariant capacity analysis and four HVS models.

In this section, we focus on the zero-error capacity of digital images. Shannon defined the zero-error capacity of a noisy channel as the least upper bound of rates at which it is possible to transmit information with zero probability of error (Shannon, 1956). In contrast, here we will show that rather than a probability of error approaching zero with increasing code length, the probability of error can be actually zero under the conditions described above. This property is especially needed in applications in which no errors can be tolerated. For instance, in multimedia authentication, it is required that no false alarm occurs under manipulations such as JPEG compression. In some applications, we need to correctly retrieve all the hidden information in the watermarked image within a pre-selected range of acceptable compression quality factors.

In this section, we will also show that the semi-fragile watermarking method that we proposed in Lin and Chang (2000) is, in fact, one way of achieving the zero-error capacity. We will also show two sets of curves that represent the zero-error capacity. Although most of our discussion will focus on image watermarking subject to JPEG manipulation, the zero-error capacity we showed here can be applied to other domains as long as the noise magnitude is constrained.

We first discuss the meaning and classification of channels in an image. Then, we will discuss a theoretical derivation of zero-error capacity of a discrete memoryless channel and an image. We will then show the capacity curves and some experiments results.

Number of Channels in an Image

Here we consider the case that the maximal acceptable level of lossy compression is pre-determined. In JPEG, maximum distortion of each DCT coefficient is determined by the quantization step size. Since JPEG uses the same quantization table in all blocks, maximum distortion just depends on the position in the block and is the same for all coefficients from different blocks but at the same position. If we define a pre-selected lower bound of acceptable compression quality factors, then all the quantization step size at any specific position of blocks will be smaller than or equal to the quantization step size from the selected lowest quality factor (Lin &Chang, 2000).

Assume a digital image ***X*** has $M \times N$ pixels that are divided into B blocks. Here, in the blocked-based DCT domain, ***X*** may be considered as

- *Case 1.* A variant-state discrete memoryless channel (DMC). Transmission utilizes this channel for $M \times N$ times.
- *Case 2.* A product of 64 static-state DMCs, in which all coefficients in the same position of blocks form a DMC. Each channel can be at most transmitted B times. In other words, the maximum codeword length is B for each channel.
- *Case 3.* A product of $M \times N$ static-state DMCs, in which each coefficient forms a DMC. Each channel can be at most transmitted once.

In most information theory research works, channel is usually considered invariant in time and has uniform power and noise constraint, which is usually valid in communication. Time variant cases have been addressed (e.g., Csiszar & Narayan, 1991), called *arbitrarily varying channel* (AVC). However, such a work on AVC may not be adequate to the watermarking problem because the channel does not vary in a statistically arbitrary way.

We think that Case 2 is the best candidate for the capacity analysis problem if the image is only manipulated by JPEG. However, assuming no error correction codes are used in this zero-error environment, the codes in Case 2 will be sensitive to local changes. Any local changes may cause loss of the whole transmitted information in each channel. In applications in which information bits have to be extracted separately from each block, Case 3 may be the best candidate. For instance, in the authentication case, some blocks of the image may be manipulated. By treating each coefficient as a separate channel (as in Case 3), we can detect such manipulations in a local range.

A general watermarking model is shown in Figure 4. Here, a message, $\boldsymbol{W}$, is encoded to $\boldsymbol{X}$, which is added to the source multimedia data, $\boldsymbol{S}$. The encoding process may apply some perceptual model of $\boldsymbol{S}$ to control the formation of the watermark codeword $\boldsymbol{X}$. The resulted watermarked image, $\boldsymbol{S}_W$, can always be considered as a summation of the source image and a watermark $\boldsymbol{X}$. At the receiver end, this watermarked image may have suffered from some distortions, for example, additive noise, geometric distortion, nonlinear magnitude distortion, and so forth. The decoder uses the received watermarked image, $\hat{\boldsymbol{S}}_W$, to reconstruct the message, $\hat{\boldsymbol{W}}$.

In general, we call the watermarking method "private" if the decoder needs the original source image $\boldsymbol{S}$, and "public" or "blind" if $\boldsymbol{S}$ is not required in the decoding process. Watermarking capacity refers to the amount of message bits in $\boldsymbol{W}$ that can be reliably transmitted.

Zero-Error Capacity of a Discrete Memoryless Channel and a Digital Image

The zero-error capacity of discrete memoryless channel can be determined by applying adjacency-reducing mapping on the adjacency graph of the DMC (Theorem 3 in Shannon, 1956). For a discrete-value channel, Shannon defined that two input letters are adjacent if there is a common output letter that can be caused by either of these two 0. Here, in the JPEG cases, a letter means an integer value within the range of the DCT coefficient. Adjacency-reducing mapping means a mapping of letters to other letters, $i \rightarrow \alpha_i$, with the property that if i and j are not adjacent in the channel (or graph) then α_i and α_j are not adjacent. In other words, it tries to reduce the number of adjacent states in the input based on the adjacency of their outputs. Adjacency means that i and j can be mapped to the same state after transmission. We should note that the problem of determining such a mapping function for an arbitrary graph is still wide open. Also, it is sometimes difficult to determine the zero-error capacity of even some simple channels (Korner & Orlitsky, 1998).

Fortunately, we can find an adjacency-reducing mapping and the zero-error capacity in the JPEG case. Assume the just noticeable change on a DCT coefficient is $\frac{1}{2} \cdot Q_w$ [1] and assume the largest applicable JPEG quantization step to this coefficient is Q_m, then the zero-capacity of this channel will be:

Figure 5. Adjacency-reducing mapping of discrete values given bounded quantization noise

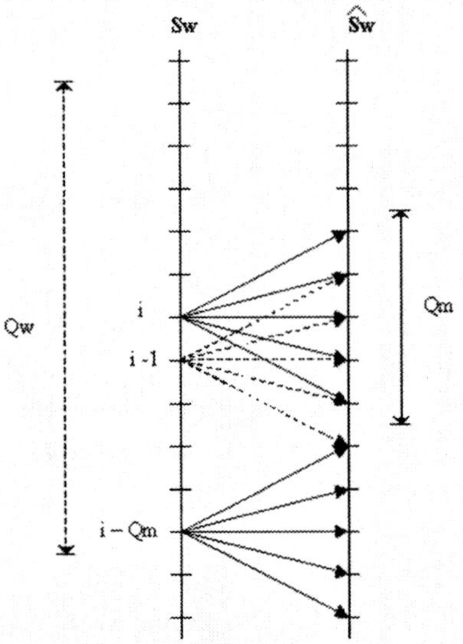

$$\tilde{C}(Q_w, Q_m) = \log_2(\lfloor Q_w / Q_m \rfloor + 1). \qquad \textbf{(7)}$$

Equation (7) can be proved by using the adjacency-reducing mapping as in Shannon (1956). Figure 5 shows an example to reduce adjacency points. Given a Q_m, which is the maximum quantization step that may be applied to the watermarked coefficient S_w, then the possible value $\hat{S}_W$ at the receiver end will be constrained in a range of Q_m possible states. According to Shannon's adjacency-reducing mapping, we can find that the non-adjacent states have to separate from each other for a minimum of Q_m. For instance, assume the source coefficient value is *i*, then its closest non-adjacency states of *i* are $i + Q_m$ and $i - Q_m$. To find out the private watermarking capacity, we assume that all the states within the just-noticeable range of $i - ½\, Q_w$, $i + ½\, Q_w$ are invisible. Therefore, there are *Qw* candidate watermarking states in this range. Since we have shown that the non-adjacent states have to separate from each other by Q_m, then there will be $\lfloor Q_w / Q_m \rfloor + 1$ applicable states in the Q_w ranges that can be used to represent information without noticeable change. Therefore, from the information theory, we can get the capacity of this channel in Equation 7. For instance, in Figure 6, $Q_w = 11$ and $Q_m = 5$. Using Equation (7), we can obtain the capacity rate to be *1.59* bits/sample.

Equation (7) is a bound for private watermarking with known source values in the receiver. However, in the public watermarking cases, *i* is unknown at the receiver end. In this case, we can fix the central position of the applicable states in the $\hat{S}_W$ axis. Then, the number of applicable states in the just-noticeable range, $[\, i - ½\, Q_w,\, i + ½\, Q_w)$, will be either $\lfloor Q_w / Q_m \rfloor + 1$ or $\lfloor Q_w / Q_m \rfloor$ if $Q_w \geq Q_m$, or only *1* state if $Q_w < Q_m$. The number of states can be represented as $\lfloor \max(Q_w - Q_m, 0) / Q_m \rfloor + 1$. Therefore, we can get the minimum capacity of public watermarking:

$$\tilde{C}(Q_w, Q_m) = \log_2(\lfloor \max(Q_w - Q_m, 0) / Q_m \rfloor + 1). \tag{8}$$

In Case 2, information is transmitted through *B* parallel channels, whose capacity can be summed up (Shannon, 1956). The total zero-error capacity of an image surviving JPEG compression is, therefore:

$$C = \left\lfloor B \times \sum_{v \in V} \tilde{C}_v (Q_w, Q_m) \right\rfloor, \tag{9}$$

where *V* is a subset of {1..64}. Intuitively, *V* is equals to the set of {1..64}. However, in practical situation, even though the changes are all within the JND of each coefficient, the more coefficients changed, the more possible the changes are visible. Also, not all the 64 coefficients can be used. We found that *V* = {1..28} is an empirically reliable set that all coefficients are quantized as recommended in the JPEG standard by using some commercial software such as Photoshop and xv[2]. Therefore, we suggest estimating the capacity based on this subset. An empirical solution of Q_w is Q_{50}, as recommended as invisible distortion bound in the JPEG standard. Although practical invisible distortion bounds may vary depending on viewing conditions and image content, this bound is considered valid in most cases (Pennebaker & Mitchell, 1993). Figure 6(a) shows the zero-error capacity of a gray-level *256×256* image.

In Case 3, we want to extract information through each transmission channel. Because the transmission can only be used once in this case, the information each channel can transmit is therefore $\lfloor \tilde{C} \rfloor$. Similar to the previous case, summing up the parallel channels, then we can get the zero-error capacity of public watermarking in Case 3 to be:

$$C = B \times \sum_{v \in V} \lfloor \tilde{C}_v (Q_w, Q_m) \rfloor. \tag{10}$$

A figure of Equation (10) is shown in Figure 6(b). These bits can be restored independently at each utilized coefficient. In other words, changes in a specific block would only affect its hidden information in that block.

Figures of Zero-Error Capacity Curve of Digital Images

In Figure 6, we show the zero-error capacity of any *256×256* gray level image. Three different just-noticeable changes in the DCT coefficients are used. The curve $Q_w = Q_{50}$ is the just-noticeable distortion suggested by JPEG. In Figure 6(a), we can see that if the image is quantized by a JPEG quality factor

Figure 6. Zero-error capacity of a 256×256 gray-level image for (a) Channel Case 2 and (b) Channel Case 3

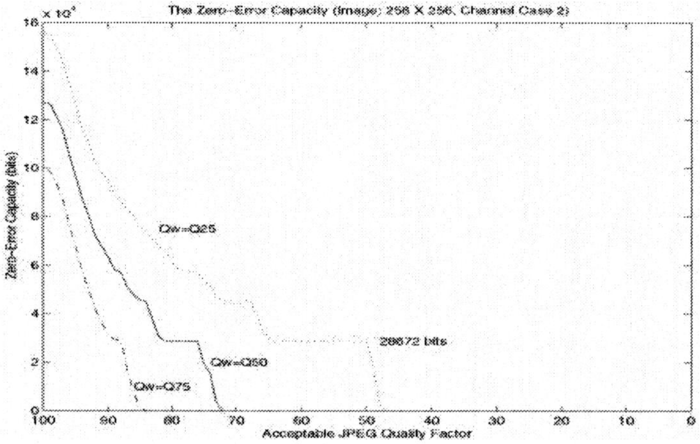

(a)

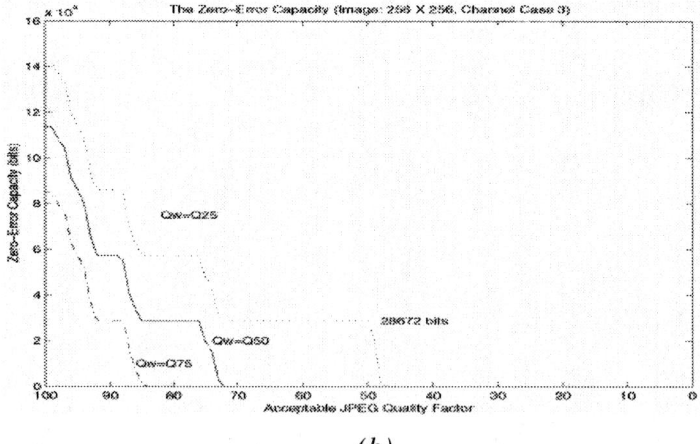

(b)

larger or equal to *75*, (i.e., $Q_m \leq Q_{75} = ½ \cdot Q_{50}$) then the zero-error capacity of this image is at least *28672* bits, which is equal to *28* bits/block. We can notice that when $75 < m \leq 72$, the capacity is not zero because some of their quantization steps in the quantization table are still the same as Q_{75}.

Comparing Equation 10 with Theorem 1 in Lin and Chang (2000), we can see the watermarking technique proposed in Lin and Chang (2000) is a method of utilizing the zero-error capacity. The only difference is that, in Lin and Chang (2000), we fixed the ratio of $Q_w = 2 \cdot Q_m$ and embed one or zero bit in each channel. For the convenience of readers, we rewrite the Theorem 1 of Lin and Chang (2000) as Theorem 2:

Theorem 2

Assume $\mathbf{F}_p$ *is an N-coefficient vector and* $\mathbf{Q}_m$ *is a pre-selected quantization table. For any integer* $\upsilon \in \{1,..,N\}$ *and* $p \in \{1,...,\zeta\}$, *where* ζ *is the total number of blocks in the image, if* $\mathbf{F}_p(\upsilon)$ *is modified to* $\mathbf{F'}_p(\upsilon)$ *s.t.* $\mathbf{F'}_p(\upsilon)/\mathbf{Q'}_m(\upsilon) \in Z$ *where* $\mathbf{Q'}_m(\upsilon) \geq \mathbf{Q}_m(\upsilon)$, *and define* $\tilde{F}_p(\upsilon) \equiv$ *Integer Round* $(\mathbf{F'}_p(\upsilon)/\mathbf{Q}(\upsilon)) \cdot \mathbf{Q}(\upsilon)$ *for any* $\mathbf{Q}(\upsilon) \leq \mathbf{Q}_m(\upsilon)$, *the following property holds:*

$$\text{Integer Round } (\tilde{F}_p(\upsilon) / \mathbf{Q'}_m(\upsilon)) \cdot \mathbf{Q'}_m(\upsilon) = \mathbf{F'}_p(\upsilon)$$

Theorem 2 shows that if a coefficient is modified to an integral multiple of a pre-selected quantization step, $\mathbf{Q'}_m(\upsilon)$, which is larger than or equal to all possible quantization steps in subsequent re-quantization, then this modified coefficient can be *exactly reconstructed* after future quantizations. It is reconstructed by quantizing the subsequent coefficient again using the same quantization step, $\mathbf{Q'}_m(\upsilon)$. We call such exactly reconstructible coefficients, $\mathbf{F'}_p(\upsilon)$, *reference coefficients.* Once a coefficient is modified to its reference value, we can guarantee this coefficient would be reconstructible in any amplitude-bounded noisy environment.

Our experiments have shown that the estimated capacity bound described in this section can be achieved in realistic applications. We tested nine images by embedding 28 bits in each block based on 0. Given $Q_w = Q_{50}$, these messages can be reconstructed without any error if the image is compressed by JPEG with quality factor larger than or equal to 75 using xv. Given $Q_w = 2 \cdot Q_{67}$, these messages can be totally reconstructed after JPEG compression using Photoshop *5.0* quality scale *10 - 4*.

In summary, we derived and demonstrated the zero-error capacity for private and public watermarking in environments with magnitude-bounded noise. Because this capacity can be realized without using the infinite codeword length and can actually accomplish zero error, it is very useful in real applications.

SELF-AUTHENTICATION-AND-RECOVERY IMAGES

SARI (Self-Authentication-and-Recovery Images, demos and test software at http://www.ee.columbia.edu/sari) is a semi-fragile watermarking technique that gives "life" to digital images (Lin & Chang, 2001). An example of a SARI system is shown in Figure 7. Like a gecko can recover its cut tail, a watermarked SARI image can detect malicious manipulations (e.g., crop-and-replacement) and approximately recover the original content in the altered area. Another important feature of SARI is its compatibility to JPEG lossy compression within an acceptable quality range. A SARI authenticator can sensitively detect malicious changes while accepting alteration introduced by JPEG lossy compression. The lowest acceptable JPEG quality factor depends on an adjustable watermarking strength controlled in the embedder. SARI images are secure because the embedded watermarks are dependent on the image content (and on their owner's private key).

Traditional digital signatures, which utilize cryptographic hashing and public key techniques, have been used to protect the authenticity of traditional data and documents (Barni, Barolini, De Rosa, & Piva, 1999). However, such schemes protect every bit of the data and do not allow any manipulation or processing of the data, including acceptable ones such as lossy compression. To the best of our knowledge, the SARI technique is the only solution that can verify the authen-

Figure 7. Embedding robust digital signatures to generate self-authentication-and-recovery images

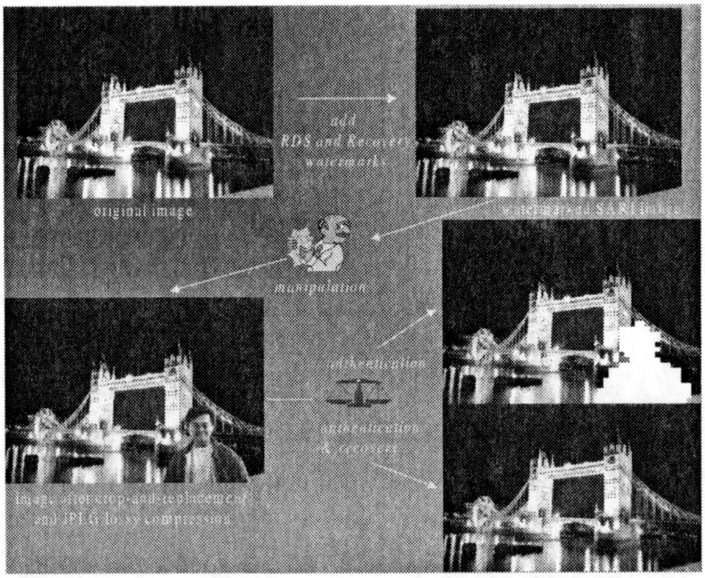

ticity of images/videos and at the same time accept desired manipulations such as JPEG compression and brightness adjustment. It also has the unique capability to sensitively detect unacceptable manipulations, correctly locate the manipulated positions and partially recover the corrupted area. This technique differs from traditional digital signatures in that (1) it uses invisible watermarking, which becomes an integral part of the image, rather than external signatures, (2) it allows some pre-defined acceptable manipulations, (3) it locates the manipulation areas, and (4) it can partly recover the corrupted areas in the image. A comparison of SARI and traditional digital signature method is shown in Table 1.

System Description

SARI is based on the following techniques. Basically, two invariant properties of quantization-based lossy compression are the core techniques in SARI. The first property (Theorem 2) shows that if a transform-domain (such as DCT in JPEG) coefficient is modified to an integral multiple of a quantization step, which is larger than the steps used in later JPEG compressions, then this coefficient can be exactly reconstructed after later JPEG compression. The second one (Theorem 1) is the invariant relationships between two coefficients in a block pair before and after JPEG compression. In SARI, we use the second property to generate authentication signature, and use the first property to embed it as watermarks. These properties provide solutions to two major challenges in

Table 1. Comparison of digital signature and SARI

	Digital Signature	**SARI**
Characteristic	*Single-stage authentication*	*End-to-end, content-based authentication*
Robustness	*No single bit of the data can be changed*	*Accept various content-preserving manipulations*
Sensitivity	*Detect any change*	*Detect malicious changes, e.g., crop-and-replacement*
Security	*Use public key methods*	*Use secret mapping function and/or public key methods*
Localization	*Cannot localize manipulated areas.*	*Can localize the manipulated areas.*
Convenience	*Need a separate digital signature file.*	*No additional file is required.*
Recovery	*Not feasible.*	*Corrupted regions can be approx. recovered.*
Visual Quality	*Not affected.*	*Not affected, but may degrade if require strong robustness*

developing authentication watermarks (aka, integrity watermarks): how to extract short, invariant, and robust information to substitute fragile hash function, and how to embed information that is guaranteed to survive quantization-based lossy compression to an acceptable extent. In additional to authentication signatures, we also embed the recovery bits for recovering approximate pixel values in corrupted areas. SARI authenticator utilizes the compressed bitstream, and thus avoids rounding errors in reconstructing transform domain coefficients.

The SARI system was implemented in the Java platform and is currently operational on-line. Users can download the embedder from the SARI website and use it to add the semi-fragile watermark into their images. He can then distribute or publish the watermarked SARI images. The counterpart of the embedder is the authenticator, which can be used in the client side or deployed on a third-party site. Currently, we maintain the authenticator at the same website so that any user can check the authenticity and/or recover original content by uploading the images they received.

The whole space of DCT coefficients is divided into three subspaces: *signature generating, watermarking,* and *ignorable* zones. Zones can be overlapped or non-overlapped. Coefficients in the signature-generating zone are used to generate authentication bits. The watermarking zone is used for embedding signature back to image as watermark. The last zone is negligible. Manipulations of coefficients in this zone do not affect the processes of signature generation and verification. In our system, we use non-overlapping zones to generate and embed authentication bits. For security, the division method of zones should be kept secret or be indicated by a secret mapping method using a seed that is time-dependent and/or location-dependent.

A very important issue in implementing this system is to use integer-based DCT and inverse DCT in all applicable situations. These algorithms control the precision of the values in both spatial and frequency domains, and thus guarantee all 8-bit integer values in the spatial domain will be exactly the same as their original values even after DCT and inverse DCT. Using integer-based operations is a critical reason why our implementation of the SARI system can achieve no false alarm and high manipulation detection probability. Details of the SARI system are shown in Lin (2000).

Figure 8(a) shows the user interface of the embedder in which the user can open image files in various formats, adjust the acceptable compression level, embed the watermarks, check the quality of the watermarked images and save them to files in desired formats (compressed or uncompressed). The user interface of the authenticator includes the functions that open image files in various formats, automatically examine the existence of the SARI watermark, and authenticate and recover the manipulated areas.

Figure 8. (a) User interface of the SARI embedder, (b) Example of the watermarked SARI image (size: 256x384, PSNR = 41.25 dB, embedded semi-fragile info bits: 20727)

(a) *(b)*

Example and Experiments

Figure 9 and 10 show an example of using SARI. In Figure 9, we first embed watermarks in the image, and then use Photoshop 5.0 to manipulate it and save it as a JPEG file. Figure 10 shows the authentication result of such manipulations. We can clearly see that the manipulated areas can be located by the SARI authenticator. In Figure 10(b), we can see that the corrupted area has been recovered.

We also conducted subjective tests to examine the quality of watermarked image toward human observers. Four viewers are used for this test. Their background and monitor types are listed in Table 2. We use the average of subjective tests to show the maximum embedding strength for each image. This is shown in Table 3. From this table, we can see the number of bits embedded

Figure 9. (a) Original image after adding SARI watermark, (b) Manipulated image by crop-and-replacement and JPEG lossy compression

(a) *(b)*

Figure 10. (a) Authentication result of the image in Figure 9(b), (b) Authentication and recovery result of the image in Figure 9(b)

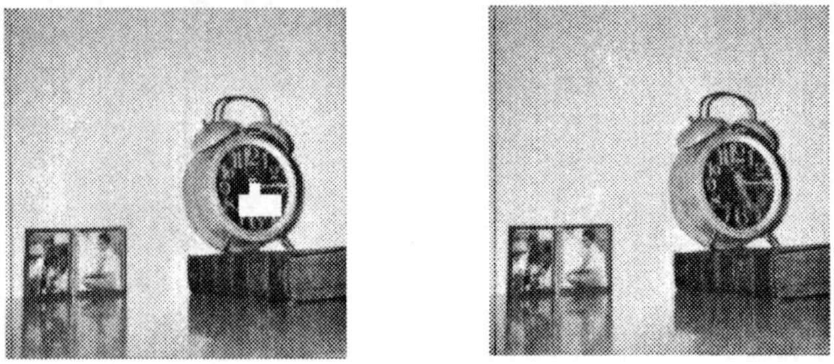

(a) *(b)*

in each image. The number of authentication bits per 8×8 block is 3 bits, and the average number of recovery bits is 13.1 bits/block. We can also see that the maximum acceptable QR or PSNR varies according different image type. Through the objective and subjective tests, we observed that:

- The changes are almost imperceptible for minimal or modest watermark strength $QR = 0 - 2$.
- The embedding capacity of a natural image is generally larger than that of a synthetic image. This is because the former has more textural areas; thus the slight modification caused by authentication bits is less visible. The image quality of human, nature, and still object is generally better than that

Table 2. Viewers in the SARI subjective visual quality test

	image-processing expert	Trinitron 17' monitor
Viewer 2	image-processing expert	Laptop LCD monitor
Viewer 3	no image-processing background	Trinitron 17' monitor
Viewer 4	image-processing expert	Trinitron 17' monitor

Figure 11. Test set for SARI benchmarking

Table 3. SARI embedded bits and max invisible (MI) embedding strength observed in the subjective test (Auth: embedding auth. bits, A+R: embedding auth. and recovery bits)

Image Name	Lena	Tokio	Cafe	Library	Fruit	Clock	Reading	Strike	Insurance
Image Type	Color	Color	Color	Color	Color	Gray	Color Graphics	Color	Color
Image Size	512x 512	768x 960	480x 592	560x 384	400x 320	256x 256	336x 352	256x 192	792x 576
Embedded Bits, Auth	12,288	34,560	13,320	10,080	6,000	3,072	5,544	2,304	21,384
Embedded Bits, A+R	47,240	109,514	88,751	52,868	24,616	11,686	34,033	10,474	90,968
Max Invis. QR, Auth	3	3	4	2	4	3	2	3	3
Max Invis. PSNR, Auth	43.0	42.3	40.2	45.0	39.8	44.7	42.5	43.8	45.0
Max Invis. QR, A+R	1	1	3	1	3	0	0	1	1
Max Invis. PSNR, A+R	41.9	42.5	33.2	39.3	36.9	36.2	34.2	39.6	41.3

of synthetic and document image, and both the objective and subjective tests show the same phenomenon.

- The quality judgments vary among different viewers. This is because users pay attention to different features of an image and their tolerance bounds can be quite different. Moreover, different types of monitors have different display effects'; for example, the images that appear not acceptable on a Dell PC look just fine on a Sun Workstation.

Two types of tests are applied: (1) the viewer randomly makes visible change on one pixel of the image, or (2) the viewer randomly changes the visual meaning of the image by crop-and-replacement (C&R). In both cases, watermarks are embedded under maximum invisible embedding strength. SARI detects all the changes conducted by the subjects.

Table 4 and Table 5 show the benchmarking result of robustness and sensitivity. We tested the robustness against JPEG lossy compression by embedding the watermarks in two different QR modes. For JPEG compression, we found that all the information bits embedded in the image can be exactly reconstructed without any false alarm after JPEG compression. We observed similar results from other JPEG testing using XV, PhotoShop *3.0*, PaintShop Pro, MS Paint, ACD See32, Kodak Imaging, and so forth. Statistics here conform to the designed robustness chart (*QR* 0 - 4). For instance, for image Lena,

Table 4. SARI robustness performance on JPEG compression measured by the quality factor in Photoshop 5.0 (Two kinds of embedding strength are applied: (1) MED: maximum invisible embedding strength, which is a variant SARI quality-and-recovery setting parameter based on subjective test results, and (2) A fixed SARI quality and recovery (QR) setting = 4)

Image Name	Lena	Tokio	Cafe	Library	Fruit	Clock	Reading	Strike	Insurance
Survive QF, MED	3	3	3	4	1	4	3	3	4
Survive QF, QR	4	1	2	2	1	2	2	2	2

Table 5. SARI sensitivity test under the maximum subjective embedding strength (Two types of test are applied: (1) the viewer randomly makes visible change on a pixel of the image, (2) the viewer randomly changes the visual meaning of the image by crop-and-replacement (C&R). In both cases, watermarks are embedded under maximum invisible embedding strength. SARI detects all the changes conducted by the subjects.)

Image Name	Lena	Tokio	Cafe	Library	Fruit	Clock	Reading	Strike	Insurance
Detect M., 1-pix	Y	Y	Y	Y	Y	Y	Y	Y	Y
Detect M., C\&R	Y	Y	Y	Y	Y	Y	Y	Y	Y

watermark with strength *QR* = 4 survives Photoshop *5.0* Quality Factor *1 - 10*. Watermarks embedded by using maximum invisible subjective embedding strength (MED) can survive JPEG compression Quality Factor *3 - 10*. This result is even better than predicted. We embedded the watermarks in the *QR = 4* mode to test its sensitivity to malicious manipulations. *QR = 4* is the most robust mode to compression and is the least sensitive mode in detecting manipulations[3]. We found that even in this worst case, SARI authenticator is quite sensitive to malicious manipulation. It is very effective in detecting crop-and-replacement manipulations up to one-pixel value changes. During the test, each subject randomly selected a pixel and changed its RGB value. The subject was told to arbitrarily change the values as long as the changes are visible. Each subject tested three times on each benchmark image. After the change is made, the subjects apply the SARI detectors to test whether the changes can be detected. The result in Table 5 shows that SARI detectors can detect all of them.

In our second test, the subjects manually use Photoshop to manipulate the image by the crop-and-replacement process. They can arbitrarily choose the range of manipulation up to half of the image. Results also show that SARI authenticator successfully identified these changes. For recovery tests, we found that in all malicious manipulation cases, an approximation of the original pixels in the corrupted area can be properly reconstructed.

We also tested other image processing manipulations. The authenticator detects changes resulted by blurring and median filtering. For Gaussian noises, the authenticator detected those changes. But, if further compressed by JPEG, usually no changes were detected because compression cancelled out the slight changes introduced by it. We also found that the robustness of noises or filtering can be increased through setting larger tolerance bound in the authentication process. Namely, rather than checking the coefficient relationships described in Theorem 2, the authenticator allows for a minor change of the coefficient difference up to some tolerance level. Examples of using tolerance bounds are in Lin and Chang (2001).

This technology could help multimedia data to regain their trustworthiness. Hopefully we can say "seeing is believing" again in this digital era!!

SEMANTIC AUTHENTICATION SYSTEM

In this section, we first describe the proposed system structure for multimedia semantic authentication, followed by the details and the experimental results.

A multimedia semantic authentication system architecture overview is shown in Figure 12. The system includes two parts: a watermark embedder and an authenticator. In the watermark embedding process, our objective is to embed a watermark, which includes the information of the models, such as objects, that are included in a video clip or image. We use either the automatic segmentation and classification result (the solid line in Figure 12) or the manual/semi-automatic annotation (the dotted line in Figure 12) to decide what the objects are. For the first scenario, the classifier learns the knowledge of objects using statistical learning, which needs training from the previous annotated video clips. We built a video annotation tool, VideoAnnEx, for the task of associating labels to the video shots on the region levelLin and Tseng (n.d.). VideoAnnEx uses three kinds of labels: background scene, foreground object, and events in the lexicon. This lexicon can be pre-defined or added to VideoAnnEx by the annotator. Based on the annotation result of a large video corpus, we can build models for each of the labels, for example, sky, or bird. After the models are built, the classifier will be able to recognize the objects in a video clip based on the result of visual object segmentation and feature extraction.

Because the capability of classifier is limited to the models that were previously built, the second scenario — manual annotation of unrecognized objects — is sometimes necessary for classifier retraining. The classifier can learn new models or modify existing models if there is annotation associated with

Figure 12. Framework for multimedia semantic authentication

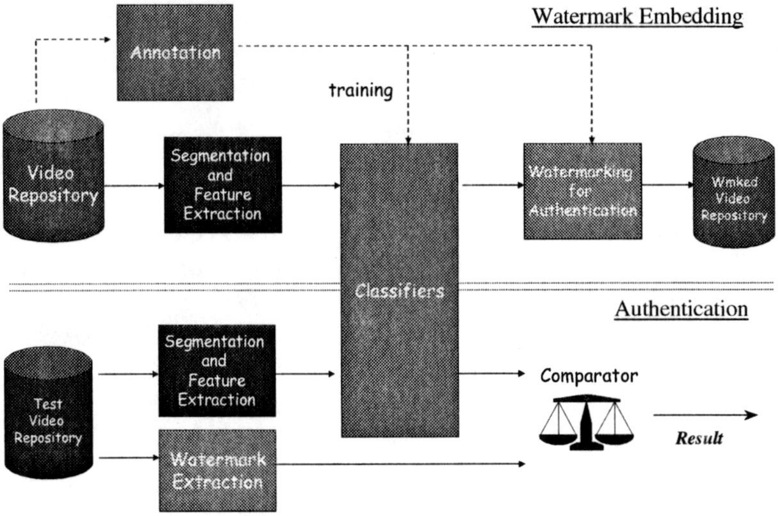

the new video. In this scenario, the annotation, which includes the label of regions, can be directly fed into the watermarking process.

The authentication process is executed by comparing the classification result with the information carried by the watermark. This process shares the same classifier of the watermark embedder (through the Internet or operating the embedding and authentication process on the same Web site). The classification result is a matrix of confidence value of each model. And the model information hidden in the watermarks can be extracted without error in most cases (Lin, Wu, Bloom, Miller, Cox & Lui, 2001). Thus, the authentication alarm flag will be trigged once the confidence value of a model indicated by the watermark is under a certain threshold.

Learning and Modeling Semantic Concepts

We have developed models for nearly 30 concepts that were pre-determined in the lexicon. Examples include:

- *Events.* Fire, smoke, launch, and so forth;
- *Scenes.* Greenery, land, outdoors, outer space, rock, sand, sky, water, and so forth;
- *Objects.* Airplane, boat, rocket, vehicle, bird, and so forth.

For modeling the semantics, statistical models were used for two-class classification using Gaussian Mixture Model (GMM) classifiers or Support Vector Machine (SVM). For this purpose, labeled training data obtained from

VideoAnnEx were used. The feature vectors associated with training data corresponding to each label were modeled by polynomial kernel of SVM, which performs better than GMM classifiers in our experiments. The rest of the training data were used to build a negative model corresponding to that label in a similar way. The difference of log-likelihoods of the feature vectors associated with a test image for each of these two models was then taken as a measure of the confidence with which the test image can be classified to the labeled class under consideration.

We analyze the videos at the temporal resolution of shots. Shot boundaries are detected using IBM CueVideo. Key-frames are automatically selected from

Figure 13. Automatic segmentation: (a) Original image, (b) Scene segmentation based on color, edge, and texture information, (c) Object segmentation based on motion vectors

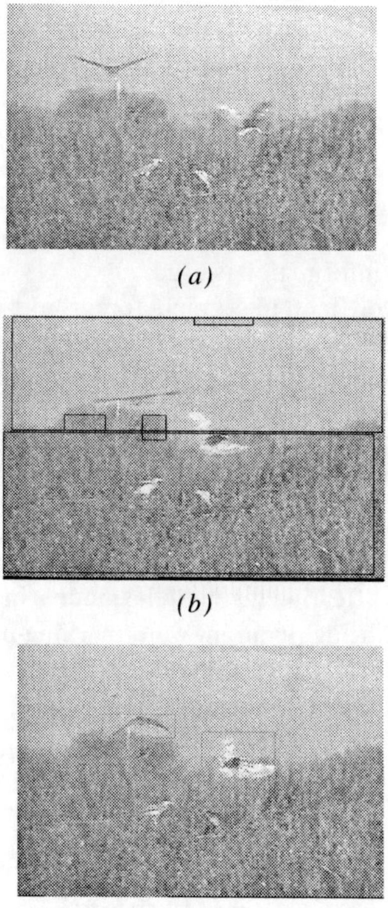

(a)

(b)

(c)

each shot. From each key-frame we extract features representing color, texture, structure, and shape. Color is represented by 24-dimensional linearized HSV histograms and color moments. Structure is captured by computing edge direction histograms. Texture is captured by gray-level co-occurrence matrix properties. Shape is captured using Dudani's moment invariants (Dudani, Breeding, & McGhee, 1977).

Segmentation

We built a sub real-time automatic segmentation for visual object segmentation. It can segment the visual object for every I- and P- frames in real time. To segment a background scene object, we use a block-based region growing method on each decoded I- or P- frame in the video clip. The criteria of region growing are based on the color histogram, edge histogram, and Tamura's texture directionality index (Tamura, Mori, & Yamawaki, 1978) of the block.

To find out the foreground object, we calculate the motion vectors of I- and P- frames, and use them to determine objects with region growing in the spatial domain and additional tracking constraints in the time domain. We tried to use the MPEG motion vectors in our system. However, those motion vectors were too noisy to be useful in our experiments. Therefore, our system calculates the motion vectors using a spiral searching technique, which can be calculated in real time if only I- and P- frames are used. Through our experiments, we find out a combination of the motion vectors with the color, edge, and texture information usually does not generate good results for foreground object segmentation. Therefore, only motion information is used.

Note that it is very difficult to segment foreground object if only an image, not a video clip, is available. Therefore, for images, only background scene objects can be reliably segmented. Thus, in our semantic authentication system, we can allow users to draw the regions corresponding to foreground objects in both the watermark embedding and authentication processes to enhance the system performance.

Watermarking

We embed the classification result of the models into the original image. A rotation, scaling, and shifting invariant watermarking method proposed in Lin, Wu, Bloom, Miller, Cox and Lui (2001) is used. The basic idea of this algorithm is using a shaping algorithm to modify a feature vector, which is a projection of log-polar map of Fourier magnitudes (a.k.a. the Fourier-Mellin Transform, FMT) of images along the log-radius axis. As shown in Figure 14, the blue signal is the original feature vector, whose distribution is similar to a Gaussian noise. Our objective is to modify the feature vector to make it closer to the pre-defined watermark signal (red). Because the FMT and inverse FMT are not one-to-one mapping, we cannot directly change the FM coefficients and apply inverse FMT

Figure 14. Example of watermarking based on feature vector shaping: Line with points that do not reach as high — Original feature vector; Line with flat tops — Watermark vector; Line with highest points — Modified featured vector (mixed signal)

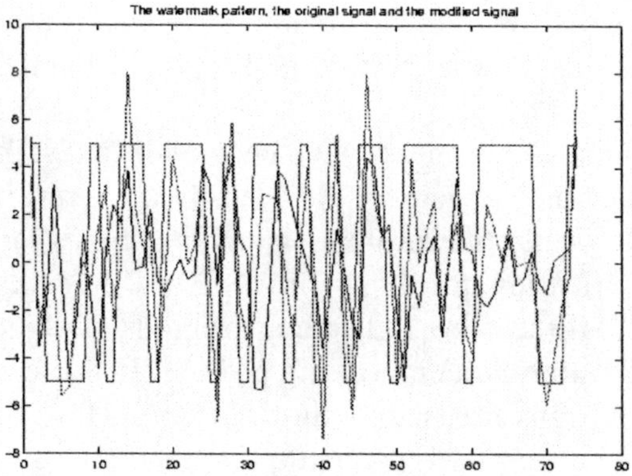

to get the watermarked DFT coefficients. We can only modify coefficients in the DFT domain to make the modified feature vector to be close to the watermark vector. This process is iterated for about three to five times. Then, the final modified feature vector (aka, mixed signal) would be similar to the watermark vector. Feature vector shaping works better than the traditional spread spectrum watermarking method on the absence of original signal in watermarking retrieval (i.e., public watermarking). In the traditional spread spectrum method:

$$T(Sw) = T(S) + X$$

where *T(.)* is a specific transform (e.g., DCT) defined by system, *S* is the source signal, *X* is the watermark signal, and *T(Sw)* is the watermarked signal. The extraction of watermark is based on a correlation value of *T(Sw)* and *X*. While in feature vector shaping, *T(Sw)* is approximately equal to *X*:

$$T(Sw) \approx X$$

Comparing these two equations, we can see that the original signal has far less effect in the correlation value using the feature vector shaping. Thus, this method (or called mixed signal) performs better in public watermarking cases (Lin, Wu, Bloom, Miller, Cox, & Lui, 2001).

Experimental Results

We have annotated on the 14 hours of video clips from the TREC video retrieval benchmarking 2001 corpus. These video clips include 5,783 shots. The lexicon is shown in Lin and Tseng (n.d.). This corpus includes mostly commentary videos of various natural, scientific, and indoor scenarios. We built nearly 30 models based on the annotated lexicon. Each model is assigned an ID, which can be as long as 42-bits watermark vectors (Lin, Wu, Bloom, Miller, Cox, & Lui, 2001).

Some preliminary experiments have been done to test the efficiency of the system. First, we test the precision of the classification result when the video is not manipulated. If we use the automatic bounding boxes for classification, the precision of classification result is 72.1%. This precision number can be increased to 98.3%, if the users indicate the regions of objects in the authentication process and watermark embedding process. In this case, because similar manual annotated regions are used for the training and testing process, the SVM classifier can achieve very high precision accuracy (Burges, 1998).

In another experiment, we extract the key-frames of shots and recompress them using a JPEG compression quality factor of 50. We then get a 98.1% of precision when the same manual bounding boxes are used, and 69.2% of authentication precision when automatic segmentation is applied. This experiment shows the classification may be affected by lossy compression. The degradation of system performance is basically affected by the segmentation algorithm. In both cases, the model information hidden in the watermarks can be extracted without any error.

We proposed a novel watermarking system for image/video semantic authentication. Our preliminary experiments show the promising effectiveness of this method. In this section, we did not address the security issues, which will be a primary direction in our future research. We will investigate on the segmentation, learning and statistical classification algorithms to improve the system precision rates on classification. And we will also conduct more experiments to test the system performance under various situations.

CONCLUSIONS

A new economy based on information technology has emerged. People create, sell, and interact with multimedia content. The Internet provides a ubiquitous infrastructure for e-commerce; however, it does not provide enough protection for its participants. Lacking adequate protection mechanisms, content providers are reluctant to distribute their digital content, because it can be easily re-distributed. Content receivers are skeptical about the source and integrity of content. Current technology in network security protects content during one stage of transmission. But, it cannot protect multimedia data through multiple stages of transmission, involving both people and machines. These concerns have hindered the universal acceptance of digital multimedia. At the same time, they also stimulate a new research field: multimedia security.

In this chapter, we described a robust digital signature algorithm and a semi-fragile watermarking algorithm. These algorithms help design the Self-Authentication-and-Recovery Images (SARI) system, demonstrating unique authentication capacities missing in existing systems. SARI is a semi-fragile watermarking technique that gives "life" to digital images. Like a gecko can recover its cut tail, a watermarked SARI image can detect malicious crop-and-replacement manipulations and recover an approximated original image in the altered area. Another important feature of SARI is its compatibility to JPEG lossy compression. SARI authenticator is the only system that can sensitively detect malicious changes while accepting alteration introduced by JPEG lossy compression. The lowest acceptable JPEG quality factor depends on an adjustable watermarking strength controlled in the embedder. SARI images are secure because the embedded watermarks are dependent on their own content (and on their owner).

There are many more topics waiting to be solved in the field of multimedia security. In the area of *multimedia authentication,* open issues include:

- *Document Authentication.* Documents include combinations of text, pictures, and graphics. This task may include two directions: authentication of digital documents after they are printed-and-scanned, and authentication of paper documents after they are scanned-and-printed or photocopied. The first direction is to develop watermarking or digital signature techniques for the continuous-tone images, color graphs, and text. The second direction is to develop half-toning techniques that can hide information in the bi-level half-tone document representations.
- *Audio Authentication.* The idea here is to study the state-of-the-art speech and speaker recognition techniques, and to embed the speaker (or his/her vocal characteristics) and speech content in the audio signal. This research also includes the development of audio watermarking techniques surviving lossy compression.
- *Image/Video/Graph Authentication.* The idea is to focus on developing authentication techniques to accept new compression standards (such as JPEG-2000) and general image/video processing operations, and reject malicious manipulations. In some cases, blind authentication schemes that directly analyze the homogeneous properties of multimedia data itself, without any prior digital signature or watermarks, are desired in several applications.

Our works in developing watermarking and digital signature techniques for multimedia authentication and copyright protection have demonstrated that, although there are still a lot of open issues, trustworthy multimedia data is a realistic achievable goal.

ACKNOWLEDGMENTS

We would like to thank Professor Shih-Fu Chang and Ms. Lexing Xie for their assistance with the content of this chapter.

REFERENCES

Barni, M., Bartolini, F., De Rosa, A., & Piva, A. (1999, January). Capacity of the watermark-channel: How many bits can be hidden within a digital image? *Proceedings of SPIE, 3657.*

Bhattacharjee, S., & Kutter, M. (1998, October). Compression tolerant image authentication. *IEEE ICIP,* Chicago, IL.

Burges, C. (1998). A tutorial on support vector machines for pattern recognition. *Data Mining and Knowledge Discovery, 2,* 121-167.

Carlin, B., & Louis, T. (1996). Bayes and empirical Bayes methods for data analysis. *Monographs on Statistics and Applied Probability, 69.* Chapman & Hall.

Csiszar, I., & Narayan, P. (1991, January). Capacity of the Gaussian arbitrarily varying channel. *IEEE Trans. on Information Theory, 37*(1), 18-26.

Diffle, W., & Hellman, M.E. (1976, November). New directions in cryptography. *IEEE Trans. on Information Theory, 22*(6), 644-654.

Dudani, S., Breeding, K., & McGhee, R. (1977, January). Aircraft identification by moment invariants. *IEEE Trans. on Computers, C-26*(1), 390-45.

Fridirch, J. (1998, October). Image watermarking for tamper detection. *IEEE ICIP,* Chicago.

Heckerman, D. (1996, November). *A tutorial on learning with Bayesian networks.* Technical Report MSR-TR-95-06. Microsoft Research.

Jaimes, A., & Chang, S.-F. (2000, January). A conceptual framework for indexing visual information at multiple levels. *SPIE Internet Imaging.* San Jose, CA.

Korner, J., & Orlitsky, A. (1998, October). Zero-error information theory. *IEEE Trans. on Information Theory, 44*(6).

Lin, C.-Y. (2000). *Watermarking and digital signature techniques for multimedia authentication and copyright protection.* PhD thesis, Columbia University.

Lin, C.-Y., & Chang, S.-F. (2000, January). Semi-fragile watermarking for authenticating JPEG visual content. *Proceedings of SPIE, 3971.*

Lin, C.-Y., & Chang, S.-F. (2001, February). A robust image authentication method distinguishing JPEG compression from malicious manipulation. *IEEE Trans. on Circuit and System for Video Technology, 11*(2), 153-168.

Lin, C.-Y., & Chang, S.-F. (2001, April). Watermarking capacity of digital images based on domain-specific masking effects. *IEEE Intl. Conf. on Information Technology: Coding and Computing*, Las Vegas.

Lin, C.-Y., & Chang, S.-F. (2001, October). SARI: Self-authentication-and-recovery watermarking system. *ACM Multimedia 2001,* Ottawa, Canada.

Lin, C.-Y., Sow, D., & Chang, S.-F. (2001, August). Using self-authentication-and- recovery for error concealment in wireless environments. *Proceedings of SPIE, 4518.*

Lin, C.-Y., & Tseng, B.L. (n.d.). VideoAnnEx: MPEG-7 video annotation. Available online: http://www.research.ibm.com/VideoAnnEx.

Lin, C.-Y., Wu, M., Bloom, J.A., Miller, M.L., Cox, I.J., & Lui, Y.M. (2001, May). Rotation, Scale, and Translation Resilient Public Watermarking for Images. *IEEE Trans. on IP,* May 2001.

Lu, C.-S., & Mark Liao, H.-Y. (2001, October). Multipurpose watermarking for image authentication and protection. *IEEE Trans. on Image Processing, 1010,* 1579-1592.

Lu, C.-S., & Mark Liao, H.-Y. (2003, February). Structural digital signature for image authentication: An incidental distortion resistant scheme. *IEEE Trans. on Multimedia, 5*(2), 161-173.

Lubin, J. (1993). The use of psychophysical data and models in the analysis of display system performance. In A.B. Watson (Ed.), *Digital images and human vision* (pp. 163-178). MIT Press.

Pennebaker, W.B., & Mitchell, J.L. (1993). JPEG: Still image data compression standard. *Van Nostrand Reinhold.* New York: Tomson Publishing.

Queluz, M.P. (1999, January). Content-based integrity protection of digital images. *SPIE Conf. on Security and Watermarking of Multimedia Contents, 3657,* San Jose.

Ramkumar, M., & Akansu, A.N. (1999, May). A capacity estimate for data hiding in Internet multimedia. *Symposium on Content Security and Data Hiding in Digital Media,* NJIT, Jersey City.

Schneider, M., & Chang, S.-F. (1996, October). A robust content based digital signature for image authentication. *IEEE ICIP,* Laussane, Switzerland.

Schneier, B. (1996). *Applied cryptography.* John Wiley & Sons.

Servetto, S.D., Podilchuk, C.I., & Ramchandran, K. (1998, October). Capacity issues in digital image watermarking. *IEEE Intl. Conf. on Image Processing.*

Shannon, C.E. (1948). A mathematical theory of communication. *Bell System Technical Journal, 27,* 373-423, 623-656.

Shannon, C.E. (1956). The zero-error capacity of a noisy channel. *IRE Trans. on Information Theory, IT-2,* 8-19.

Tamura, H., Mori, S., & Yamawaki, T. (1978). Texture features corresponding to visual perception. *IEEE Trans. on Sys. Man., and Cybemetics, 8*(6).

Watson, A.B. (1993). DCT quantization matrices visually optimized for individual images. *Proceeding of SPIE, 1913,* 202-216.

ENDNOTES

1. Note that Q_w can be assumed to be uniform in all coefficients in the same DCT frequency position, or they can be non-uniform if we adopt some human perceptual properties. For Case 2, we assume the uniform property, while whether Q_w is uniform or non-uniform does not affect our discussion in Case 3.
2. Some application software may discard all the 29th .. 64th DCT coefficients regardless of their magnitudes.
3. We use *QR = 2* for the Insurance image because the visual degradation of *QR = 4* is clearly visible.

Chapter VII

Digital Signature-Based Image Authentication

Der-Chyuan Lou, National Defense University, Taiwan

Jiang-Lung Liu, National Defense University, Taiwan

Chang-Tsun Li, University of Warwick, UK

ABSTRACT

This chapter is intended to disseminate the concept of digital signature-based image authentication. Capabilities of digital signature-based image authentication and its superiority over watermarking-based approaches are described first. Subsequently, general models of this technique — strict authentication and non-strict authentication are introduced. Specific schemes of the two general models are also reviewed and compared. Finally, based on the review, design issues faced by the researchers and developers are outlined.

INTRODUCTION

In the past decades, the technological advances of international communication networks have facilitated efficient digital image exchanges. However, the availability of versatile digital signal/image processing tools has also made image duplication trivial and manipulations discernable for the human visual system (HVS). Therefore, image authentication and integrity verification have become a popular research area in recent years. Generally, image authentication is projected as a procedure of guaranteeing that the image content has not been altered, or at least that the visual (or semantic) characteristics of the image are maintained after incidental manipulations such as JPEG compression. In other words, one of the objectives of image authentication is to verify the integrity of the image. For many applications such as medical archiving, news reporting and political events, the capability of detecting manipulations of digital images is often required. Another need for image authentication arises from the requirement of checking the identity of the image sender. In the scenario that a buyer wants to purchase and receive an image over the networks, the buyer may obtain the image via e-mails or from the Internet-attached servers that may give a malicious third party the opportunities to intercept and manipulate the original image. So the buyer needs to assure that the received image is indeed the original image sent by the seller. This requirement is referred to as the *legitimacy* requirement in this chapter.

To address both the integrity and legitimacy issues, a wide variety of techniques have been proposed for image authentication recently. Depending on the ways chosen to convey the authentication data, these techniques can be roughly divided into two categories: *labeling-based techniques* (e.g., the method proposed by Friedman, 1993) and *watermarking-based techniques* (e.g., the method proposed by Walton, 1995). The main difference between these two categories of techniques is that labeling-based techniques create the authentication data in a separate file while watermarking-based authentication can be accomplished without the overhead of a separate file. However, compared to watermarking-based techniques, labeling-based techniques potentially have the following advantages.

- They can detect the change of every single bit of the image data if strict integrity has to be assured.
- The image authentication can be performed in a secure and robust way in public domain (e.g., the Internet).
- The data hiding capacity of labeling-based techniques is higher than that of watermarking.

Given its advantages on watermarking-based techniques, we will focus on labeling-based authentication techniques.

In labeling-based techniques, the authentication information is conveyed in a separate file called *label.* A label is additional information associated with the image content and can be used to identify the image. In order to associate the label content with the image content, two different ways can be employed and are stated as follows.

- The first methodology uses the functions commonly adopted in message authentication schemes to generate the authentication data. The authentication data are then encrypted with secret keys or private keys depending on what cryptographic authentication protocol is employed. When applying to two different bit-streams (i.e., different authentication data), these functions can produce two different bit sequences, in such a way that the change of every single bit of authentication data can be detected. In this chapter, image authentication schemes of this class are referred to as *strict authentication.*

- The second methodology uses some special-purpose functions to extract essential image characteristics (or *features*) and encrypt them with senders' private keys (Li, Lou & Chen, 2000; Li, Lou & Liu, 2003). This procedure is the same as the digital signature protocol except that the features must be designed to compromise with some specific image processing techniques such as JPEG compression (Wallace, 1991). In this chapter, image authentication techniques of this class are referred to as *non-strict authentication.*

The strict authentication approaches should be used when strict image integrity is required and no modification is allowed. The functions used to produce such authentication data (or *authenticators*) can be grouped into three classes: *message encryption, message authentication code* (MAC), and *hash function* (Stallings, 2002). For *message encryption,* the original message is encrypted. The encrypted result (or cipher-text) of the entire message serves as its authenticator. To authenticate the content of an image, both the sender and receiver share the same secret key. *Message authentication code* is a fixed-length value (authenticator) that is generated by a public function with a secret key. The sender and receiver also share the same secret key that is used to generate the authenticator. A *hash function* is a public function that maps a message of any length to a fixed-length hash value that serves as the authenticator. Because there is no secret key adopted in creating an authenticator, the hash functions have to be included in the procedure of digital signature for the electronic exchange of message. The details of how to perform those labeling-based authentication schemes and how to obtain the authentication data are described in the second section.

The non-strict authentication approaches must be chosen when some forms of image modifications (e.g., JPEG lossy compression) are permitted, while malicious manipulation (e.g., objects' deletion and modification) must be detected. This task can be accomplished by extracting features that are invariant to predefined image modifications. Most of the proposed techniques in the literature adopted the same authentication procedure as that performed in digital signature to resolve the legitimacy problem, and exploited invariant features of images to resolve the non-strict authentication. These techniques are often regarded as digital signature-based techniques and will be further discussed in the rest of this chapter. To make the chapter self-contained, some labeling-based techniques that do not follow the standard digital-signature procedures are also introduced in this chapter.

This chapter is organized as follows. Following the introduction in the first section, the second section presents some generic models including strict and non-strict ones for digital signature-based image authentication. This is followed by a section discussing various techniques for image authentication. Next, the chapter addresses the challenges for designing secure digital signature-based image authentication methods. The final section concludes this chapter.

GENERIC MODELS

The digital signature-based image authentication is based on the concept of digital signature, which is derived from a cryptographic technique called public-key cryptosystem (Diffie & Hellman, 1976; Rivest, Shamir & Adleman, 1978). Figure 1 shows the basic model of digital signature. The sender first uses a hash function, such as MD5 (Rivest, 1992), to hash the content of the original data (or *plaintext*) to a small file (called *digest*). Then the digest is encrypted with the sender's private key. The encrypted digest can form a unique "signature" because only the sender has the knowledge of the private key. The signature is then sent to the receiver along with the original information. The receiver can use the sender's public key to decrypt the signature, and obtain the original digest. Of course, the received information can be hashed by using the same hash function in the sender side. If the decrypted digest matches the newly created digest, the legitimacy and the integrity of the message are therefore authenticated.

There are two points worth noting in the process of digital signature. First, the plaintext is not limited to text file. In fact, any types of digital data, such as digitized audio data, can be the original data. Therefore, the original data in Figure 1 can be replaced with a digital image, and the process of digital signature can then be used to verify the legitimacy and integrity of the image. The concept of trustworthy digital camera (Friedman, 1993) for image authentication is based on this idea. In this chapter, this type of image authentication is referred to as *digital signature-based image authentication.* Second, the hash function is a mathematical digest function. If a single bit of the original image is changed, it may result in a different hash output. Therefore, the strict integrity of the image can be verified, and this is called strict authentication in this chapter. The framework of strict authentication is described in the following subsection.

Figure 1. Process of digital signature

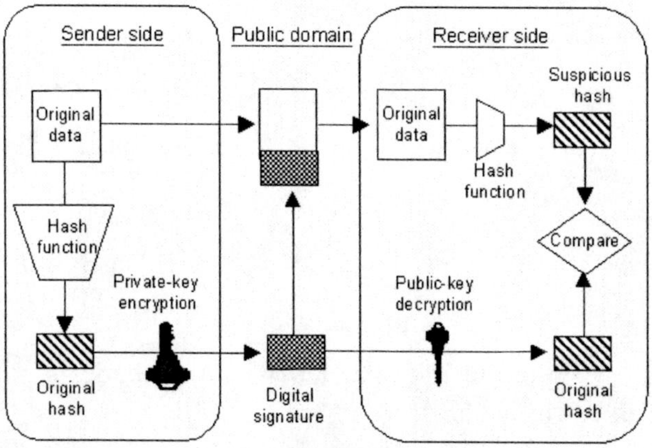

Strict Authentication

Figure 2 shows the main elements and their interactions in a generic digital signature-based model for image authentication. Assume that the sender wants to send an image I to the receiver, and the legitimate receiver needs to assure the legitimacy and integrity of I. The image I is first hashed to a small file h. Accordingly:

$$h = \mathrm{H}(I), \quad \textbf{(1)}$$

where $\mathrm{H}(\cdot)$ denotes hash operator. The hashed result h is then encrypted (signed) with the sender's private key K_R to generate the signature:

$$S = \mathrm{E}_{K_R}(h), \quad \textbf{(2)}$$

where $\mathrm{E}(\cdot)$ denotes the public-key encryption operator. The digital signature S is then attached to the original image to form a composite message:

$$M = I \,||\, S, \quad \textbf{(3)}$$

where "||" denotes concatenation operator.

If the legitimacy and integrity of the received image I' needs to be verified, the receiver first separates the suspicious image I' from the composite message, and hashes it to obtain the new hashed result, that is:

$$h' = \mathrm{H}(I'). \quad \textbf{(4)}$$

Figure 2. Process of digital signature-based strict authentication

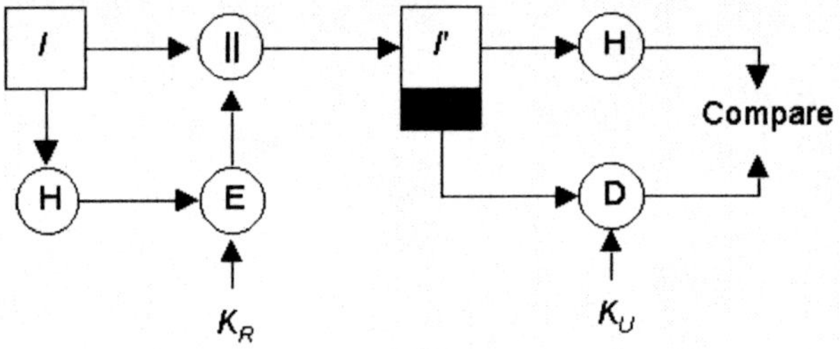

The attached signature is decrypted with the sender's public-key K_p to obtain the possible original hash code:

$$\hat{h} = \mathrm{D}_{Kp}(\hat{S}), \qquad (5)$$

where $\mathrm{D}(\cdot)$ denotes the public-key decryption operator. Note that we use $\hat{S}$ and $\hat{h}$ respectively to represent the received signature and its hash result because the received signature may be a forged one. The legitimacy and integrity can be confirmed by comparing the newly created hash h' and the possible original hash $\hat{h}$. If they match with each other, we can claim that the received image I' is authentic.

The above framework can be employed to make certain the strict integrity of an image because of the characteristics of the hash functions. In the process of digital signature, one can easily create the hash of an image, but it is difficult to reengineer a hash to obtain the original image. This can be also referred to "*one-way*" property. Therefore, the hash functions used in digital signature are also called *one-way hash* functions. MD5 and SHA (NIST FIPS PUB, 1993) are two good examples of one-way hash functions. Besides one-way hash functions, there are other authentication functions that can be utilized to perform the strict authentication. Those authentication functions can be classified into two broad categories: conventional encryption functions and message authentication code (MAC) functions.

Figure 3 illustrates the basic authentication framework for using conventional encryption functions. An image, *I*, transmitted from the sender to the receiver, is encrypted using a secret key *K* that was shared by both sides. If the decrypted image *I'* is meaningful, then the image is authentic. This is because only the legitimate sender has the shared secret key. Although this is a very straightforward method for strict image authentication, it also provides oppo-

Figure 3. Process of encryption function-based strict authentication

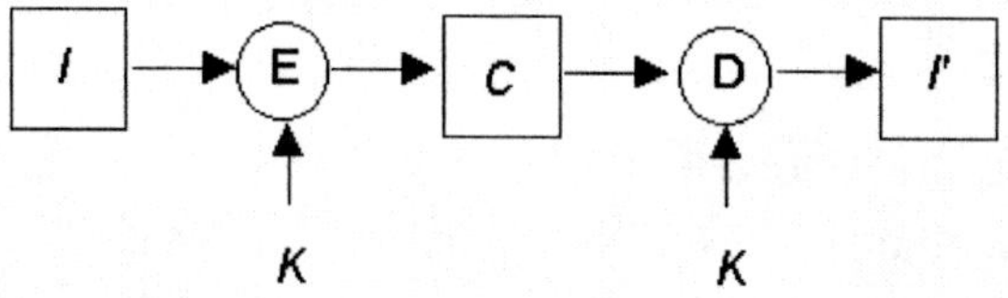

nents opportunities to forge a meaningful image. For example, if an opponent has the pair of (I, C), he/she can forge an intelligible image I' by the *cutting and pasting* method (Li, Lou & Liu, 2003). One solution to this problem is to use the message authentication code (MAC).

Figure 4 demonstrates the basic model of MAC-based strict authentication. The MAC is a cryptographic checksum that is first generated with a shared secret key before the transmission of the original image I. The MAC is then transmitted to the receiver along with the original image. In order to assure the integrity, the receiver conducts the same calculation on the received image I' using the same secret key to generate a new MAC. If the received MAC matches the calculated MAC, then the integrity of the received image is verified. This is because if an attacker alters the original image without changing the MAC, then the newly calculated MAC will still differ from the received MAC.

The MAC function is similar to the encryption one. One difference is that the MAC algorithm does not need to be reversible. Nevertheless, the decryption formula must be reversible. It results from the mathematical properties of the authentication function. It is less vulnerable to be broken than the encryption function. Although MAC-based strict authentication can detect the fake image created by an attacker, it cannot avoid "legitimate" forgery. This is because both the sender and the receiver share the same secret key. Therefore, the receiver can create a fake image with the shared secret key, and claim that this created image is received from the legitimate sender.

With the existing problems of encryption and MAC functions, the digital signature-based method seems a better way to perform strict authentication.

Figure 4. Process of MAC-based strict authentication

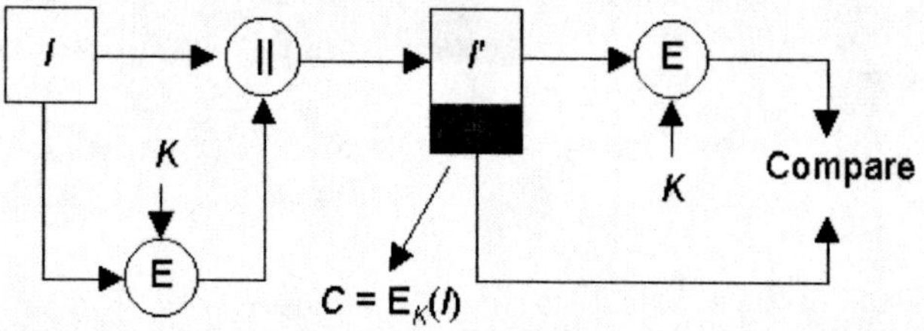

Following the increasing applications that can tolerate one or more content-preserving manipulations, non-strict authentication becomes more and more important nowadays.

Non-Strict Authentication

Figure 5 shows the process of non-strict authentication. As we can see, the procedure of non-strict authentication is similar to that of strict authentication except that the function here used to digest the image is a special-design feature extraction function f_C.

Assume that the sender wants to deliver an image I to the receiver. A feature extraction function f_C is used to extract the image feature and to encode it to a small feature code:

$$C = f_C(I), \quad \textbf{(6)}$$

where $f_C(\cdot)$ denotes feature extraction and coding operator. The extracted feature code has three significant properties. First, the size of extracted feature code is relatively small compared to the size of the original image. Second, it preserves the characteristics of the original image. Third, it can tolerate incidental modifications of the original image. The feature code C is then encrypted (signed) with the sender's private key K_R to generate the signature:

$$S = \mathrm{E}_{K_R}(C). \quad \textbf{(7)}$$

The digital signature S is then attached to the original image to form a composite message:

$$M = I \,||\, S. \quad \textbf{(8)}$$

Figure 5. Process of non-strict authentication

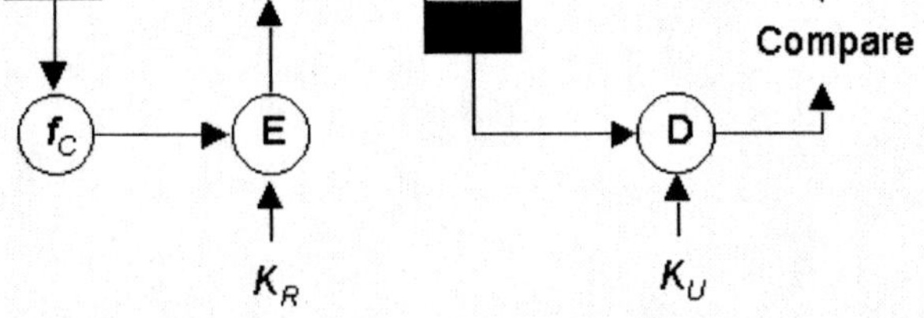

Then the composite message M is forwarded to the receiver. The original image may be lossy compressed, decompressed, or tampered during transmission. Therefore, the received composite message may include a corrupted image I'. The original I may be compressed prior to the concatenation operation. If a lossy compression strategy is adopted, the original image I in the composite message can be considered as a corrupted one.

In order to verify the legitimacy and integrity of the received image I', the receiver first separates the corrupted image I' from the composite message, and generates a feature code C' by using the same feature extraction function in the sender side, that is:

$$C' = f_C(I'). \tag{9}$$

The attached signature is decrypted with the sender's public-key K_U to obtain the original feature code:

$$\hat{C} = \mathrm{D}_{K_U}(\hat{S}). \tag{10}$$

Note that we use $\hat{S}$ and $\hat{C}$ to represent the received signature and feature code here because the signature may be forged.

The legitimacy and integrity can be verified by comparing the newly generated feature C' and the received feature code $\hat{C}$. To differentiate the errors caused by authorized modifications from the errors of malevolent manipulations, let $d(C, C')$ be the measurement of similarity between the extracted features and the original. Let T denote a tolerable threshold value for examining the values of $d(C, C')$ (e.g., it can be obtained by performing a maximum compression to an image). The received image may be considered authentic if the condition $< T$ is met.

Defining a suitable function to generate a feature code that satisfies the requirements for non-strict authentication is another issue. Ideally, employing a feature code should be able to detect content-changing modifications and tolerate content-preserving modifications. The content-changing modifications may include cropping, object addition, deletion, and modification, and so forth, while the content-preserving modifications may include lossy compression, format conversion and contrast *enhancing,* etc.

It is difficult to devise a feature code that is sensitive to all the content-changing modifications, while it remains insensitive to all the content-preserving modifications. A practical approach to design a feature extraction function would be based on the manipulation methods (e.g., JPEG lossy compression). As we will see in the next section, most of the proposed non-strict authentication techniques are based on this idea.

STATE OF THE ART

In this section, several existing digital signature-based image authentication schemes are detailed. Specifically, works related strict authentication is described in the first subsection and non-strict ones in the second subsection. Note that the intention of this section is to describe the methodology of the techniques. Some related problems about these techniques will be further discussed in the fourth section, in which some issues of designing practical schemes of digital signature-based image authentication are also discussed.

Strict Authentication

Friedman (1993) associated the idea of digital signature with digital camera, and proposed a "trustworthy digital camera," which is illustrated as Figure 6. The proposed digital camera uses a digital sensor instead of film, and delivers the image directly in a computer-compatible format. A secure microprocessor is assumed to be built in the digital camera and be programmed with the private key at the factory for the encryption of the digital signature. The public key necessary for later authentication appears on the camera body as well as the image's border. Once the digital camera captures the objective image, it produces two output files. One is an all-digital industry-standard file format representing the captured image; the other is an encrypted digital signature generated by applying the camera's unique private key (embedded in the camera's secure microprocessor) to a hash of the captured image file, a procedure described in the second

Figure 6. Idea of the trustworthy digital camera

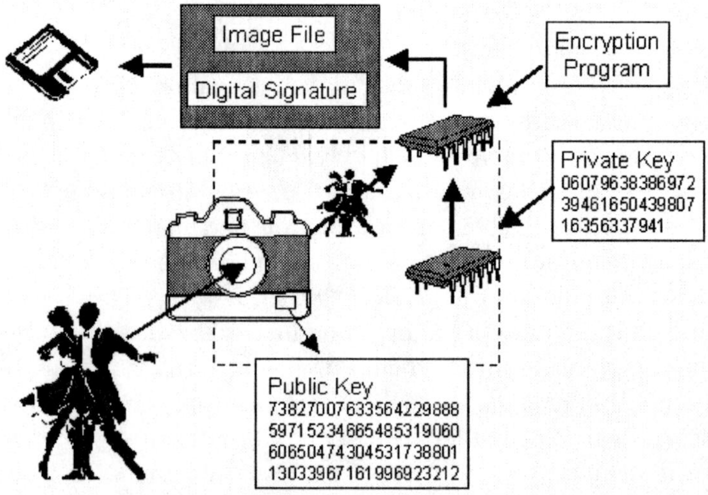

Figure 7. Verification process of Friedman's idea

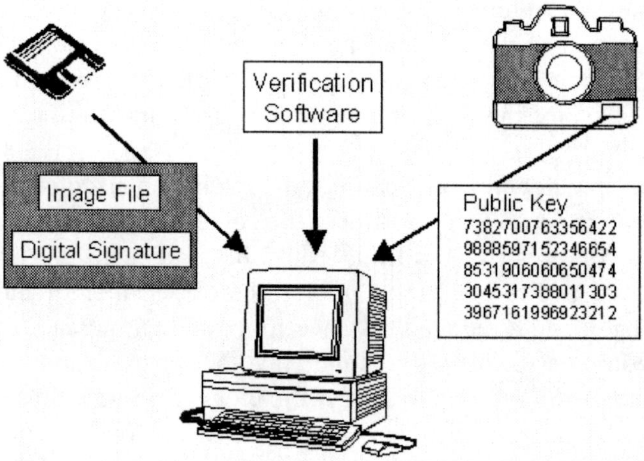

section. The digital image file and the digital signature can later be distributed freely and safely.

The verification process of Friedman's idea is illustrated in Figure 7. The image authentication can be accomplished with the assistance of the public domain verification software. To authenticate a digital image file, the digital image, its accompanying digital signature file, and the public key are needed by the verification software running on a standard computer platform. The program then calculates the hash of the input image, and uses the public key to decode the digital signature to reveal the original hash. If these two hash values match, the image is considered to be authentic. If these two hash values are different, the integrity of this image is questionable.

It should be noted that the hash values produced by using the cryptographic algorithm such as MD5 will not match if a single bit of the image file is changed. This is the characteristic of the strict authentication, but it may not be suitable for authenticating images that undergo lossy compression. In this case, the strict authentication code (hash values) should be generated in a non-strict way. Non-strict authentication schemes have been proposed for developing such algorithms.

Non-Strict Authentication

Instead of using a strict authentication code, Schneider and Chang (1996) used content-based data as the authentication code. Specifically, the content-based data can be considered to be the image feature. As the image feature is invariant for some content-preserving transformation, the original image can also be authenticated although it may be manipulated by some allowable image transformations. The edge information, DCT coefficients, color, and intensity histograms are regarded as potentially invariant features. In Schneider and Chang's method, the intensity histogram is employed as the invariant feature in the implementation of the content-based image authentication scheme. To be effective, the image is divided into blocks of variable sizes and the intensity histogram of each block is computed separately and is used as the authentication code.

To tolerate incidental modifications, the Euclidean distance between intensity histograms was used as a measure of the content of the image. It is reported that the lossy compression ratio that could be applied to the image without producing a false positive is limited to 4:1 at most. Schneider and Chang also pointed out that using a reduced distance function can increase the maximum permissible compression ratio. It is found that the alarm was not triggered even at a high compression ratio up to 14:1 if the block average intensity is used for detecting image content manipulation. Several works have been proposed in the literature based on this idea. They will be introduced in the rest of this subsection.

Feature-Based Methods

The major purpose of using the image digest (hash values) as the signature is to speed up the signing procedure. It will violate the principle of the digital signature if large-size image features were adopted in the authentication scheme. Bhattacharjee and Kutter (1998) proposed another algorithm to extract a smaller size feature of an image. Their feature extraction algorithm is based on the so-called *scale interaction model.* Instead of using Gabor wavelets, they adopted Mexican-Hat wavelets as the filter for detecting the feature points. The algorithm for detecting feature-points is depicted as follows.

- Define the feature-detection function, $P_{ij}(\cdot)$ as:

$$P_{ij}(\vec{x}) = |M_i(\vec{x}) - \gamma \cdot M_j(\vec{x})| \qquad \textbf{(11)}$$

where $M_i(\vec{x})$ and $M_j(\vec{x})$ represent the responses of Mexican-Hat wavelets at the image-location $\vec{x}$ for scales i and j, respectively. For the image A, the wavelet response $M_i(\vec{x})$ is given by:

$$M_i(\vec{x}) = \langle (2^{-i}\psi(2^{-i} \cdot \vec{x})); A \rangle \qquad \textbf{(12)}$$

where <·;·> denotes the convolution of its operands. The normalizing constant γ is given by $\gamma = 2^{-(i-j)}$, the operator $|\cdot|$ returns the absolute value of its parameter, and the $\psi(\vec{x})$ represents the response of the Mexican-Hat mother wavelet, and is defined as:

$$\psi(\vec{x}) = (2 - |\vec{x}|^2)\exp(-\frac{\vec{x}^2}{2}) \quad \textbf{(13)}$$

- Determine points of local maximum of $P_{ij}(\cdot)$. These points correspond to the set of potential feature points.
- Accept a point of local maximum in $P_{ij}(\cdot)$ as a feature-point if the variance of the image-pixels in the neighborhood of the point is higher than a threshold. This criterion eliminates suspicious local maximum in featureless regions of the image.

The column-positions and row-positions of the resulting feature points are concatenated to form a string of digits, and then encrypted to generate the image signature. It is not hard to imagine that the file constructed in this way can have a smaller size compared to that constructed by recording the block histogram.

In order to determine whether an image *A* is authentic with another known image *B*, the feature set S_A of *A* is computed. The feature set S_A is then compared with the feature set S_B of *B* that is decrypted from the signature of *B*. The following rules are adopted to authenticate the image *A*.

- Verify that each feature location is present both in S_B and in S_A.
- Verify that no feature location is present in S_A but absent in S_B.
- Two feature points with coordinates $\vec{x}$ and $\vec{y}$ are said to match if:

$$|\vec{x} - \vec{y}| < 2 \quad \textbf{(14)}$$

Edge-Based Methods

The edges in an image are the boundaries or contours where the significant changes occur in some physical aspects of an image, such as the surface reflectance, illumination, or the distances of the visible surfaces from the viewer. Edges are kinds of strong content features for an image. However, for common picture formats, coding edges value and position produces a huge overhead. One way to resolve this problem is to use a binary map to represent the edge. For example, Li, Lou and Liu (2003) used a binary map to encode the edges of an image in their watermarking-based image authentication scheme. It should be concerned that edges (both their position and value, and also the resulting binary image) might be modified if high compression ratios are used. Consequently, the success of using edges as the authentication code is greatly dependent on the

Figure 8. Process of edge extraction proposed by Queluz (2001)

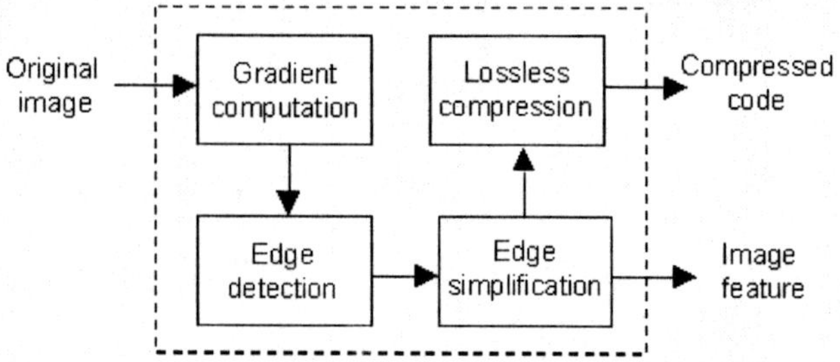

capacity of the authentication system to discriminate the differences the edges produced by content-preserving manipulations from those content-changing manipulations. Queluz (2001) proposed an algorithm for edges extraction and edges integrity evaluation.

The block diagram of the edge extraction process of Queluz's method is shown as Figure 8. The gradient is first computed at each pixel position with an edge extraction operator. The result is then compared with an image-dependent threshold obtained from the image gradient histogram to obtain a binary image marking edge and no-edge pixels. Depending on the specifications for label size, the bit-map could be sub-sampled with the purpose of reducing its spatial resolution. Finally, the edges of the bit-map are encoded (compressed).

Edges integrity evaluation process is shown as Figure 9. In the *edges difference computation* block, the suspicious error pixels that have differences between the original and computed edge bit-maps and a certitude value associated with each error pixel are produced. These suspicious error pixels are evaluated in an *error relaxation* block. This is done by iteratively changing low certitude errors to high certitude errors if necessary, until no further change occurs. At the end, all high certitude errors are considered to be true errors and

Figure 9. Process of edges integrity evaluation proposed by Queluz (2001)

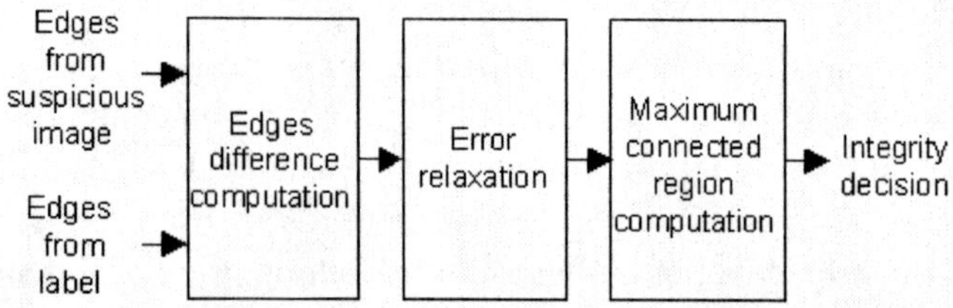

low certitude errors are eliminated. After error relaxation, the maximum connected region is computed according to a predefined threshold.

A similar idea was also proposed by Dittmann, Steinmetz and Steinmetz (1999). The feature-extraction process starts with extracting the edge characteristics C_I of the image I with the Canny edge detector E (Canny, 1986). The C_I is then transformed to a binary edge pattern EP_{CI}. The variable length coding is then used to compress EP_{CI} into a feature code. This process is formulated as follows:

- Feature extraction: $C_I = E(I)$;
- Binary edge pattern: $EP_{CI} = f(C_I)$;
- Feature code: $VLC(EP_{CI})$.

The verification process begins with calculating the actual image edge characteristic C_T and the binary edge pattern EP_{CT}. The original binary edge pattern EP_{CI} is obtained by decompressing the received $VLC(EP_{CI})$. The EP_{CI} and CP_{CT} are then compared to obtain the error map. These steps can also be formulated as follows:

- Extract feature: $C_T = E(T)$, $EP_{CT} = f(C_T)$;
- Extract the original binary pattern: EP_{CI} = Decompress($VLC(EP_{CI})$);
- Check $EP_{CI} = EP_{CT}$.

Mean-Based Methods

Using local mean as the image feature may be the simplest and most practical way to represent the content character of an image. For example, Lou and Liu (2000) proposed an algorithm to generate a mean-based feature code. Figure 10 shows the process of feature code generation. The original image is first divided into non-overlapping blocks. The mean of each block is then calculated and quantized according to a predefined parameter. All the calculated results are then encoded (compressed) to form the authentication code. Figure 11 shows an example of this process. Figure 11(a) is a 256×256 gray image, and is used as the original image. It is first divided into 8×8 non-overlapping blocks. The mean of each block is then computed and is shown as Figure 11(b). Figure 11(c) also shows the 16-step quantized block-means of Figure 11(b). The quantized block-means are further encoded to form the authentication code. It should be noted that Figure 11(c) is visually close to Figure 11(b). It means that the feature of the image is still preserved even though only the quantized block-means are encoded.

The verification process starts with calculating the quantized block-means of the received image. The quantized code is then compared with the original quantized code by using a sophisticated comparison algorithm. A binary error

Figure 10. Process of generation of image feature proposed by Lou and Liu (2000)

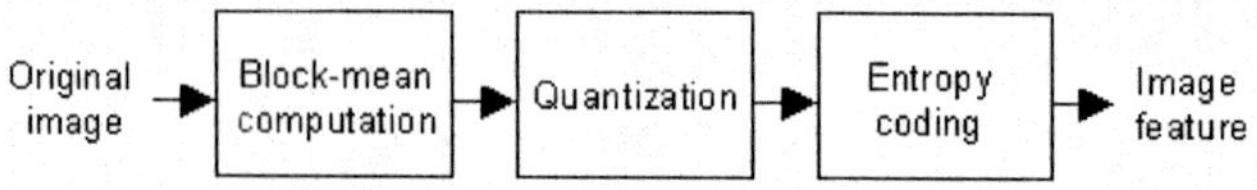

Figure 11. (a) Original image, (b) Map of block-means, (c) Map of 16-step quantized block-means

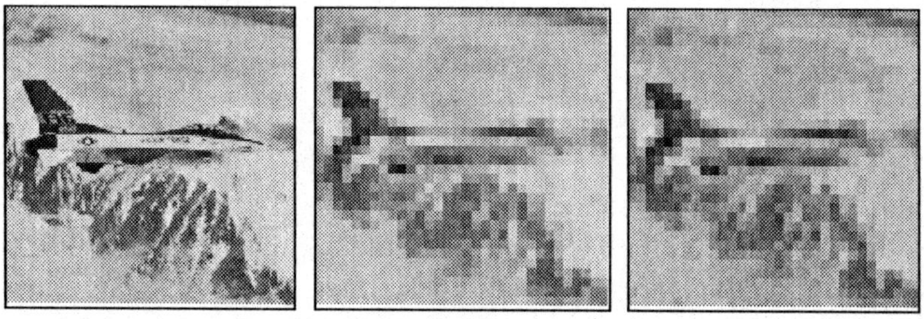

(a) (b) (c)

map is then produced as an output, with "1" denoting *match* and "0" denoting *mismatch.* The verifier can thus tell the possibly tampered blocks by inspecting the error map. It is worth mentioning that the quantized block-means can be used to repair the tampered blocks. This feasibility is attractive in the applications of the real-time image such as the video.

A similar idea was adopted in the process of generating the AIMAC (Approximate Image Message Authentication Codes) (Xie, Arce & Graveman, 2001). In order to construct a robust IMAC, an image is divided into non-overlapping 8×8 blocks, and the block mean of each block is computed. Then the most significant bit (MSB) of each block mean is extracted to form a binary map. The AIMAC is then generated according to this binary map. It should be noted that the histogram of the pixels in each block should be adjusted to preserve a gap of 127 gray levels for each block mean. In such a way, the MSB is robust enough to distinguish content-preserving manipulations from content-changing manipulations. This part has a similar effectiveness to the sophisticated comparison part of the algorithm proposed by Lou and Liu (2000).

Relation-Based Methods

Unlike the methods introduced above, relation-based methods divide the original image into non-overlapping blocks, and use the relation between blocks as the feature code. The method proposed by Lin and Chang (1998, 2001) is called SARI. The feature code in SARI is generated to survive the JPEG compression. To serve this purpose, the process of the feature code generation starts with dividing the original image into 8×8 non-overlapping blocks. Each block is then DCT transformed. The transformed DCT blocks are further grouped into two non-overlapping sets. There are equal numbers of DCT blocks in each set (i.e., there are *N*/2 DCT blocks in each set if the original image is divided into *N* blocks). A secret key-dependent mapping function then one-to-one maps each DCT block in one set into another DCT block in the other set, and generates *N*/2 DCT block pairs. For each block pair, a number of DCT coefficients are then selected and compared. The feature code is then generated by comparing the corresponding coefficients of the paired blocks. For example, if the coefficient in the first DCT block is greater than the coefficient in the second DCT block, then code is generated as "1". Otherwise, a "0" is generated. The process of generating the feature code is illustrated as Figure 12.

To extract the feature code of the received image, the same secret key should be applied in the verification process. The extracted feature code is then compared with the original feature code. If either block in each block pair has not been maliciously manipulated, the relation between the selected coefficients is maintained. Otherwise, the relation between the selected coefficients may be changed.

It can be proven that the relationship between the selected DCT coefficients of two given image blocks is maintained even after the JPEG compression by using the same quantization matrix for the whole image. Consequently, SARI authentication system can distinguish JPEG compression from other malicious manipulations. Moreover, SARI can locate the tampered blocks because it is a block-wise method.

Figure 12. Feature code generated with SARI authentication scheme

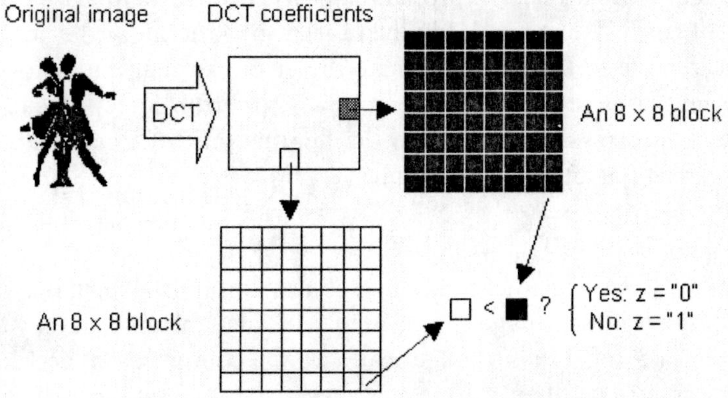

Structure-Based Methods

Lu and Liao (2000, 2003) proposed another kind of method to generate the feature code. The feature code is generated according to the structure of the image content. More specifically, the content structure of an image is composed of parent-child pairs in the wavelet domain. Let $w_{s,o}(x, y)$ be a wavelet coefficient at the scale s. Orientation o denotes horizontal, vertical, or diagonal direction. The inter-scale relationship of wavelet coefficients is defined for the parent node $w_{s+1,o}(x, y)$ and its four children nodes $w_{s,o}(2x+i, 2y+j)$ as either $|w_{s+1,o}(x, y)| \geq |w_{s,o}(2x+i, 2y+j)|$ or $|w_{s+1,o}(x, y)| \leq |w_{s,o}(2x+i, 2y+j)|$, where $0 \leq i, j \leq 1$.

The authentication code is generated by recording the parent-child pair that satisfies $||w_{s+1,o}(x, y)| - |w_{s,o}(2x+i, 2y+j)|| > \rho$, where $\rho > 0$. Clearly, the threshold ρ is used to determine the size of the authentication code, and plays a trade-off role between robustness and fragility. It is proven that the inter-scale relationship is difficult to be destroyed by content-preserving manipulations and is hard to be preserved by content-changing manipulations.

DESIGN ISSUES

Digital signature-based image authentication is an important element in the applications of image communication. Usually, the content verifiers are not the creator or the sender of the original image. That means the original image is not available during the authentication process. Therefore, one of the fundamental requirements for digital signature-based image authentication schemes is *blind authentication,* or *obliviousness,* as it is sometimes called. Other requirements depend on the applications that may be based on strict authentication or non-strict authentication. In this section, we will discuss some issues about designing effective digital signature-based image authentication schemes.

Error Detection

In some applications, it is proper if modification of an image can be detected by authentication schemes. However, it is beneficial if the authentication schemes are able to detect or estimate the errors so that the distortion can be compensated or even corrected. Techniques for error detection can be categorized into two classes according to the applications of image authentication; namely, error type and error location.

Error Type

Generally, strict authentication schemes can only determine whether the content of the original image is modified. This also means that they are not able to differentiate the types of distortion (e.g., compression or filtering). By contrast, non-strict authentication schemes tend to tolerate some form of errors.

The key to developing a non-strict authentication scheme is to examine what the digital signature should protect. Ideally, the authentication code should protect the message conveyed by the content of the image, but not the particular representation of that content of the image. Therefore, the authentication code can be used to verify the authenticity of an image that has been incidentally modified, leaving the value and meaning of its contents unaffected. Ideally, one can define an authenticity versus modification curve such as the method proposed by Schneider and Chang (1996) to achieve the desired authenticity. Based on the authenticity versus modification curve, authentication is no longer a yes-or-no question. Instead, it is a continuous interpretation. An image that is bit by bit identical to the original image has an authenticity measure of 1.0 and is considered to be completely authentic. An image that has nothing in common with the original image has an authenticity measure of 0.0 and is considered unauthentic. Each of the other images would have authenticity measure between the range (0.0, 1.0) and be partially authentic.

Error Location

Another desirable requirement for error detection in most applications is errors localization. This can be achieved by block-oriented approaches. Before transmission, an image is usually partitioned into blocks. The authentication code of each block is calculated (either for strict or non-strict authentication). The authentication codes of the original image are concatenated, signed, and transmitted as a separate file. To locate the distorted regions during the authenticating process, the received image is partitioned into blocks first. The authentication code of each block is calculated and compared with the authentication code recovered from the received digital signature. Therefore, the smaller the block size is, the better the localization accuracy is. However, the higher accuracy is gained at the expense of the larger authentication code file and the longer process of signing and decoding. The trade-off needs to be taken into account at the designing stage of an authentication scheme.

Error Correction

The purpose of error correction is to recover the original images from their manipulated version. This requirement is essential in the applications of military intelligence and motion pictures (Dittmann, Steinmetz & Steinmetz, 1999; Queluz, 2001). Error correction can be achieved by means of error correction code (ECC) (Lin & Costello, 1983). However, encrypting ECC along with feature code may result in a lengthy signature. Therefore, it is more advantageous to enable the authentication code itself to be the power of error correction. Unfortunately, the authentication code generated by strict authentication schemes is meaningless and cannot be used to correct the errors. Compared to strict authentication, the authentication code generated by non-strict authentication schemes is potentially capable of error correction. This is because the authentication code generated by the non-strict authentication is usually derived from the image feature and is highly content dependent.

An example of using authentication code for image error correction can be found in Xie, Arce and Graveman (2001). This work uses quantized image gray values as authentication code. The authenticated code is potentially capable of error correcting since image features are usually closely related to image gray values. It should be noted that the smaller the quantization step is, the better the performance of error correction is. However, a smaller quantization step also means a longer signature. Therefore, trade-off between the performance of error correction and the length of signature has to be made as well. This is, without doubt, an acute challenge, and worth further researching.

Security

With the protection of public-key encryption, the security of the digital signature-based image authentication is reduced to the security of the image digest function that is used to produce the authentication code. For strict authentication, the attacks on hash functions can be grouped into two categories: brute-force attacks and cryptanalysis attacks.

Brute-force Attacks

It is believed that, for a general-purpose secure hash code, the strength of a hash function against brute-force attacks depends solely on the length of the hash code produced by the algorithm. For a code of length *n,* the level of effort required is proportional to $2^{n/2}$. This is also known as *birthday attack.* For example, the length of the hash code of MD5 (Rivest, 1992) is 128 bits. If an attacker has 2^{64} different samples, he or she has more than 50% of chances to find the same hash code. In other words, to create a fake image that has the same hash result as the original image, an attacker only needs to prepare 2^{64} visually equivalent fake images. This can be accomplished by first creating a fake image and then varying the least significant bit of each of 64 arbitrarily chosen pixels of the fake image. It has been proved that we could find a collision in 24 days by using a $10 million collision search machine for MD5 (Stallings, 2002). A simple solution to this problem is to use a hash function to produce a longer hash code. For example, SHA-1 (NIST FIPS PUB 180, 1993) and RIPEMD-160 (Stallings, 2002) can provide 160-bit hash code. It is believed that over 4,000 years would be required if we used the same search machine to find a collision (Oorschot & Wiener, 1994). Another way to resolve this problem is to link the authentication code with the image feature such as the strategy adopted by non-strict authentication.

Non-strict authentication employs image feature as the image digest. This makes it harder to create enough visually equivalent fake images to forge a legal one. It should be noted that, mathematically, the relationship between the original image and the authentication code is many-to-one mapping. To serve the purpose of error tolerance, non-strict authentication schemes may have one authentication code corresponding to more images. This phenomenon makes non-strict authentication approaches vulnerable and remains as a serious design issue.

Cryptanalysis Attacks

Cryptanalysis attacks on digest function seek to exploit some property of the algorithm to perform some attack rather than an exhaustive search. Cryptanalysis on the strict authentication scheme is to exploit the internal structure of the hash function. Therefore, we have to select a secure hash function that can resist cryptanalysis performed by attackers. Fortunately, so far, SHA-1 and RIPEMD-160 are still secure for various cryptanalyses and can be included in strict authentication schemes. Cryptanalysis on non-strict authentication has not been defined so far. It may refer to the analysis of key-dependent digital signature-based schemes. In this case, an attacker tries to derive the secret key from multiple feature codes, which is performed in a SARI image authentication system (Radhakrisnan & Memon, 2001). As defined in the second section, there is no secret key involved in a digital signature-based authentication scheme. This means that the secrecy of the digital signature-based authentication schemes depends on the robustness of the algorithm itself and needs to be noted for designing a secure authentication scheme.

CONCLUSIONS

With the advantages of the digital signature (Agnew, Mullin & Vanstone, 1990; ElGamal, 1985; Harn, 1994; ISO/IEC 9796, 1991; NIST FIPS PUB, 1993; Nyberg & Rueppel, 1994; Yen & Laih, 1995), digital signature-based schemes are more applicable than any other schemes in image authentication. Depending on applications, digital signature-based authentication schemes are divided into strict and non-strict categories and are described in great detail in this chapter. For strict authentication, the authentication code derived from the calculation of traditional hash function is sufficiently short. This property enables fast creation of the digital signature. In another aspect, the arithmetic-calculated hash is very sensitive to the modification of image content. Some tiny changes to a single bit in an image may result in a different hash. This results in that strict authentication can provide binary authentication (i.e., yes or no). The trustworthy camera is a typical example of this type of authentication scheme.

For some image authentication applications, the authentication code should be sensitive for content-changing modification and can tolerate some content-preserving modification. In this case, the authentication code is asked to satisfy some basic requirements. Those requirements include locating modification regions and tolerating some forms of image processing operations (e.g., JPEG lossy compression). Many non-strict authentication techniques are also described in this chapter. Most of them are designed to employ a special-purpose authentication code to satisfy those basic requirements shown above. However, few of them are capable of recovering some certain errors. This special-purpose authentication code may be the modern and useful aspect for non-strict authentication.

Under the quick evolution of image processing techniques, existing digital signature-based image authentication schemes will be further improved to meet new requirements. New requirements pose new challenges for designing effective digital signature-based authentication schemes. These challenges may include using large-size authentication code and tolerating more image-processing operations without compromising security. This means that new approaches have to balance the trade-off among these requirements. Moreover, more modern techniques combining the watermark and digital signature techniques may be proposed for new image authentication generations. Those new image authentication techniques may result in some changes of the watermark and digital signature framework, as demonstrated in Sun and Chang (2002), Sun, Chang, Maeno and Suto (2002a, 2002b) and Lou and Sung (to appear).

REFERENCES

Agnew, G.B., Mullin, R.C., & Vanstone, S.A. (1990). Improved digital signature scheme based on discrete exponentiation. *IEEE Electronics Letters, 26,* 1024-1025.

Bhattacharjee, S., & Kutter, M. (1998). Compression tolerant image authentication. *Proceedings of the International Conference on Image Processing, 1,* 435-439.

Canny, J. (1986). A computational approach to edge detection. *IEEE Transactions on Pattern Analysis and Machine Intelligence, PAMI-8*(6), 679-698.

Diffie, W., & Hellman, M.E. (1976). New directions in cryptography. *IEEE Transactions on Information Theory, IT-22*(6), 644-654.

Dittmann, J., Steinmetz, A., & Steinmetz, R. (1999). Content-based digital signature for motion pictures authentication and content-fragile watermarking. *Proceedings of the IEEE International Conference On Multimedia Computing and Systems, 2,* 209-213.

ElGamal, T. (1985). A public-key cryptosystem and a signature scheme based on discrete logarithms. *IEEE Transactions on Information Theory, IT-31*(4), 469-472.

Friedman, G.L. (1993). The trustworthy digital camera: Restoring credibility to the photographic image. *IEEE Transactions on Consumer Electronics, 39*(4), 905-910.

Harn, L. (1994). New digital signature scheme based on discrete logarithm. *IEE Electronics Letters, 30*(5), 396-398.

ISO/IEC 9796. (1991). Information technology security techniques digital signature scheme giving message recovery. *International Organization for Standardization.*

Li, C.-T., Lou, D.-C., & Chen, T.-H. (2000). Image authentication via content-based watermarks and a public key cryptosystem. *Proceedings of the IEEE International Conference on Image Processing, 3,* 694-697.

Li, C.-T., Lou, D.-C., & Liu, J.-L. (2003). Image integrity and authenticity verification via content-based watermarks and a public key cryptosystem. *Journal of the Chinese Institute of Electrical Engineering, 10*(1), 99-106.

Lin, C.-Y., & Chang, S.-F. (1998). A robust image authentication method surviving JPEG lossy compression. *SPIE storage and retrieval of image/ video databases.* San Jose.

Lin, C.-Y., & Chang, S.-F. (2001). A robust image authentication method distinguishing JPEG Compression from malicious manipulation. *IEEE Transactions on Circuits and Systems of Video Technology, 11*(2), 153-168.

Lin, S., & Costello, D.J. (1983). *Error control coding: Fundamentals and applications.* NJ: Prentice-Hall.

Lou, D.-C., & Liu, J.-L. (2000). Fault resilient and compression tolerant digital signature for image authentication. *IEEE Transactions on Consumer Electronics, 46*(1), 31-39.

Lou, D.-C., & Sung, C.-H. (to appear). A steganographic scheme for secure communications based on the chaos and Euler theorem. *IEEE Transactions on Multimedia.*

Lu, C.-S., & Liao, M.H.-Y. (2000). Structural digital signature for image authentication: An incidental distortion resistant scheme. *Proceedings of Multimedia and Security Workshop at the ACM International Conference On Multimedia,* pp. 115-118.

Lu, C.-S., & Liao, M.H.-Y. (2003). Structural digital signature for image authentication: An incidental distortion resistant scheme. *IEEE Transactions on Multimedia, 5*(2), 161-173.

NIST FIPS PUB. (1993). *Digital signature standard.* National Institute of Standards and Technology, U.S. Department of Commerce, DRAFT.

NIST FIPS PUB 180. (1993). *Secure hash standard.* National Institute of Standards and Technology, U.S. Department of Commerce, DRAFT.

Nyberg, K., & Rueppel, R. (1994). Message recovery for signature schemes based on the discrete logarithm problem. *Proceedings of Eurocrypt'94,* 175-190.

Oorschot, P.V., & Wiener, M.J. (1994). Parallel collision search with application to hash functions and discrete logarithms. *Proceedings of the Second ACM Conference on Computer and Communication Security,* 210-218.

Queluz, M.P. (2001). Authentication of digital images and video: Generic models and a new contribution. *Signal Processing: Image Communication, 16,* 461-475.

Radhakrisnan, R., & Memon, N. (2001). On the security of the SARI image authentication system. *Proceedings of the IEEE International Conference on Image Processing, 3,* 971-974.

Rivest, R.L. (1992). The MD5 message digest algorithm. *Internet Request For Comments 1321.*

Rivest, R.L., Shamir, A., & Adleman, L. (1978). A method for obtaining digital signatures and public-key cryptosystems. *Communications of the ACM, 21*(2), 120-126.

Schneider, M., & Chang, S.-F. (1996). Robust content based digital signature for image authentication. *Proceedings of the IEEE International Conference on Image Processing, 3,* 227-230.

Stallings, W. (2002). *Cryptography and network security: Principles and practice* (3rd ed.). New Jersey: Prentice-Hall.

Sun, Q., & Chang, S.-F. (2002). Semi-fragile image authentication using generic wavelet domain features and ECC. *Proceedings of the 2002 International Conference on Image Processing, 2,* 901-904.

Sun, Q., Chang, S.-F., Maeno, K., & Suto, M. (2002a). A new semi-fragile image authentication framework combining ECC and PKI infrastructures. *Proceedings of the 2002 IEEE International Symposium on Circuits and Systems, 2,* 440-443.

Sun, Q., Chang, S.-F., Maeno, K., & Suto, M. (2002b). A quantitive semi-fragile JPEG2000 image authentication system. *Proceedings of the 2002 International Conference on Image Processing, 2,* 921-924.

Wallace, G.K. (1991, April). The JPEG still picture compression standard. *Communications of the ACM, 33,* 30-44.

Walton, S. (1995). Image authentication for a slippery new age. *Dr. Dobb's Journal, 20*(4), 18-26.

Xie, L., Arce, G.R., & Graveman, R.F. (2001). Approximate image message authentication codes. *IEEE Transactions on Multimedia, 3*(2), 242-252.

Yen, S.-M., & Laih, C.-S. (1995). Improved digital signature algorithm. *IEEE Transactions on Computers, 44*(5), 729-730.

Chapter VIII

Data Hiding in Document Images

Minya Chen, Polytechnic University, USA

Nasir Memon, Polytechnic University, USA

Edward K. Wong, Polytechnic University, USA

ABSTRACT

With the proliferation of digital media such as images, audio, and video, robust digital watermarking and data hiding techniques are needed for copyright protection, copy control, annotation, and authentication of document images. While many techniques have been proposed for digital color and grayscale images, not all of them can be directly applied to binary images in general and document images in particular. The difficulty lies in the fact that changing pixel values in a binary image could introduce irregularities that are very visually noticeable. Over the last few years, we have seen a growing but limited number of papers proposing new techniques and ideas for binary image watermarking and data hiding. In this chapter we present an overview and summary of recent developments on this important topic, and discuss important issues such as robustness and data hiding capacity of the different techniques.

INTRODUCTION

Given the increasing availability of cheap yet high quality scanners, digital cameras, digital copiers, printers and mass storage media the use of document images in practical applications is becoming more widespread. However, the same technology that allows for creation, storage and processing of documents in digital form, also provides means for mass copying and tampering of documents. Given the fact that digital documents need to be exchanged in printed format for many practical applications, any security mechanism for protecting digital documents would have to be compatible with the paper-based infrastructure. Consider for example the problem of authentication. Clearly an authentication tag embedded in the document should survive the printing process. That means that the authentication tag should be embedded inside the document data rather than appended to the bitstream representing the document. The reason is that if the authentication tag is appended to the bitstream, a forger could easily scan the document, remove the tag, and make changes to the scanned copy and then print the modified document.

The process of embedding information into digital content without causing perceptual degradation is called *data hiding*. A special case of data hiding is *digital watermarking* where the embedded signal can depend on a secret key. One main difference between data hiding and watermarking is in whether an active adversary is present. In watermarking applications like copyright protection and authentication, there is an active adversary that would attempt to remove, invalidate or forge watermarks. In data hiding there is no such active adversary as there is no value associated with the act of removing the hidden information. Nevertheless, data hiding techniques need to be robust against accidental distortions.

A special case of data hiding is *steganography* (meaning *covered writing* in Greek), which is the science and art of secret communication. Although steganography has been studied as part of cryptography for many decades, the focus of steganography is secret communication. In fact, the modern formulation of the problem goes by the name of the *prisoner's problem.* Here Alice and Bob are trying to hatch an escape plan while in prison. The problem is that all communication between them is examined by a warden, Wendy, who will place both of them in solitary confinement at the first hint of any suspicious communication. Hence, Alice and Bob must trade seemingly inconspicuous messages that actually contain hidden messages involving the escape plan. There are two versions of the problem that are usually discussed — one where the warden is *passive,* and only observes messages, and the other where the warden is *active* and modifies messages in a limited manner to guard against hidden messages. The most important issue in steganography is that the very presence of a hidden message must be concealed. Such a requirement is not critical in general data hiding and watermarking problems.

Before we describe the different techniques that have been devised for data hiding, digital watermarking and steganography for document images, we briefly list different applications that would be enabled by such techniques.

1. *Ownership assertion.* To assert ownership of a document, Alice can generate a watermarking signal using a secret private key, and embed it into the original document. She can then make the watermarked document publicly available. Later, when Bob contends the ownership of a copy derived from Alice's original, Alice can produce the unmarked original and also demonstrate the presence of her watermark in Bob's copy. Since Alice's original is unavailable to Bob, he cannot do the same provided Alice has embedded her watermark in the proper manner (Holliman & Memon, 2000). For such a scheme to work, the watermark has to survive operations aimed at malicious removal. In addition, the watermark should be inserted in such a manner that it cannot be forged, as Alice would not want to be held accountable for a document that she does not own (Craver et al., 1998).
2. *Fingerprinting.* In applications where documents are to be electronically distributed over a network, the document owner would like to discourage unauthorized duplication and distribution by embedding a distinct watermark (or a fingerprint) in each copy of the data. If, at a later point in time, unauthorized copies of the document are found, then the origin of the copy can be determined by retrieving the fingerprint. In this application the watermark needs to be invisible and must also be invulnerable to deliberate attempts to forge, remove or invalidate. The watermark should also be resistant to collusion. That is, a group of *k* users with the same document but containing different fingerprints should not be able to collude and invalidate any fingerprint or create a copy without any fingerprint.
3. *Copy prevention or control.* Watermarks can also be used for copy prevention and control. For example, every copy machine in an organization can include special software that looks for a watermark in documents that are copied. On finding a watermark the copier can refuse to create a copy of the document. In fact it is rumored that many modern currencies contain digital watermarks which when detected by a compliant copier will disallow copying of the currency. The watermark can also be used to control the number of copy generations permitted. For example a copier can insert a watermark in every copy it makes and then it would not allow further copying when presented a document that already contains a watermark.
4. *Authentication.* Given the increasing availability of cheap yet high quality scanners, digital cameras, digital copiers and printers, the authenticity of documents has become difficult to ascertain. Especially troubling is the threat that is posed to conventional and well established document based mechanisms for identity authentication, like passports, birth certificates, immigration papers, driver's license and picture IDs. It is becoming increasingly easier for individuals or groups that engage in criminal or terrorist activities to forge documents using off-the-shelf equipment and limited resources. Hence it is important to ensure that a given document

was originated from a specific source and that it has not been changed, manipulated or falsified. This can be achieved by embedding a watermark in the document. Subsequently, when the document is checked, the watermark is extracted using a unique key associated with the source, and the integrity of the data is verified through the integrity of the extracted watermark. The watermark can also include information from the original document that can aid in undoing any modification and recovering the original. Clearly a watermark used for authentication purposes should not affect the quality of the document and should be resistant to forgeries. Robustness is not critical, as removal of the watermark renders the content inauthentic and hence is of no value.

5. *Metadata Binding.* Metadata information embedded in an image can serve many purposes. For example, a business can embed the Web site URL for a specific product in a picture that shows an advertisement for that product. The user holds the magazine photo in front of a low-cost CMOS camera that is integrated into a personal computer, cellular phone, or a personal digital assistant. The data are extracted from the low-quality picture and is used to take the browser to the designated Web site. For example, in the mediabridge application (*http://www.digimarc.com*), the information embedded in the document image needs to be extracted despite distortions incurred in the print and scan process. However, these distortions are just a part of a process and not caused by an active and malicious adversary.

The above list represents example applications where data hiding and digital watermarks could potentially be of use. In addition, there are many other applications in digital rights management (DRM) and protection that can benefit from data hiding and watermarking technology. Examples include tracking the use of documents, automatic billing for viewing documents, and so forth. From the variety of potential applications exemplified above it is clear that a digital watermarking technique needs to satisfy a number of requirements. Since the specific requirements vary with the application, data hiding and watermarking techniques need to be designed within the context of the entire system in which they are to be employed. Each application imposes different requirements and would require different types of watermarking schemes.

Over the last few years, a variety of digital watermarking and data hiding techniques have been proposed for such purposes. However, most of the methods developed today are for grayscale and color images (Swanson et al., 1998), where the gray level or color value of a selected group of pixels is changed by a small amount without causing visually noticeable artifacts. These techniques cannot be directly applied to binary document images where the pixels have either a 0 or a 1 value. Arbitrarily changing pixels on a binary image causes very

Figure 1. Effect of arbitrarily changing pixel values on a binary image

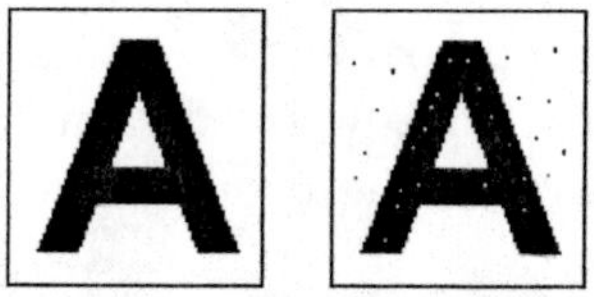

noticeable artifacts (see Figure 1 for an example). A different class of embedding techniques must therefore be developed. These would have important applications in a wide variety of document images that are represented as binary foreground and background; for example, bank checks, financial instruments, legal documents, driver licenses, birth certificates, digital books, engineering maps, architectural drawings, road maps, and so forth. Until recently, there has been little work on watermarking and data hiding techniques for binary document images. In the remaining portion of this chapter we describe some general principles and techniques for document image watermarking and data hiding. Our aim is to give the reader a better understanding of the basic principles, inherent trade-offs, strengths, and weaknesses of document image watermarking and data hiding techniques that have been developed in recent years.

Most document images are binary in nature and consist of a foreground and a background color. The foreground could be printed characters of different fonts and sizes in text documents, handwritten letters and numbers in a bank check, or lines and symbols in engineering and architectural drawings. Some documents have multiple gray levels or colors, but the number of gray levels and colors is usually few and each local region usually has a uniform gray level or color, as opposed to the different gray levels and colors you find at individual pixels of a continuous-tone image. Some binary documents also contain grayscale images represented as half-tone images, for example the photos in a newspaper. In such images, *nxn* binary patterns are used to approximate gray level values of a gray scale image, where *n* typically ranges from two to four. The human visual system performs spatial integration of the fine binary patterns within local regions and perceives them as different intensities (Foley et al., 1990).

Many applications require that the information embedded in a document be recovered despite accidental or malicious distortions they may undergo. Robustness to printing, scanning, photocopying, and facsimile transmission is an important consideration when hardcopy distributions of documents are involved. There are many applications where robust extraction of the embedded data is not required. Such embedding techniques are called *fragile* embedding techniques. For example, fragile embedding is used for authentication whereby any modification made to the document can be detected due to a change in the watermark itself or a change in the relationship between the content and the watermark. Fragile embedding techniques could also be used for steganography applications.

In the second section, of this chapter, we summarize recent developments in binary document image watermarking and data hiding techniques. In the third section, we present a discussion on these techniques, and in the fourth section we give our concluding remarks.

DATA HIDING TECHNIQUES FOR DOCUMENTS IMAGES

Watermarking and data hiding techniques for binary document images can be classified according to one of the following embedding methods: text line, word, or character shifting, fixed partitioning of the image into blocks, boundary modifications, modification of character features, modification of run-length patterns, and modifications of half-tone images. In the rest of this section we describe representative techniques for each of these methods.

Text Line, Word or Character Shifting

One class of robust embedding methods shifts a text line, a group of words, or a group of characters by a small amount to embed data. They are applicable to documents with formatted text.

S. Low and co-authors have published a series of papers on document watermarking based on line and word shifting (Low et al., 1995a, 1995b, 1998; Low & Maxemchuk, 1998; Maxemchuk & Low, 1997). These methods are applicable to documents that contain paragraphs of printed text. Data is embedded in text documents by shifting lines and words spacing by a small amount (1/150 inch.) For instance, a text line can be moved up to encode a '1' or down to encode a '0,' a word can be moved left to encode a '1' or right to encode '0'. The techniques are robust to printing, photocopying, and scanning. In the decoding process, distortions and noise introduced by printing, photocopying and scanning are corrected and removed as much as possible. Detection is by use of maximum-likelihood detectors. In the system they implemented, line shifts are detected by the change in the distance of the marked line and two control lines — the lines immediately above and below the marked line. In computing the distance between two lines, the estimated centroids of the horizontal profiles (projections) of the two lines are used as reference points. Vertical profiles (projections) of words are used for detecting word shifts. The block of words to be marked (shifted) is situated between two control blocks of words. Shifting is detected by computing the correlation between the received profile and the uncorrupted marked profile. The line shifting approach has low embedding capacity but the embedded data are robust to severe distortions introduced by processes such as printing, photocopying, scanning, and facsimile transmission. The word shifting approach has better data embedding capacity but reduced robustness to printing, photocopying and scanning.

In Liu et al. (1999), a combined approach that marks a text document by line or word shifting, and detects the watermark in the frequency domain by Cox et al.'s algorithm (Cox et al., 1996) was proposed. It attempts to combine the unobtrusiveness of spatial domain techniques and the good detection performance of frequency domain techniques. Marking is performed according to the line and word shifting method described above. The frequency watermark X is then computed as the largest N values of the absolute differences in the transforms of the original document and the marked document. In the detection process, the transform of the corrupted document is first computed. The corrupted frequency watermark X^* is then computed as the largest N values of the absolute differences in the transform of the corrupted document and the original document. The detection of watermark is by computing a similarity between X and X^*. This method assumes that the transform of the original document, and the frequency watermark X computed from the original document and the marked document (before corruption) is available during the detection process.

In Brassil and O'Gorman (1996), it is shown that the height of a bounding box enclosing a group of words can be used to embed data. The height of the bounding box is increased by either shifting certain words or characters upward, or by adding pixels to end lines of characters with ascenders or descenders. The method was proposed to increase the data embedding capacity over the line and/or word shifting methods described above. Experimental results show that bounding box expansions as small as 1/300 inch can be reliably detected after several iterations of photocopying. For each mark, one or more adjacent words on an encodable text line are selected for displacement according to a selection criterion. The words immediately before and after the shifted word(s), and a block of words on the text line immediately above or below the shifted word(s), remain unchanged and are used as "reference heights" in the decoding process. The box height is measured by computing a local horizontal projection profile for the bounding box. This method is very sensitive to baseline skewing. A small rotation of the text page can cause distortions in bounding box height, even after de-skewing corrections. Proper methods to deal with skewing require further research.

In Chotikakamthorn (1999), character spacing is used as the basic mechanism to hide data. A line of text is first divided into blocks of characters. A data bit is then embedded by adjusting the widths of the spaces between the characters within a block, according to a predefined rule. This method has advantage over the word spacing method above in that it can be applied to written languages that do not have spaces with sufficiently large width for word boundaries; for example, Chinese, Japanese, and Thai. The method has embedding capacity comparable to that of the word shifting method. Embedded data are detected by matching character spacing patterns corresponding to data bits '0' or '1'. Experiments show that the method can withstand document duplications. However, improvement is needed for the method to be robust against severe document degradations. This could be done by increasing the block size for embedding data bits, but this also decreases the data embedding capacity.

Fixed Partitioning of Images

One class of embedding methods partitions an image into fixed blocks of size *m* x *n,* and computes some pixel statistics or invariants from the blocks for embedding data. They can be applied to binary document images in general; for example, documents with formatted text or engineering drawings.

In Wu et al. (2000), the input binary image is divided into 3x3 (or larger) blocks. The flipping priorities of pixels in a 3x3 block are then computed and those with the lowest scores can be changed to embed data. The flipping priority of a pixel is indicative of the estimated visual distortion that would be caused by flipping the value of a pixel from 0 to 1 or from 1 to 0. It is computed by considering the change in smoothness and connectivity in a 3x3 window centered at the pixel. Smoothness is measured by the horizontal, vertical, and diagonal transitions, and connectivity is measured by the number of black and white clusters in the 3x3 window. Data are embedded in a block by modifying the total number of black pixels to be either odd or even, representing data bits 1 and 0, respectively. Shuffling is used to equalize the uneven embedding capacity over the image. It is done by random permutation of all pixels in the image after identifying the flippable pixels.

In Koch and Zhao (1995), an input binary image is divided into blocks of 8x8 pixels. The numbers of black and white pixels in each block are then altered to embed data bits 1 and 0. A data bit 1 is embedded if the percentage of white pixels is greater than a given threshold, and a data bit 0 is embedded if the percentage of white pixels is less than another threshold. A group of contiguous or distributed blocks is modified by switching white pixels to black or vice versa until such thresholds are reached. For ordinary binary images, modifications are carried out at the boundary of black and white pixels, by reversing the bits that have the most neighbors with the opposite pixel value. For dithered images, modifications are distributed throughout the whole block by reversing bits that have the most neighbors with the same pixel value. This method has some robustness against noise if the difference between the thresholds for data bits 1 and 0 is sufficiently large, but this also decreases the quality of the marked document.

In Pan et al. (2000), a data hiding scheme using a secret key matrix *K* and a weight matrix *W* is used to protect the hidden data in a host binary image. A host image *F* is first divided into blocks of size *mxn*. For each block F_i, data bits $b_1 b_2 \ldots b_r$ are embedded by ensuring the invariant

$$SUM((F_i \oplus K) \otimes W) \equiv b_1 b_2 .. b_r \pmod{2^r},$$

where $\oplus$ represents the bit-wise exclusive OR operation, $\otimes$ represents pair-wise multiplication, and SUM is the sum of all elements in a matrix. Embedded data can be easily extracted by computing:

$$SUM((F_i \oplus K) \otimes W) \pmod{2^r}$$

The scheme can hide as many as $\lfloor \log_2(mn+1) \rfloor$ bits of data in each image block by changing at most two bits in the image block. It provides high security, as long as the block size (m x n) is reasonably large. In a 256x256 test image divided into blocks of size 4x4, 16,384 bits of information were embedded. This method does not provide any measure to ensure good visual quality in the marked document.

In Tseng and Pan (2000), an enhancement was made to the method proposed in Pan et al. (2000) by imposing the constraint that every bit that is to be modified in a block is adjacent to another bit that has the opposite value. This improves the visual quality of the marked image by making the inserted bits less visible, at the expense of sacrificing some data hiding capacity. The new scheme can hide up to $\lfloor \log_2(mn+1) \rfloor - 1$ bits of data in an mxn image by changing at most two bits in the image block.

Boundary Modifications

In Mei et al. (2001), the data are embedded in the eight-connected boundary of a character. A fixed set of pairs of five-pixel long boundary patterns were used for embedding data. One of the patterns in a pair requires deletion of the center foreground pixel, whereas the other requires the addition of a foreground pixel. A unique property of the proposed method is that the two patterns in each pair are dual of each other — changing the pixel value of one pattern at the center position would result in the other. This property allows easy detection of the embedded data without referring to the original document, and without using any special enforcing techniques for detecting embedded data. Experimental results showed that the method is capable of embedding about 5.69 bits of data per character (or connected component) in a full page of text digitized at 300 dpi. The method can be applied to general document images with connected components; for example, text documents or engineering drawings.

Modifications of Character Features

This class of techniques extracts local features from text characters. Alterations are then made to the character features to embed data.

In Amamo and Misaki (1999), text areas in an image are identified first by connected component analysis, and are grouped according to spatial closeness. Each group has a bounding box that is divided into four partitions. The four partitions are divided into two sets. The average width of the horizontal strokes of characters is computed as feature. To compute average stroke width, vertical black runs with lengths less than a threshold are selected and averaged. Two operations — "make fat" and "make thin" — are defined by increasing and decreasing the lengths of the selected runs, respectively. To embed a "1" bit, the "make fat" operation is applied to partitions belonging to set 1, and the "make thin" operation is applied to partitions belongs to set 2. The opposite operations are used to embed "0" bit. In the detection process, detection of text line bounding boxes, partitioning, and grouping are performed. The stroke width features are extracted from the partitions, and added up for each set. If the difference of the sum totals is larger than a positive threshold, the detection process outputs 1. If the difference is less than a negative threshold, it outputs 0. This method could survive the distortions caused by print-and-scan (re-digitization) processes. The method's robustness to photocopying needs to be furthered investigated.

In Bhattacharjya and Ancin (1999), a scheme is presented to embed secret messages in the scanned grayscale image of a document. Small sub-character-sized regions that consist of pixels that meet criteria of text-character parts are identified first, and the lightness of these regions are modulated to embed data. The method employs two scans of the document — a low resolution scan and a high resolution scan. The low-resolution scan is used to identify the various components of the document and establish a coordinate system based on the paragraphs, lines and words found in the document. A list of sites for embedding data is selected from the low resolution scanned image. Two site selection methods were presented in the paper. In the first method, a text paragraph is partitioned into grids of 3x3 pixels. Grid cells that contain predominately text-type pixels are selected. In the second method, characters with long strokes are identified. Sites are selected at locations along the stroke. The second scan is a full-resolution scan that is used to generate the document copy. The pixels from the site lists generated in the low-resolution scan are identified and modulated by the data bits to be embedded. Two or more candidate sites are required for embedding each bit. For example, if the difference between the average luminance of the pixels belonging to the current site and the next one is positive, the bit is a 1; else, the bit is a 0. For robustness, the data to be embedded are first coded using an error correcting code. The resulting bits are then scrambled and dispersed uniformly across the document page. For data retrieval, the average luminance for the pixels in each site is computed and the data are retrieved according to the embedding scheme and the input site list. This method was claimed to be robust against printing and scanning. However, this method requires that the scanned grayscale image of a document be available. The data hiding capacity of this method depends on the number of sites available on the image, and in some cases, there might not be enough sites available to embed large messages.

Modification of Run-Length

In Matsui and Tanaka (1994), a method was proposed to embed data in the run-lengths of facsimile images. A facsimile document contains 1,728 pixels in each horizontal scan line. Each run length of black (or foreground) pixels is coded using modified Huffman coding scheme according to the statistical distribution of run-lengths. In the proposed method, each run length of black pixels is shortened or lengthened by one pixel according to a sequence of signature bits. The signature bits are embedded at the boundary of the run lengths according to some pre-defined rules.

Modifications of Half-Toned Images

Several watermarking techniques have been developed for half-tone images that can be found routinely in printed matters such as books, magazines, newspapers, printer outputs, and so forth. This class of methods can only be used for half-tone images, and are not suitable for other types of document images. The methods described in Baharav and Shaked (1999) and Wang (2001) embed data during the half-toning process. This requires the original grayscale image. The methods described in Koch and Zhao (1995) and Fu and Au (2000a, 2000b, 2001) embed data directly into the half-tone images after they have been generated. The original grayscale image is therefore not required.

In Baharav and Shaked (1999), a sequence of two different dither matrices (instead of one) was used in the half-toning process to encode the watermark information. The order in which the two matrices are applied is the binary representation of the watermark. In Knox (United States Patent) and Wang (United States Patent), two screens were used to form two halftone images and data were embedded through the correlations between the two screens.

In Fu and Au (2000a, 2000b), three methods were proposed to embedded data at pseudo-random locations in half-tone images without knowledge of the original multi-tone image and the half-toning method. The three methods, named DHST, DHPT, and DHSPT, use one half-tone pixel to store one data bit. In DHST, N data bits are hidden at N pseudo-random locations by forced toggling. That is, when the original half-tone pixel at the pseudo-random locations differs from the desired value, it is forced to toggle. This method results in undesirable clusters of white or black pixels. In the detection process, the data are simply read from the *N* pseudo-random locations. In DHPT, a pair of white and black pixels (instead of one in DHST) is chosen to toggle at the pseudo-random locations. This improves over DHST by preserving local intensity and reducing the number of undesirable clusters of white or black pixels. DHSPT improves upon DHPT by choosing pairs of white and black pixels that are maximally connected with neighboring pixels before toggling. The chosen maximally connected pixels will become least connected after toggling and the resulting clusters will be smaller, thus improving visual quality.

In Fu and Au (2001), an algorithm called *intensity selection* (IS) is proposed to select the best location, out of a set of candidate locations, for the application of the DHST, DHPT and DHSPT algorithms. By doing so, significant improvement in visual quality can be obtained in the output images without sacrificing data hiding capacity. In general, the algorithm chooses pixel locations that are either very bright or very dark. It represents a data bit as the parity of the sum of the half-tone pixels at *M* pseudo-random locations and selects the best out of the *M* possible locations. This algorithm, however, requires the original grayscale image or computation of the inverse-half-toned image.

In Wang (2001), two data hiding techniques for digital half-tone images were described: *modified ordered dithering* and *modified multiscale error diffusion*. In the first method, one of the 16 neighboring pixels used in the dithering process is replaced in an ordered or pre-programmed manner. The method was claimed to be similar to replacing the insignificant one or two bits of a grayscale image, and is capable of embedding 4,096 bits in an image of size 256 x 256 pixels. The second method is a modification of the *multi-scale error diffusion* (MSED) algorithm for half-toning as proposed in Katsavounidis and Kuo (97), which alters the binarization sequence of the error diffusion process based on the global and local properties of intensity in the input image. The modified algorithm uses fewer floors (e.g., three or four) in the image pyramid and displays the binarization sequence in a more uniform and progressive way. After 50% of binarization is completed, the other 50% is used for encoding the hidden data. It is feasible that edge information can be retained with this method.

Kacker and Allebach propose a joint halftoning and watermarking approach (Kacker & Allebach, 2003), that combines optimization based halftoning with a spread spectrum robust watermark. The method uses a joint metric to account for the distortion between a continuous tone and a halftone (FWMSE), as well as a watermark detectability criterion (correlation). The direct binary search method (Allebach et al., 1994) is used for searching a halftone that minimizes the metric. This method is obviously extendable in that other distortion metric and/or watermarking algorithms can be used.

DISCUSSION

Robustness to printing, scanning, photocopying, and facsimile transmission is an important consideration when hardcopy distributions of documents are involved. Of the methods described above, the line and word shifting approaches described in Low et al. (1995a, 1995b, 1998), Maxemchuk and Low (1997), Low and Maxemchuk (1998), and Liu et al. (1999), and the method using intensity modulation of character parts (Bhattacharjya & Ancin, 1999) are reportedly robust to printing, scanning, and photocopying operations. These methods, however, have low data capacity. The method described in Amamo and Misaki (1999) reportedly can survive printing and scanning (re-digitization) if the strokes remain in the image. This method's robustness to photocopying still needs to be determined. The bounding box expansion method described in Brassil and O'Gorman (1996) is a robust technique, but further research is needed to develop an appropriate document de-skewing technique for the method to be useful. The character spacing width sequence coding method described in Chotikakamthorn (1999) can withstand a modest amount of document duplications.

The methods described in Wu et al. (2000), Pan et al. (2000), Tseng and Pan (2000), Mei et al. (2001), Matsui and Tanaka(1994), Wang (2001), and Fu and Au (2000a, 200b, 2001) are not robust to printing, scanning and copying operations but they offer high data embedding capacity. These methods are useful in applications when documents are distributed in electronic form, when no printing, photocopying, and scanning of hardcopies are involved. The method

Table 1. Comparison of techniques

Techniques	Robustness	Advantages (+) / Disadvantages (-)	Capacity	Limitations
Line shifting	High		Low	Formatted text only
Word shifting	Medium		Low/Medium	Formatted text only
Bounding box expansion	Medium	- Sensitive to document skewing	Low/Medium	Formatted text only
Character spacing	Medium	+ Can be applied to languages with no clear-cut word boundaries	Low/Medium	Formatted text only
Fixed partitioning -- Odd/Even pixels	None	+ Can be applied to binary images in general	High	
Fixed partitioning -- Percentage of white/black pixels	Low/Medium	+ Can be applied to binary images in general - Image quality may be reduced	High	
Fixed partitioning -- Logical invariant	None	+ Embed multiple bits within each block + Use of a secret key	High	
Boundary modifications	None	+ Can be applied to general binary images + Direct control on image quality	High	

Table 1. Comparison of techniques (continued)

Techniques	Robustness	Advantages (+) / Disadvantages (-)	Capacity	Limitations
Modification of horizontal stroke widths	Medium		Low/Medium	Languages rich in horizontal strokes only
Intensity modulations of sub-character regions	Medium		Medium	Grayscale images of scanned documents only
Run-length modifications	None	- Image quality may be reduced	High	
Use two-dithering matrices	None			Half-tone images only
Embed data at pseudo-random locations	None		High	Half-tone images only
Modified ordered dithering	None		High	Half -tone images only
Modified error diffusion	None		High	Half-tone images only

in Koch and Zhao (1995) also has high embedding capacity. It offers some amount of robustness if the two thresholds are chosen sufficiently apart, but this also decreases image quality.

Methods based on character feature modifications require reliable extraction of the features. For example, the methods described in Amamo and Misaki (1999) and one of the two site-selection methods presented in Bhattacharjya and Anci (1999) require reliable extraction of character strokes. The boundary modification method presented in Mei et al. (2001) traces the boundary of a character (or connected-component), which can always be reliably extracted in binary images. This method also provides direct and good image quality control. The method described in Matsui and Tanaka (1994) was originally developed for facsimile images, but could be applied to regular binary document images. The resulting image quality, however, may be reduced.

A comparison of the above methods shows that there is a trade off between embedding capacity and robustness. Data embedding capacity tends to decrease with increased robustness. We also observed that for a method to be robust, data must be embedded based on computing some statistics over a reasonably large set of pixels, preferably spread out over a large region, instead of based on the exact locations of some specific pixels. For example, in the line shifting method, data are embedded by computing centroid position from a horizontal line of text pixels, whereas in the boundary modification method, data are embedded based on specific configurations of a few boundary pixel patterns.

In addition to robustness and capacity, another important characteristic of a data hiding technique is its "security" from a steganographic point of view. That is, whether documents that contain an embedded message can be distinguished from documents that do not contain any message. Unfortunately, this aspect has not been investigated in the literature. However, for any of the above techniques to be useful in a covert communication application, the ability of a technique to be indistinguishable is quite critical. For example, a marked document created using line and word shifting can easily be spotted as it has characteristics that are not expected to be found in "normal" documents. The block-based techniques and boundary-based technique presented in the second section may produce marked documents that are distinguishable if they introduce too many irregularities or artifacts. This needs to be further investigated. A similar comment applies to the techniques presented in the second section. In general, it appears that the development of "secure" steganography techniques for binary documents has not received enough attention in the research community and much work remains to be done in this area.

Table 1 summarizes the different methods in terms of embedding techniques, robustness, advantages/disadvantages, data embedding capacity, and limitations. Robustness here refers to robustness to printing, photocopying, scanning, and facsimile transmission.

CONCLUSIONS

We have presented an overview and summary of recent developments in binary document image watermarking and data hiding research. Although there has been little work done on this topic until recent years, we are seeing a growing number of papers proposing a variety of new techniques and ideas. Research on binary document watermarking and data hiding is still not as mature as for color and grayscale images. More effort is needed to address this important topic. Future research should aim at finding methods that offer robustness to printing, scanning, and copying, yet provide good data embedding capacity. Quantitative methods should also be developed to evaluate the quality of marked images. The steganographic capability of different techniques needs to be investigated and techniques that can be used in covert communication applications need to be developed.

REFERENCES

Allebach, J.P., Flohr, T.J., Hilgenberg, D.P., & Atkins, C.B. (1994, May). Model-based halftoning via direct binary search. *Proceedings of IS&T's 47th Annual Conference*, (pp. 476-482), Rochester, NY.

Amamo, T., & Misaki, D. (1999). Feature calibration method for watermarking of document images. *Proceedings of 5th Int'l Conf on Document Analysis and Recognition,* (pp. 91-94), Bangalore, India.

Baharav, Z., & Shaked, D. (1999, January). Watermarking of dither half-toned images. *Proc. of SPIE Security and Watermarking of Multimedia Contents, 1,*307-313.

Bhattacharjya, A.K., & Ancin, H. (1999). Data embedding in text for a copier system. *Proceedings of IEEE International Conference on Image Processing, 2,* 245-249.

Brassil, J., & O'Gorman, L. (1996, May). Watermarking document images with bounding box expansion. *Proceedings of 1st Int'l Workshop on Information Hiding,* (pp. 227-235). Newton Institute, Cambridge, UK.

Chotikakamthorn, N. (1999). Document image data hiding techniques using character spacing width sequence coding. *Proc. IEEE Intl. Conf. Image Processing,* Japan.

Cox, I., Kilian, J., Leighton, T., & Shamoon, T. (1996, May/June). Secure spread spectrum watermarking for multimedia. In R. Anderson (Ed.), *Proc. First Int. Workshop Information Hiding* (pp. 183-206). Cambridge, UK: Springer-Verlag.

Craver, S., Memon, N., Yeo, B., & Yeung, M. (1998, May). Resolving rightful ownership with invisible watermarking techniques: Limitations, attacks, and implications. *IEEE Journal on Selected Areas in Communications, 16*(4), 573-586.

Digimarc Corporation. http://www.digimarc.com.

Foley, J.D., Van Dam, A., Feiner, S.K., & Hughes, J.F. (1990). *Computer graphics: Principles and practice* (2nd ed.). Addison-Wesley.

Fu, M.S., & Au, O.C. (2000a, January). Data hiding for halftone images. *Proc of SPIE Conf. On Security and Watermarking of Multimedia Contents II, 3971,* 228-236.

Fu, M.S., & Au, O.C. (2000b, June 5-9). Data hiding by smart pair toggling for halftone images. *Proc. of IEEE Int'l Conf. Acoustics, Speech, and Signal Processing, 4,* (pp. 2318-2321).

Fu, M.S., & Au, O.C. (2001). Improved halftone image data hiding with intensity selection. *Proc. IEEE International Symposium on Circuits and Systems, 5,* 243-246.

Holliman, M., & Memon, N. (2000, March). Counterfeiting attacks and blockwise independent watermarking techniques. *IEEE Transactions on Image Processing, 9*(3), 432-441.

Kacker, D., & Allebach, J.P. (2003, April). Joint halftoning and watermarking. *IEEE Trans. Signal Processing, 51,* 1054-1068.

Katsavounidis, I., & Jay Kuo, C.C. (1997, March). A multiscale error diffusion technique for digital half–toning. *IEEE Trans. on Image Processing, 6*(3), 483-490.

Knox, K.T. *Digital watermarking using stochastic screen patterns,* United States Patent Number 5,734,752.

Koch, E., & Zhao, J. (1995, August). Embedding robust labels into images for copyright protection. *Proc. International Congress on Intellectual Property Rights for Specialized Information, Knowledge & New Technologies,* Vienna.

Liu, Y., Mant, J., Wong, E., & Low, S.H. (1999, January).Marking and detection of text documents using transform-domain techniques. *Proc. SPIE Conf. on Security and Watermarking of Multimedia Contents,* (pp. 317-328), San Jose, CA.

Low, S.H., Lapone, A.M., & Maxmchuk, N.F. (1995, November 13-17). Document identification to discourage illicit copying. *IEEE GlobeCom 95,* Singapore.

Low, S.H., & Maxemchuk, N.F. (1998, May). Performance comparison of two text marking methods. *IEEE Journal on Selected Areas in Communications, 16*(4).

Low, S.H., Maxemchuk, N.F., Brassil, J.T., & O'Gorman, L. (1995). Document marking and identification using both line and word shifting. *Infocom 95.* Los Alamitos, CA: IEEE Computer Society Press.

Low, S.H., Maxemchuk, N.F., & Lapone, A.M. (1998, March). Document identification for copyright protection using centroid detection. *IEEE Trans. on Comm., 46*(3), 372-83.

Matsui, K. & Tanaka, K. (1994). Video-steganography: How to secretly embed a signature in a picture. *Proceedings of IMA Intellectual Property Project, 1*(1), 187-206.

Maxemchuk, N.F., & Low, S.H. (1997, October). Marking text documents. *Proceedings of IEEE Intl Conference on Image Processing.*

Mei, Q., Wong, E.K., & Memon, N. (2001, January). Data hiding in binary text documents. *SPIE Proc Security and Watermarking of Multimedia Contents III,* San Jose, CA.

Pan, H.-K., Chen, Y.-Y., & Tseng, Y.-C. (2000). A secure data hiding scheme for two-color images. *IEEE Symposium on Computers and Communications.*

Swanson, M., Kobayashi, M., & Tewfik, A. (1998, June). Multimedia data embedding and watermarking technologies. *IEEE Proceedings, 86*(6), 1064-1087.

Tseng, Y., & Pan, H. (2000). Secure and invisible data hiding in 2-color images. *IEEE Symposium on Computers and Communications.*

Wang, H.-C.A. (2001, April 2-4). Data hiding techniques for printed binary images. *The International Conference on Information Technology: Coding and Computing.*

Wang, S.G. *Digital watermarking using conjugate halftone screens,* United States Patent Number 5,790,703.

Wu, M., Tang, E., & Liu, B. (2000, July 31-August 2). Data hiding in digital binary images. *Proc. IEEE Int'l Conf. on Multimedia and Expo,* New York.

About the Authors

Chun-Shien Lu received a PhD in Electrical Engineering from the National Cheng-Kung University, Taiwan, ROC (1998). From October 1998 through July 2002, he joined the Institute of Information Science, Academia Sinica, Taiwan, as a postdoctoral fellow for his army service. Since August 2002, he has been an assistant research fellow at the same institute. His current research interests mainly focus on topics of multimedia and time-frequency analysis of signals and images (including security, networking and signal processing). Dr. Lu received the paper award of the Image Processing and Pattern Recognition Society of Taiwan many times for his work on data hiding. He organized and chaired a special session on multimedia security in the Second and Third IEEE Pacific-Rim Conference on Multimedia (2001-2002). He will co-organize two special sessions in the Fifth IEEE International Conference on Multimedia and Expo (ICME) (2004). He holds one U.S. and one ROC patent on digital watermarking. He is a member of the IEEE Signal Processing Society and the IEEE Circuits and Systems Society.

* * *

Andrés Garay Acevedo was born in Bogotá, Colombia, where he studied systems engineering at the University of Los Andes. After graduation he pursued a Master's in Communication, Culture and Technology at Georgetown University, where he worked on topics related to audio watermarking. Other research interests include sound synthesis, algorithmic composition, and music information retrieval. He currently works for the Colombian Embassy in Washington, DC, where he is implementing several projects in the field of information and network security.

Mauro Barni was born in Prato in 1965. He graduated in electronic engineering at the University of Florence (1991). He received a PhD in Informatics and

Telecommunications (October 1995). From 1991 to 1998, he was with the Department of Electronic Engineering, University of Florence, Italy, where he worked as a postdoc researcher. Since September 1998, he has been with the Department of Information Engineering of the University of Siena, Italy, where he works as associate professor. His main interests are in the field of digital image processing and computer vision. His research activity is focused on the application of image processing techniques to copyright protection and authentication of multimedia data (digital watermarking), and on the transmission of image and video signals in error-prone, wireless environments. He is author/co-author of more than 150 papers published in international journals and conference proceedings. Mauro Barni is member of the IEEE, where he serves as member of the Multimedia Signal Processing Technical Committee (MMSP-TC). He is associate editor of the *IEEE Transactions on Multimedia.*

Franco Bartolini was born in Rome, Italy, in 1965. In 1991, he graduated (cum laude) in electronic engineering from the University of Florence, Italy. In November 1996, he received a PhD in Informatics and Telecommunications from the University of Florence. Since November 2001, he has been assistant professor at the University of Florence. His research interests include digital image sequence processing, still and moving image compression, nonlinear filtering techniques, image protection and authentication (watermarking), image processing applications for the cultural heritage field, signal compression by neural networks, and secure communication protocols. He has published more than 130 papers on these topics in international journals and conferences. He holds three Italian and one European patent in the field of digital watermarking. Dr. Bartolini is a member of IEEE, SPIE and IAPR. He is a member of the program committee of the SPIE/IST Workshop on Security, Steganography, and Watermarking of Multimedia Contents.

Minya Chen is a PhD student in the Computer Science Department at Polytechnic University, New York (USA). She received her BS in Computer Science from University of Science and Technology of China, Hefei, China, and received her MS in Computer Science from Polytechnic University, New York. Her research interests include document image analysis, watermarking, and pattern recognition, and she has published papers in these areas.

Alessia De Rosa was born in Florence, Italy, in 1972. In 1998, she graduated in electronic engineering from the University of Florence, Italy. In February 2002, she received a PhD in Informatics and Telecommunications from the University of Florence. At present, she is involved in the research activities of the Image Processing and Communications Laboratory of the Department of Electronic and Telecommunications of the University of Florence, where she works as a postdoc researcher. Her main research interests are in the fields of digital watermarking, human perception models for digital image watermarking and quality assessment, and image processing for cultural heritage applications. She holds an Italian patent in the field of digital watermarking.

Jana Dittmann was born in Dessau, Germany. She studied Computer Science and Economy at the Technical University in Darmstadt. In 1999, she received her PhD from the Technical University of Darmstadt. She has been a full professor in the field of multimedia and security at the University of Otto-von-Guericke University Magdeburg since September 2002. Dr. Dittmann specializes in the field of Multimedia Security. Her research is mainly focused on digital watermarking and content-based digital signatures for data authentication and for copyright protection. She has many national and international publications, is a member of several conference PCs, and organizes workshops and conferences in the field of multimedia and security issues. She was involved in all of the last five Multimedia and Security Workshops at ACM Multimedia and she has initiated this workshop as a standalone ACM event since 2004. In 2001, she was a co-chair of the CMS2001 conference that took place in May 2002 in Darmstadt, Germany. She is an associate editor for the *ACM Multimedia Systems Journal* and a guest editor for the *IEEE Transaction on Signal Processing Journal for Secure Media.* Dr. Dittmann is a member of the ACM and GI Informatik.

Chang-Tsun Li received a BS in Electrical Engineering from the Chung Cheng Institute of Technology (CCIT), National Defense University, Taiwan (1987), an MS in Computer Science from the U.S. Naval Postgraduate School (1992), and a PhD in Computer Science from the University of Warwick, UK (1998). He was an associate professor during 1999-2002 in the Department of Electrical Engineering at CCIT and a visiting professor in the Department of Computer Science at the U.S. Naval Postgraduate School in the second half of 2001. He is currently a lecturer in the Department of Computer Science at the University of Warwick. His research interests include image processing, pattern recognition, computer vision, multimedia security, and content-based image retrieval.

Ching-Yung Lin received his PhD from Columbia University. Since 2000, he has been a research staff member in the IBM T.J. Watson Research Center (USA). His current research interests include multimedia understanding and multimedia security. Dr. Lin has pioneered the design of video/image content authentication systems. His IBM multimedia semantic mining project team performs best in the NIST TREC video semantic concept detection benchingmarking in 2002 and 2003. Dr. Lin has led a semantic annotation project, which involves 23 worldwide research institutes, since 2003. He is a guest editor of the *Proceedings of IEEE,* technical program chair of IEEE ITRE 2003, and chair of Watson Workshop on Multimedia 2003. Dr. Lin received the 2003 IEEE

Circuits and Systems Society Outstanding Young Author award, and is an affiliate assistant professor at the University of Washington.

Jiang-Lung Liu received a BS (1988) and a PhD (2002), both in Electrical Engineering, from the Chung Cheng Institute of Technology (CCIT), National Defense University, Taiwan. He is currently an assistant professor in the Department of Electrical Engineering at CCIT. His research interests include cryptology, steganography, multimedia security, and image processing.

Der-Chyuan Lou received a PhD (1997) from the Department of Computer Science and Information Engineering at National Chung Cheng University, Taiwan, ROC. Since 1987, he has been with the Department of Electrical Engineering at Chung Cheng Institute of Technology, National Defense University, Taiwan, ROC, where he is currently a professor and a vice chairman. His research interests include cryptography, steganography, algorithm design and analysis, computer arithmetic, and parallel and distributed systems. Professor Lou is currently area editor for Security Technology of Elsevier Science's *Journal of Systems and Software.* He is an honorary member of the Phi Tau Phi Scholastic Honor Society. He has been selected and included in the 15th and 18th editions of *Who's Who in the World,* published in 1998 and 2001, respectively.

Nasir Memon is an associate professor in the Computer Science Department at Polytechnic University, New York (USA). He received his BE in Chemical Engineering and MSc in Mathematics from the Birla Institute of Technology, Pilani, India, and received his MS and PhD in Computer Science from the University of Nebraska. His research interests include data compression, computer and network security, multimedia data security and multimedia communications. He has published more than 150 articles in journals and conference proceedings. He was an associate editor for *IEEE Transactions on Image Processing* from 1999 to 2002 and is currently an associate editor for the *ACM Multimedia Systems Journal* and the *Journal of Electronic Imaging.* He received the Jacobs Excellence in Education award in 2002.

Martin Steinebach is a research assistant at Fraunhofer IPSI (Integrated Publication and Information Systems Institute). His main research topic is digital audio watermarking. He studied computer science at the Technical University of Darmstadt and finished his diploma thesis on copyright protection for digital audio in 1999. Martin Steinebach had the organizing committee chair of CMS 2001 and co-organizes the Watermarking Quality Evaluation Special Session at ITCC International Conference on Information Technology: Coding and Computing 2002. Since 2002 he has been the head of the department MERIT

(Media Security in IT) and of the C4M Competence Centre for Media Security.

Mohamed Abdulla Suhail received his PhD from the University of Bradford (UK), School of Informatics in Digital Watermarking for Multimedia Copyright Protection. Currently, he is working as a project manager for IT and telecommunications projects in an international development bank. Having worked for several years in project management, Dr. Suhail retains close links with the industry. He has spoken at conferences and guest seminars worldwide and is known for his research work in the area of information systems and digital watermarking. He has published more than 16 papers in international refereed journals and conferences. He also contributed to two books published by international publishers. Dr. Suhail has received several awards from different academic organizations.

Qi Tian is a principal scientist in the Media Division, Institute for Infocomm Research (I2R), Singapore. His main research interests include image/video/audio analysis, indexing and retrieval, media content identification and security, computer vision, and pattern recognition. He received a BS and an MS from the Tsinghua University in China, and a PhD from the University of South Carolina (USA). All of these degrees were in electrical and computer engineering. He is an IEEE senior member and has served on editorial boards of international journals and as chairs and members of technical committees of international conferences on multimedia.

Edward K. Wong received his BE from the State University of New York at Stony Brook, his ScM from Brown University, and his PhD from Purdue University, all in Electrical Engineering. He is currently associate professor in the Department of Computer and Information Science at Polytechnic University, Brooklyn, New York (USA). His current research interests include content-based image/video retrieval, document image analysis and watermarking, and pattern recognition. He has published extensively in these areas, and his research has been funded by federal and state agencies, as well as private industries.

Changsheng Xu received his PhD from Tsinghua University, China (1996). From 1996 to 1998, he was a research associate professor in the National Lab of Pattern Recognition, Institute of Automation, Chinese Academy of Sciences. He joined the Institute for Infocomm Research (I2R) of Singapore in March 1998. Currently, he is a senior scientist and head of the Media Adaptation Lab at I2R. His research interests include digital watermarking, multimedia processing and analysis, computer vision and pattern recognition. He is an IEEE senior member.

Index

E

F

H

I

J

L

M

N

O

P

R

S

T

V

W